The publication of *Portraits of John Quincy Adams and His Wife* makes available [a rec]ord which both affords unique visual [docu]mentation of the most varied political c[areer] in American history and exemplifies the work of the principal American portraitists from the days of Copley and Stuart to the dawn of the daguerrean era.

Included in the volume's 159 illustrations are all the known life portraits, busts, and silhouettes of John Quincy and Louisa Catherine Adams, along with important replicas, copies, engravings, and representative likenesses of their siblings. The book is organized into seven chapters which generally coincide with the major divisions of John Quincy Adams' political career. Within each chapter are discussed the artists, their relationships with the Adamses, and the provenance of each of their works. A comprehensive chronology of John Quincy Adams' life for each period accompanies the chapter to which it pertains. All important information about the size of each likeness, the inscriptions if any, the date executed, and present ownership where known is summarized in the List of Illustrations.

The Adamses, as they watched themselves age over the years in the marble, ink, or oil of the artists who portrayed them, recorded much by way of commentary on the artistic talent and process at hand. Mr. Oliver, in his detailed and lively discussions of each likeness, makes full use of the diaries and correspondence preserved in the Adams

Andrew Oliver, long a student and collector of American portraits, has been a distinguished member of the bar in New York City. Chancellor of the Episcopal Diocese of New York, he holds the honorary D.Cn.L. from the General Theological Seminary. He is First Vice President of The New-York Historical Society, a member of the Council of the Massachusetts Historical Society, a Commissioner of the National Portrait Gallery, and author of *Faces of a Family* (1960) and *Portraits of John and Abigail Adams* (HUP, 1967).

The Adams Papers

L. H. BUTTERFIELD, EDITOR IN CHIEF

SERIES IV

PORTRAITS

John Quincy Adams and His Wife

Portraits of John Quincy Adams and His Wife

by
ANDREW OLIVER

———————— ☆ ————————

THE BELKNAP PRESS
OF HARVARD UNIVERSITY PRESS
CAMBRIDGE, MASSACHUSETTS

1970

Distributed in Great Britain by Oxford University Press · London

Funds for editing *The Adams Papers* were originally furnished by Time, Inc., on behalf of *Life*, to the Massachusetts Historical Society, under whose supervision the editorial work is being done. Further funds have been provided by a grant from the Ford Foundation to the National Archives Trust Fund Board in support of this and four other major documentary publications. In common with these and many other enterprises like them, *The Adams Papers* benefits from the continuing and indispensable cooperation and aid of the National Historical Publications Commission, whose chairman is the Archivist of the United States.

Library of Congress Catalog Card Number 70-128349
SBN 674-69152-0
Printed in the United States of America

This edition of *The Adams Papers*
is sponsored by the MASSACHUSETTS HISTORICAL SOCIETY
to which the ADAMS MANUSCRIPT TRUST
by a deed of gift dated 4 April 1956
gave ultimate custody of the personal and public papers
written, accumulated, and preserved over a span of three centuries
by the Adams family of Massachusetts

The Adams Papers

The acorn and oakleaf device on the preceding page is redrawn from a seal cut for John Quincy Adams after 1830. The motto is from Cæcilius Statius as quoted by Cicero in the First Tusculan Disputation: *Serit arbores quæ alteri seculo prosint* ("He plants trees for the benefit of later generations").

Foreword

With Remarks on John Quincy Adams and the Fine Arts

Few statesmen can have served their country as long and in as varied capacities as John Quincy Adams, and for probably no other does there survive so extended a record of likenesses from life. The boy painted at The Hague in 1783, looking very Dutch in features and costume, was only sixteen, but he had already lived in several European capitals and acted in a quasi-diplomatic role at the Empress Catherine's court in St. Petersburg. His last likeness taken from life that can be dated with certainty was painted by William Henry Powell in Washington sixty-four years later. This volume is as full a record as can be provided of what John Quincy Adams looked like during that long span.

Aesthetically, as the illustrations show, the results were mixed. But on other grounds they are separately and collectively of the highest interest. They bring to life again and make more credible a figure of such force and individuality that he sometimes seems more of a phenomenon of nature, like Niagara Falls or an earthquake, than a human being. He was, said his grandson, the second Charles Francis Adams, "a whale." Others who found it hard to encompass him in words tended to resort to comparisons with the gigantic. Adams was a short man and physically unimpressive, but one who watched him fight the slave power in Congress to a standstill said that the repeated attacks upon him by numerous, able, and determined adversaries were "like the sting of so many musquitoes upon the hide of a rhinoceros." Another, whose admiration was more qualified, remarked that he resembled the elephants used in battle in ancient times, because one could not be certain whether he would inflict greater damage on his foes or on his friends.

Happily, the iconographic record brings out other qualities. John Quincy Adams was not an adversary in all the relations of life. Copley presents a suitor handsome enough to seem, for one brief moment, a true romantic; Stuart and Sully give us a Secretary of State and President who is grave but not unamiable. Hints, however, of something more than the expected ravages of time begin to appear in other likenesses taken during the Presidency. Browere's life mask perpetuates the lineaments of the man of whom Anne Royall wondered if "he [had] ever laughed in his life"; and in Greenough's busts appears the iron sternness which a combination of public disasters and private suffering wrought on Adams' countenance and bearing during middle life. Here, at least by anticipation, is the man who could say—and mean it—that "Perhaps the severest trial of righteousness is the patient Fortitude which endures, without yielding to, the perverseness of mankind," and who could write in a young lady's autograph album, "This world, to me, is but the Lions' den." This attitude settled into the standard mood of Adams' later years, a kind of quizzical gloom which is caught with perfect fidelity in the series of daguerreotypes presented in Mr. Oliver's sixth chapter. Yet even this mood is sometimes relieved by the kindly if not idealized representations of Durand and Healy, and by an occasional humorist like the Quaker primitive Marcus Mote and the silhouettists Edouart and Brown.

A matter of keen regret to those engaged in the production of this book is the lack of a greater number of likenesses of the woman who shared John Quincy Adams' fortunes for more than half a century, Louisa Catherine (Johnson) Adams. All that could be done to make her a less shadowy figure than she has always been, Mr. Oliver has done. Yet, considering her highly cultivated interest in poetry, drama, and music, and also how handsomely she was rendered by several of the few artists who painted her, it is remarkable that she was not painted more often. It may seem still more remarkable that the last recorded oil portrait of her is that painted by Charles Bird King before she became First Lady, and that the only later likenesses known are silhouettes by Hubard and Hanks. Because she lived for almost a quarter of a century after Hanks cut his shade, it is a great temptation to believe that one or more late portraits of Mrs. Adams remain to be discovered.

To compensate for this major gap we have from her grandson Henry one of the most vivid and touching pen portraits among many from his hand. Who that has read *The Education of Henry Adams* can forget the cadences of the early pages devoted to the President's wife? "By that time [the early 1840's] she was seventy years old or more, and thoroughly weary of being beaten about a stormy world. To the boy she seemed singularly peaceful, a vision of silver gray, presiding over her old President and her Queen Anne mahogany; an exotic, like her Sèvres china; an object of deference to every one."

But to return to our behemoth, John Quincy Adams. Even from raw quantitative data—the number of portraits executed in the differ-

ent periods of his career as summarized in Mr. Oliver's Introduction—
there is much to be learned about Adams' standing in the eye and
mind of the American public. This was the more true for the time and
place in which he lived because, as a number of recent writers have
pointed out, the patronage of art shifted radically in the United States
during the early 19th century from wealthy connoisseurs, who still
almost exclusively supported European artists, to the people themselves as buyers of what they liked. "Maecenas might be lacking,"
Charles Coleman Sellers remarks in *Charles Willson Peale with
Patron and Populace*, "but not the sedulous multitude." Whether or
not John Quincy Adams understood this phenomenon, he must have
sensed that a rough equation existed between the frequency of artists'
demands to paint his features and his popularity in the country. But
he had a kind of self-interest—or inverted self-interest—in *not* recog-
nizing it. To do so would have violated his code; it would be stooping
to the popular arts that he despised in others. And so he went on
affecting, to an almost exaggerated degree, indifference as to whether
he was painted or not, how often, or how well or badly, and at the
same time submitting with astonishing complaisance to the outrageous
demands upon his time by "daubers" (as he called them) whose pro-
ductions he declared the more "hideous" as they were the more "like."
As an Adams he would have been embarrassed to admit to any vanity
or pride in his "image." These conditions greatly complicated his relations with the painters and sculptors for whom he sat, and of course
his opinions of their work.

Externally, with no apparent exceptions, his relations with artists
were of the happiest sort, as Mr. Oliver's pages make amply clear.
Those, like Horatio Greenough, who left testimony concurred in
finding him a good subject to work with. George Healy recorded much
of Adams' conversation, while sitting, about the characters and methods
of artists whom he had earlier sat for or seen at work, the galleries he
had visited, and the great paintings he especially admired.

Adams' interest in the world of art was genuine, long-standing,
and wide-ranging, though it could not by any stretching of words be
called profound. It grew out of his reading, his travels, and his unusually early and constant association with older people of taste as
well as with artists and their works. John Adams did not exaggerate
when he wrote from the Netherlands to his wife, on her arrival in
London in the summer of 1784, that he was sending to meet her "a
son who is the greatest Traveller, of his Age." This lad, just seventeen, had crossed the ocean three times, had traveled in France, Spain,

the Low Countries, England, the German states, Russia, and Sweden, and had spent enough time in most if not all of these countries to visit churches, galleries, royal collections, and other repositories of fine art. He was shortly to return to Paris for a year during which he would see so much of Mr. Jefferson, the first American connoisseur of art, that John Adams remembered feeling that John Quincy was almost as much Jefferson's son as his own.

He was, then, no raw American when he returned to the scene of Europe just a decade later to serve successively as President Washington's envoy to The Hague and as President John Adams' minister at Berlin. European diplomats who supposed they could talk down to him on matters of taste usually found themselves mistaken. Thus, in 1795 M. Richard, the French representative to the new Batavian Republic, asked Adams if there were any living American painters who were worthy of attention; Adams, who was personally acquainted with West, Copley, and Trumbull and their works, undertook to satisfy him. Richard shifted the subject a little and asked whether "any originals of the greatest masters of the schools" were to be found in the United States. When told that there were very few, he put his finger to his forehead and said, "vous me faites venir un idée.... We will send you some; you must form a national Gallery.... How do you think such a present would be received?" "No doubt it would be received," Adams replied, "with all the gratitude that would be due to it." But he characteristically reserved his final comment for his diary alone: "I believe my promise of gratitude is as good as his promise of pictures." Thus ended the earliest recorded proposal for a national gallery of the fine arts in the United States.

Returning from Berlin to America in 1801, Adams had a second diplomatic career in Europe ahead of him, but his views respecting the fine arts and their role in the life of the individual and in society were completely formed. Those who know the austerity of his character may be surprised to find him untroubled by the doubts his father had felt and still felt. John Adams, who during his years in Europe was sometimes strongly moved by examples of high art, never ceased to believe that the fine arts were actually or potentially corrupting to republican virtue, and took comfort in the thought that generations would pass before a craving for them, and the luxury they connoted, would threaten the American republic he had helped to found. No trace of this kind of thinking appears in John Quincy Adams. However widely conversant with art and artists he may have been, he had

little to say of the fine arts in the abstract. In an autobiographical letter
to Skelton Jones, 17 April 1809, he noted how he had

> acquired at an early period of life a taste for the fine arts. In the capitals
> of the great European nations, the monuments of Architecture and of
> sculpture continually meet the eye, and cannot escape the attention even
> of the most careless observer. Painting, Musick, the Decorations of the
> Drama, and the elegant arts which are combined in its Representations,
> have a charm to the senses and imagination of youth. . . . The exhibitions
> of excellence in all these faculties, which I had frequent opportunities of
> witnessing, at the time of life when they were calculated to make the
> strongest impression, gave me a taste for them, which has contributed so
> much to the enjoyment of my life.

No hint is given here of their possibly immoral effects on the citizen
or the state. An informed appreciation of art is simply part of a young
man's education and contributes to his enjoyment of life. This, for the
time, was a more typically European than American view. It suggests
that John Quincy Adams' education in Europe had gone further than
his parents would have wished when they solicitously sent him home
from Paris to Harvard College in 1785. It even lends a tincture of
plausibility to the argument of political critics that his "life style"
was based on European, "aristocratic," even "royalist," rather than on
sound American and good old-fashioned republican principles.

Adams' taste for the fine arts posed no threat, however, except to
his own success in politics. His interest did not extend beyond his
interest in virtually all other branches of higher human endeavor, including the sciences. His love of the theater—another product of his
European experience—went much deeper, and his lifelong passion for
literature, particularly as a reader of the classics and as a writer of
poetry, led him into indulgences that often filled him with a sense of
guilt. Such indulgences cost him only time and energy (which he self-
accusingly thought should have been devoted to public service) and a
certain outlay for books; he never had the means or apparently the
inclination to become a patron or collector of art. Though he was
never happier, as Mr. Oliver's chapters repeatedly show, than when
playing the confident critic at exhibitions, his personal interest in
painting and sculpture stopped there. Though willing to discuss the
didactic values and historical background of a work of art, he seems
rarely, if ever, to have been genuinely moved by a masterpiece. "His
enthusiasm," said Horatio Greenough, "is of the head."

Adams' views respecting the role of government patronage of art require fuller explanation. The early decades of the 19th century, particularly after the War of 1812, were marked by a great surge of nationalistic feeling that expressed itself as conspicuously in arts and letters as in politics. Despite his European background, or perhaps in part because of it, Adams shared the widespread hope for a distinctively American literature, art, and intellectual life. His whole political philosophy may be understood as an extension of Jefferson's phrase "the pursuit of happiness" and the "general Welfare" clause in the Preamble to the Constitution. In 1809 John Quincy Adams wrote a testament to his sons in which he said it should be their "ardent solicitude" to "employ [their] faculties in such a manner as shall produce the greatest quantity of human happiness." Two "modes" of doing so offered themselves: "The first, by taking a share in the public administration of the Government. The second, by cultivating the Arts and Sciences." Adams' own life had been so relentlessly devoted to public service that he knew he had contributed nothing enduring to any art or science. But the opportunity, the challenge, for others to do so was infinitely greater, he was convinced, under a government of popular institutions like the United States than under aristocratic patronage in Europe. What were the masterpieces in the great galleries at Paris and Dresden or the researches conducted at the Imperial Observatory at Pulkova in comparison with what would eventually and inevitably be achieved in a nation where, as he was fond of saying, "Liberty is Power"?

This was the philosophical theme of President Adams' State of the Union address to Congress in December 1825. It called for federal encouragement of higher education; for scientific exploration of the American continent and the seas beyond; for better communications, an astronomical observatory, and the advancement of the "Mechanic and . . . Elegant Arts" and literature generally. It justified these on the broad ground that "The great object of the institution of Civil Government, is the improvement of the condition of those who are parties to the social compact. And no government . . . can accomplish the lawful ends of its institution, but in proportion as it improves the condition of those over whom it is established." Failure to invoke such powers under the warrant of the "general Welfare" clause "would be to hide in the earth the talent committed to our charge—would be treachery to the most sacred of trusts." In a peroration setting forth his vision of American intellectual progress, Adams declared: "While foreign nations, less blessed with that freedom which is power, than ourselves, are advancing with gigantic strides in the career of public improve-

ment, were we to slumber in indolence, or fold up our arms and pro-
claim to the world that we are palsied by the will of our constituents,
would it not be to cast away the bounties of Providence, and doom ourselves to perpetual inferiority?"

From the moment it was uttered, Adams' call for a great society
was perfectly null. The leaders in Congress—ardent states'-righters
and thoroughgoing anti-intellectuals—thought talk of federal universi-
ties and observatories, to say nothing of "Elegant Arts," was, if not
merely laughable, downright subversive. Contemptuous of the President's aspirations for his country and the earnest reasoning from
which they proceeded, they agreed that he had been too long exposed
to European courts and was bent on consolidating the states into a
single national union, over which he proposed to reign as political
sovereign and artistic patron.

His program thus completely throttled, Adams had to satisfy himself with a minor role in the government's only conspicuous activity
in the arts during his Presidency—the embellishment of the Capitol
and the improvement of its site. Although Charles Bulfinch was then
serving as architect, this was a halting time for this great federal art
project. Congress, preferring mud, confusion, and discomfort to anything that suggested monarchical grandeur, struck many of Bulfinch's
proposals from its annual appropriations, and finally abolished his
office. These frustrations may not, however, fully account for Adams'
relatively small part in the building of the Capitol. He seems to have
turned an even duller eye toward the spatial forms and relations that
are the essence of architecture than he did toward the color and plastic
values of painting and sculpture. His correspondence with Bulfinch
was routine in character, and one looks in vain among his writings
for significant discussion of the art and science of building. The
clutter of his farmstead home in Quincy, described by a dozen visitors
with more or less condescension on account of its lack of elegance,
shows that, unlike his one-time mentor Jefferson, Adams never thought
of consulting the muses on how he should shelter himself from the
weather.

On the other hand, he did find congenial to his taste and talents
the problem of the symbolic ornamentation of the Capitol. At the
time he became President, the theme of the relief sculpture for the
central pediment of the East Front had not been decided on. Adams
busied himself with it immediately and at length. A competition was
held, evidently at his instigation, in which some thirty artists submitted thirty-six designs. These were "set up in the unfurnished long

room" of the President's House for examination. At a conference in May 1825 with Adams and Bulfinch, the sculptor Luigi Persico presented a scheme that must have drawn something from each of them. As described in Adams' diary, it was to include: "a personification of the United States standing on a throne, leaning upon the Roman fasces, surmounted with the cap of Liberty, with Justice at her right hand ... and Hercules at her left ... emblematical of Strength. To which were added ... Plenty seated with her Cornucopia ... and Peace, a flying angel extending a garland of Victory towards America with one hand and bearing a palm in the other."

Bulfinch reported that the President questioned whether this was "a suitable decoration for a legislative building. He disclaimed all wish to exhibit triumphal cars and emblems of victory, and all allusions to heathen mythology, and thought that the duties of the nation or its legislators should be expressed in an obvious and intelligent manner." On this commendable principle, Plenty, Peace, and their paraphernalia were banished. Hercules was replaced by "Hope, with an anchor—a scriptural Image"; Justice was to hold the text of the United States Constitution; and an American eagle was to look on approvingly. This conception was less felicitous than Adams' Lyre and Eagle design, which recurs throughout his portraits as an emblem of an harmonious American union; but it was vastly superior to anything the professionals proposed. Together with other more fragmentary evidence it lends weight to Charles Francis Adams' rather startling assertion in 1829 that "Few people in this Country are aware of the fact that [John Quincy Adams] is the source of all that is ornamental in the Statuary sculpture about the Capitol."

His response to art being so entirely "of the head," symbolic design was precisely the thing that Adams liked and did best, in part of course because it brought his classical and historical learning into play. No doubt this was a minor talent, but he worked it effectively.

As early as 1802 Adams remarked in his diary: "A politician in this Country must be the man of a party. I would fain be the man of my whole Country." Yet there were few occasions during his entire "first career," ending with his unhappy single term as President, when he could square the image he held of himself as a leader of the whole constellation of states (Orpheus leading the stars) with the ambiguous image that he knew the American people held of him. When, in the Senate, he had courageously risen above sectional loyalty to support President Jefferson's embargo, he was promptly repudiated by Federalist New England. The Treaty of Ghent was a national triumph, but in the popular mind it was utterly overshadowed by General Jackson's victory at New Orleans. The successful negotiation of the Transcontinental Treaty with Spain, which occupied so many years and so much of Adams' energy while Secretary of State, was profoundly significant for the nation and its future, but at the time it was concluded few besides Adams grasped its significance.

Tragically, he had proved himself "the ideal man," as Richard Hofstadter has said, "to unite the country—against himself." Upon being turned out of the Presidency after four years that saw the accomplishment of none of his major aims, Adams could only reflect that "The Sun of my political life sets in the deepest gloom," adding, to a friend, that he must content himself "with the slender portion of regard which may be yielded to barren good Intentions, and aspirations beyond the temper of the Age." From his own point of view and for the moment at least, all this was true enough; and it has the strongest sort of bearing on the record of his face and figure in the portraits exhibited in the middle chapters of the present volume.

Then, after a brief pause, a process set in that remains unique in our national history. To the dismay—to use no stronger word—of his family, John Quincy Adams returned to politics as a Representative in Congress from the Plymouth District. Within a decade he succeeded, simply by being his inimitable self, in winning a wider national following than he had ever attracted before.

In the course of his eight-year struggle with the successive "gags" on the discussion of slavery and in defense of the right of all to petition, Adams became the tribune of not just the Plymouth District but of New England, New York State, Pennsylvania, Ohio, and parts beyond. In 1843 he traveled for the first time through upper New York State and, on a separate trip, into Ohio to dedicate an astronomical observatory. Both trips became triumphal progresses. "Old Man Eloquent" was taken to the bosom of the great American public. Quite literally, for he reported that at Akron, after one woman—"a very pretty one"—kissed him, he kissed all the others that followed in line. "Some made faces," he truthfully admitted, "but none refused."

These demonstrations of affection came some years too late to encourage hope for a second chance at the highest office in the land. But they warmed a heart that had grown cold with the tribulations of the years. At last and for a moment John Quincy Adams tasted the sweets that his great contemporaries and rivals, Jackson, Clay, and Webster, had long enjoyed with no better claims to them than his, if as good. At last, like Orpheus in his favorite fable, he led the stars. NUNC SIDERA DUCIT. His motto had come true. The profusion and variety of the late portraits and, above all, the questioning look in the eyes of the tired but gallant old gentleman in the daguerreotypes prove it. His image of himself and the image held of him by his countrymen (always excepting "slavocrats" and Know-Nothings) were now nearly identical. Is it surprising that he looked surprised?

L. H. BUTTERFIELD
Editor in Chief

Contents

List of Illustrations

The List of Illustrations incorporates a number of elements ordinarily included in a catalogue of works. However, the formal statement of ownership of the works reproduced is given not here but in the text. The courtesy lines in the List of Illustrations commonly do indicate ownership, but in some instances indicate only the sources of photographs used for reproduction and permission to reproduce them. The absence of a courtesy line is an indication that the present whereabouts of the work is unknown. The text should be consulted for more detailed information on dating. Where no date can be assigned to a likeness, any reference to its date has been omitted from this List. For certain miniatures, engravings, and so on, the one dimension given is the height.

"Given to me by my brother Dr. Fordyce Foster / when he resided in Cohasset Mass. / Jane F. Porter / Quechee Vt. / March 9, 1886." Courtesy of the Boston Athenæum.

F. Hanks (b. 1799); 1829. Size: 11⅜ × 7¾ in. Courtesy of James B. Ames.

30½ × 25½ in. Signed: "E. D. Marchant." Courtesy of the Adams National Historic Site, National Park Service, Department of the Interior.

92. JOHN QUINCY ADAMS. Oil on canvas, modified replica of Fig. 87 or the 1840 portrait, by Edward Dalton Marchant; 1843. Size: 29½ × 24½ in. Signed: "E. D. Marchant 1843." Courtesy of the American Embassy, London.   211

93a. JOHN QUINCY ADAMS. Silhouette by Auguste Edouart (1789–1861); 1841. Inscribed: "John Quincy Adams Ex Prest. / Washington 10th March 1841." Courtesy of The New-York Historical Society.   214

93b. JOHN QUINCY ADAMS. Silhouette by Auguste Edouart; 1841. Size: 11 × 8 in. Inscribed: "John Quincy Adams Ex President / Washington 11th March 1841" and, "John Quincy Adams / 11 March 1841 [auto.]." Courtesy of a private collector.   215

94. JOHN QUINCY ADAMS. Oil on canvas by James Reid Lambdin (1807–1889); 1841. Size: 30 × 25 in. Courtesy of The Pennsylvania Academy of the Fine Arts, Philadelphia.   220

95. JOHN QUINCY ADAMS. Oil on canvas, adapted from Fig. 94, by James Reid Lambdin; 1844. Size: 30 × 25 in. Signed: "JRL 1844." Courtesy of The Union League of Philadelphia.   220

96. JOHN QUINCY ADAMS. Drawing by Marcus Mote (1817–1898); 1843. Inscribed in the artist's hand: "From Life, John Quincy Adams, Eleventh Mo. 1843, His own autograph, while speaking in Old Baptist Church. Drawn at Lebanon, O. His visit to Cinti. to lay cornerstone for Mt. Adams Observatory." Reproduced from Opal Thornburg, "Marcus Mote—Early Ohio Artist," Historical and Philosophical Society of Ohio, *Bulletin*, vol. 14, no. 3, p. 191 (July 1956).   228

97. JOHN QUINCY ADAMS. Drawing by Marcus Mote; 1843. Inscribed in the artist's hand: "From life at the Williamson Hotel, Lebanon, O. 11 Mo. 1843. Present were Tom Corwin, Judge Burnet of Cinti. O, and Hon. Jos. H. Grinnell of Bedford, Mass." Reproduced from Historical and Philosophical Society of Ohio and the University of Cincinnati, *The Centenary of the Cincinnati Observatory, 1843–1943*, Cincinnati, 1944, facing p. 19.   228

98. JOHN QUINCY ADAMS. Oil on panel by George Caleb Bingham (1811–1879); 1844. Size: 10 × 7¾ in. Courtesy of James S. Rollins.   232

99. JOHN QUINCY ADAMS. Oil on panel, modified copy or replica of Fig. 98, by George Caleb Bingham; 1850. Size: 10 × 7⅞ in. Inscribed on the reverse, in ink: "Born 1767 / [J]ohn [Quincy] Adams / Painted in his 81st year [. . .] (aetat 8[ ]) / Taken by Bingham of Washington / and presented to Rev.   234

worth; 1843. Size: 5½ × 4¼ in. Courtesy of the Metropolitan Museum of Art, Gift of I. N. Phelps Stokes, Edward S. Hawes, Alice Mary Hawes, Marion Augusta Hawes, 1937.

131. JOHN QUINCY ADAMS. Engraving by Thomas Doney; 1848. Size: 4⅛ × 3½ in. Inscribed: "Engraved by T. Doney from a Daguerreotype taken by E. Anthony—John Quincy Adams [auto.], Published by E. Anthony 247 Broadway, N. Y. / Printed by Powell & Co / Entered according to Act of Congress in the year 1848 by E. Anthony in the Clerk's Office of the District Court of the Southern District of New York." Courtesy of The New-York Historical Society.   290

132. *U.S. Senate Chamber.* Engraving, including a likeness of John Quincy Adams taken from Fig. 131 or its prototype, by Thomas Doney. Size: 27 × 36¼ in. Inscribed: "U.S. Senate Chamber / Designed by J. Whitehorne / Engraved by T. Doney / Engraved from daguerreotype likenesses in the National Miniature Gallery / Printed Powell & Co." Courtesy of The New-York Historical Society.   291

133. JOHN QUINCY ADAMS. Engraving, presumably after Fig. 131, by James Bannister (1821–1901). Size: 4 × 3¼ in. Inscribed: "Engraved by J. Bannister / John Quincy Adams / Engraved for the Columbian Magazine." Reproduced from *Columbian Magazine*, vol. 9, no. 6, frontispiece (June 1848).   292

134. JOHN QUINCY ADAMS. Engraving, probably after Fig. 131, by unknown artist. Size: 2⅝ × 1⅞ in. Inscribed, over: "John Quincy Adams / Born in Massachusetts July 11th 1767. / Died in the Capitol in Washington Feb. 23d. 1848 / Aged 81 Years"; and under: "Sold by Edwd. P. Whaites, cor Cortlandt St. & Broadway." Courtesy of The New-York Historical Society.   293

135. JOHN QUINCY ADAMS. Photographic copy of daguerreotype by Mathew B. Brady (ca. 1823–1896); 1847. Size: 3⅝ × 2⅛ in. Courtesy of the Massachusetts Historical Society.   294

136. JOHN QUINCY ADAMS. Engraving after Fig. 135 by William Wellstood (1819–1900); 1857. Size: 5⅞ × 4⅞ in. Inscribed: "Engd by W. Wellstood / John Quincy Adams [auto.] / The last Portrait taken from Life / Johnson, Fry & Co. Publishers N.Y. / Entered according to Act of Congress A D 1857 by Johnson, Fry & Co in the clerk's office of the district court of the southern district of New York." Courtesy of Andrew Oliver.   296

137. JOHN QUINCY ADAMS. Engraving, after a painting by Alonzo Chappel taken from Fig. 135 or 136, by unknown artist; 1861. Size: 7½ × 5¼ in. Inscribed: "J. Q. Adams / From the original painting by Chappel in the possession of the publishers / Johnson Fry & Co. Publishers New York / Entered according to act of Congress A D 1861 by Johnson Fry & Co in the clerks office of the district court for the southern district of   297

Acknowledgments

No volume such as this could be undertaken without expecting—or completed without receiving—aid and comfort from the many owners, librarians, curators, and historians in whose possession or within whose ken lie the portraits or rumors of portraits described herein. The ready and helpful responses of such keepers of this portion of our national heritage have been among the things that have made the task of accumulating detail a pleasure rather than a frustration. The kindness of over sixty owners of the one hundred and forty-odd likenesses reproduced is noted in the List of Illustrations and gratefully acknowledged here.

The resources of the Frick Art Reference Library, The New-York Historical Society, the Massachusetts Historical Society, the Boston Athenæum, and the New York Society Library, and the courtesy and help of their staffs have proved invaluable.

The Editor in Chief of the Adams Papers, L. H. Butterfield, his Associate Editor, Marc Friedlaender, and his predecessor as Associate Editor, Wendell D. Garrett, of *Antiques* magazine, together with their assistants from time to time, Gaspare Saladino, D. Maureen Clegg, Mrs. Sarah Morrison, Nancy Jane Simkin, Patricia O'R. Drechsler, and B. Richard Burg, have allowed me to draw not only on their seemingly limitless knowledge of the Adams Family but on their almost instant recall of where references and notations could be found and have thus on many occasions at the expense of their time and effort produced in a short time what would have taken me months to find. To each I am grateful.

The chronologies at the head of the first five chapters, selective, brief, but instructive, were prepared, in the main, by Mr. Friedlaender and wholly under his oversight. To his keen eye and wise judgment I also owe the elimination of many curious inconsistencies that had escaped me, the solving of difficult problems of dating some likenesses, and the cutting of several Gordian knots. The errors that remain are mine.

Others, whose names appear below, whose help has been generous and valuable but which cannot be stated in detail will, I hope, by this mention of them know that their kindness is appreciated: C. Kingsley Adams, J. R. Baker, Whitfield J. Bell Jr., Mrs. John Howard Benson, Francis Blake, Marion V. Brewington, Roger Butterfield, Charles D. Childs, Mary Comstock, Clement E. Conger, Louisa Dresser, Wilson

G. Duprey, Malcolm Freiberg, Donald T. Gibbs, Robert G. Goelet, James Gregory, Mrs. Wilhelmina S. Harris, Richard L. Hayes, Mrs. Henry W. Howell Jr., Mrs. Lee Jordan, Milton Kaplan, Cuthbert Lee, Martin Leifer, Thomas N. Maytham, Mrs. Ann Louise C. McLaughlin, Ray Nash, Dorothy E. Newton, the Reverend F. P. Prucha, S.J., Edgar P. Richardson, Stephen T. Riley, Stuart C. Sherman, J. George Stewart, F. Charles Taylor, Opal Thornburg, Jack L .Vrooman, Nicholas B. Wainwright, Louise Wallman, Mrs. T. J. Yost, and Joseph B. Zywicki.

Editorial Method and Apparatus

Although it stands as an independent work, this book is the second in a series of volumes treating Adams family portraits, and the Portrait series is, in turn, a part of the over-all Belknap Press edition of *The Adams Papers.* Accordingly, while the contents and structure of the present volume markedly vary from those in other published series, and while it should be cited by its own individual title, it incorporates all the features of *Adams Papers* editorial practice, as well as format, that it feasibly can.

In the first three sections (1–3) of the six sections of this Guide are listed, respectively, the arbitrary devices used for clarifying the text, the code names for designating prominent members of the Adams family, and the symbols describing the various kinds of MS originals used or referred to, that are employed throughout *The Adams Papers* in all its series and parts. In the final three sections (4–6) are listed, respectively, only those symbols designating institutions holding original materials, the various abbreviations and conventional terms, and the short titles of books and other works, that occur in *Portraits of John Quincy Adams and his Wife.*

1. TEXTUAL DEVICES

[. . .], [. . . .]	One or two words missing and not conjecturable.
[. . .]¹, [. . . .]¹	More than two words missing and not conjecturable; subjoined footnote estimates amount of missing matter.
[ ]	Number or part of a number missing or illegible. Amount of blank space inside brackets approximates the number of missing or illegible digits.
[roman]	Conjectural reading for missing or illegible matter. A question mark is inserted before the closing bracket if the conjectural reading is seriously doubtful.
⟨*italic*⟩	Matter canceled in the manuscript but restored in our text.
[*italic*]	Editorial insertion in the text.

2. ADAMS FAMILY CODE NAMES

First Generation

JA	John Adams (1735–1826)
AA	Abigail Smith (1744–1818), *m.* JA 1764

Second Generation

JQA	John Quincy Adams (1767–1848), son of JA and AA
LCA	Louisa Catherine Johnson (1775–1852), *m.* JQA 1797
CA	Charles Adams (1770–1800), son of JA and AA
Mrs. CA	Sarah Smith (1769–1828), sister of WSS, *m.* CA 1795
TBA	Thomas Boylston Adams (1772–1832), son of JA and AA
Mrs. TBA	Ann Harrod (1774–1846), *m.* TBA 1805
AA2	Abigail Adams (1765–1813), daughter of JA and AA, *m.* WSS 1786
WSS	William Stephens Smith (1755–1816), brother of Mrs. CA

Third Generation

GWA	George Washington Adams (1801–1829), son of JQA and LCA
JA2	John Adams (1803–1834), son of JQA and LCA
Mrs. JA2	Mary Catherine Hellen (1807–1870), *m.* JA2 1828
CFA	Charles Francis Adams (1807–1886), son of JQA and LCA
ABA	Abigail Brown Brooks (1808–1889), *m.* CFA 1829
ECA	Elizabeth Coombs Adams (1808–1903), daughter of TBA and Mrs. TBA

Fourth Generation

JQA2	John Quincy Adams (1833–1894), son of CFA and ABA
CFA2	Charles Francis Adams (1835–1915), son of CFA and ABA
HA	Henry Adams (1838–1918), son of CFA and ABA
MHA	Marian Hooper (1842–1885), *m.* HA 1872
BA	Brooks Adams (1848–1927), son of CFA and ABA
LCA2	Louisa Catherine Adams (1831–1870), daughter of CFA and ABA, *m.* Charles Kuhn 1854
MA	Mary Adams (1845–1928), daughter of CFA and ABA, *m.* Henry Parker Quincy 1877

Fifth Generation

CFA3	Charles Francis Adams (1866–1954), son of JQA2
HA2	Henry Adams (1875–1951), son of CFA2

3. DESCRIPTIVE SYMBOLS

Dft	draft
FC	file copy
LbC	letterbook copy
MS, MSS	manuscript, manuscripts
RC	recipient's copy

4. LOCATION SYMBOLS

DLC	Library of Congress
DNA	National Archives
MBAt	Boston Athenæum

MHi	Massachusetts Historical Society
NHi	New-York Historical Society
PHi	Historical Society of Pennsylvania
PPAmP	American Philosophical Society

5. OTHER ABBREVIATIONS AND CONVENTIONAL TERMS

Adams Papers

> Manuscripts and other materials, 1639–1889, in the Adams Manuscript Trust collection given to the Massachusetts Historical Society in 1956 and enlarged by a few additions of family papers since then. Citations in the present edition are simply by date of the original document if the original is in the main chronological series of the Papers and therefore readily found in the microfilm edition of the Adams Papers (see below). The location of materials in the Letterbooks and the Miscellany is given more fully, and often, if the original would be hard to locate, by the microfilm reel number.

Adams Papers Editorial Files

> Other materials in the Adams Papers editorial office, Massachusetts Historical Society. These include photoduplicated documents (normally cited by the location of the originals), photographs, correspondence, and bibliographical and other aids compiled and accumulated by the editorial staff.

Adams Papers, Fourth Generation

> Adams manuscripts dating 1890 or later, now separated from the Trust collection and administered by the Massachusetts Historical Society on the same footing with its other manuscript collections.

Adams Papers, Microfilms

> The corpus of the Adams Papers, 1639–1889, as published on microfilm by the Massachusetts Historical Society, 1954–1959, in 608 reels. Cited in the present work, when necessary, by reel number. Available in research libraries throughout the United States and in a few libraries in Europe.

The Adams Papers

> The present edition in letterpress, published by The Belknap Press of Harvard University Press.

6. SHORT TITLES OF WORKS FREQUENTLY CITED

AA, *Letters*, ed. CFA, 1848

> *Letters of Mrs. Adams, the Wife of John Adams. With an Introductory Memoir by Her Grandson, Charles Francis Adams*, 4th edn., Boston, 1848.

Bemis, *JQA*

Samuel Flagg Bemis, *John Quincy Adams*, New York, 1949–1956; 2 vols. [Vol. 1:] *John Quincy Adams and the Foundations of American Foreign Policy;* [vol. 2:] *John Quincy Adams and the Union.*

Boston Athenæum, *Catalogue of JQA's Books*

A Catalogue of the Books of John Quincy Adams Deposited in the Boston Athenæum, with Notes on Books, Adams Seals and Book-Plates by Henry Adams, with an Introduction by Worthington Chauncey Ford, Boston, 1948.

Cappon, ed., *Adams-Jefferson Letters*

Lester J. Cappon, ed., *The Adams-Jefferson Letters: The Complete Correspondence between Thomas Jefferson and Abigail and John Adams*, Chapel Hill, 1959; 2 vols.

CFA, *Diary*

Diary of Charles Francis Adams, Cambridge, 1964– . Vols. 1–2, ed. Aïda DiPace Donald and David Donald; vols. 3–4, ed. Marc Friedlaender and L. H. Butterfield.

Dunlap, *Arts of Design*, ed. Bayley and Goodspeed

William Dunlap, *A History of the Rise and Progress of the Arts of Design in the United States*, ed. Frank W. Bayley and Charles E. Goodspeed, Boston, 1918; 3 vols.

Groce and Wallace, *Dict. Amer. Artists*

George C. Groce and David H. Wallace, *The New-York Historical Society's Dictionary of Artists in America, 1564–1860*, New Haven and London, 1957.

HA2, *Birthplaces*

Henry Adams, *The Birthplaces of Presidents John and John Quincy Adams in Quincy, Massachusetts*, Quincy, 1936.

Jefferson, *Writings*, ed. Lipscomb and Bergh

Andrew A. Lipscomb and Albert Ellery Bergh, eds., *The Writings of Thomas Jefferson*, Washington, 1903–1904; 20 vols.

JQA, *Memoirs*

Memoirs of John Quincy Adams, Comprising Portions of His Diary from 1795–1848, ed. Charles Francis Adams, Philadelphia, 1874–1877; 12 vols.

JQA, *Writings*

The Writings of John Quincy Adams, ed. Worthington C. Ford, New York, 1913–1917; 7 vols.

Niles' Register

Niles' Weekly Register, Baltimore, 1811–1849.

NYHS, *Colls., Pubn. Fund Ser.*
New-York Historical Society, *Collections, Publication Fund Series*, New York, 1868–

NYHS, *Quart.*
New-York Historical Society, *Quarterly.*

Oliver, *Portraits of JA and AA*
Andrew Oliver, *Portraits of John and Abigail Adams*, Cambridge, 1967.

Park, *Gilbert Stuart*
Lawrence Park, comp., *Gilbert Stuart: An Illustrated Descriptive List of His Works*, New York, 1926; 4 vols.

PMHB
Pennsylvania Magazine of History and Biography.

Quincy, *Figures of the Past*
Josiah Quincy [1802–1882], *Figures of the Past, from the Leaves of Old Journals*, ed. M. A. DeWolfe Howe, Boston, 1926.

Richardson, ed., *Messages and Papers*
James Daniel Richardson, ed., *A Compilation of the Messages and Papers of the Presidents, 1789–1897*, Washington, 1896–1899; 10 vols.

F. W. Seward, *Seward*
Frederick W. Seward, *William H. Seward: An Autobiography from 1801 to 1834. With a Memoir . . . and . . . Letters, 1831–1846; Seward at Washington . . . 1846–1861; Seward at Washington . . . 1861–1872*, New York, 1891; 3 vols.

Wilson, *Where Amer. Independence Began*
Daniel Munro Wilson, *Where American Independence Began: Quincy, Its Famous Group of Patriots; Their Deeds, Homes, and Descendants*, 2d edn., Boston and New York, 1904.

Portraits of John Quincy Adams
and His Wife

Introduction

"What would not the modern student of history give," wrote the Reverend Elias Brewster Hillard in 1865, as he gathered together for publication the likenesses of the last seven surviving soldiers of the Revolution, "for the privilege of looking on the faces of the men who fought for Grecian liberty at Marathon, or stood with Leonidas at Thermopylæ. With what interest would every lover of liberty regard the pictures of the last of the Scots who were with Bruce at Bannock-burn, or of the Swiss who followed Tell, or of Cromwell's Ironsides!"[1] It is with this cry in mind that we produce here the likenesses, from youth to old age, of one of those who took such an active and vital part in the rise and progress of our Republic to a first position among the nations.

The spring of 1839 furnished, in its way, as characteristic a pattern of the activity of John Quincy Adams as any other period of his life could supply. In addition to the hectic activity normally attendant on the affairs of the Congress, Adams was engaged in preparing an address to be delivered before The New-York Historical Society on the last day of April; the occasion, the fiftieth anniversary of the inauguration of his early friend and benefactor George Washington as first President of the United States. "The subject," Adams wrote, "is rugged with insurmountable difficulties. My reputation, my age, my decaying faculties, have all warned me to decline the task. Yet I cannot resist the pressing and repeated invitations of the Society. The day was a real epocha in our history; but to seize, and present in bold relief all its peculiar characters would require a younger hand and a brighter mind." After ten more days of composition: "I shall have no quiet of mind till it is over, and perhaps then less than ever."[2]

During the whole period in which he was so occupied he was sitting regularly for his portrait. A brief note in the diary describing a last sitting just given to the painter S. M. Charles mentions the fact that he had already had thirty-four portraits painted during his life. This latter subject was fresh in his mind, despite other and clearly more pressing concerns. A list of all these portraits, prepared in his own hand on that same day, 20 April 1839, appears, not in his diary itself, but on a paper later bound up in one of his volumes of miscellany,

[1] E. B. Hillard, *The Last Men of the Revolution*, ed. Wendell D. Garrett, Barre, Mass., 1968, p. 24.
[2] JQA, Diary, 23 March, 3 April 1839.

labeled "Rubbish."[3] It was probably compiled in a moment of relaxation between his congressional duties, his sitting to Charles (which probably prompted the compilation), and the preparation of the memorial address. The list, illustrated opposite in facsimile, is without heading or any accompanying explanation.

It would be remarkable if a list, constructed under such circumstances and when Adams was seventy-two years old, were not only complete but accurate. It was neither. It omitted some portraits, it included others that had not been painted, and it contained errors in the date of certain paintings. But it is nevertheless an extraordinary register of the painting of almost three dozen portraits of one man over a period of more than half a century.

In a diary entry several years later, 15 August 1843, at the time he was sitting to Mr. Franklin White, who, as Adams said, "can scarcely claim to be called an artist," he gives the latest score of his portraits:

This is about the 45th time that I have sitten for my pictures, and I question whether another man lives who has been so wofully and so variously bedaubed as I have been. There is no picture of my childhood but from the age of 16, when I was caricatured in crayons by Mr. Schmidt for four ducats, down to this my 77th year, when Mr. White has lampooned me in oil, scarcely a year has passed away, without a crucifixion of my face and form by some painter, engraver, or sculptor. A miniature in a bracelet for my mother, painted at the Hague in 1795 by an Englishman named Parker, now in the possession of my son John's widow — Copley's Portrait of 1796 — Stuart's head of 1825, and Durand's of 1836 painted for Mr. Luman Reed, are the only ones worthy of being preserved, with the Busts by Persico, Greenough and Powers. The features of my old age are such as I have no wish to have transmitted to the memory of the next age. They are harsh and stern far beyond the true portraiture of the heart; and there is no ray of intellect in them to redeem their repulsive severity.

Despite Adams' protestations to the contrary, the 1839 list confirms his genuine, indeed overriding, interest in preserving, not only for himself and his family but for his country's history, his own likeness—as it was throughout his life, each year of which he knew was significant in the life of that country. It had been the same with his father, continually protesting, yet sitting to every artist, save one, who sought to take his likeness. The son in his turn had seen to it that the great Stuart had painted his father in his ninetieth year, to

[3] Same, 20 April 1839; "Rubbish," 4:581 (Adams Papers, Microfilms, Reel No. 52).

Schmidt	The Hague	Crayons	1783
Parker	The Hague	Miniature	1795
Copley	London	Kit Cat	1796
	London	Miniature	1796
Leslie	London		1816
	Ghent		1815
Stewart	Boston		1818
	New York		1817
Peale	Washington		1819
Cardelli	Do	Bust	1818
King	Do	Engraved	1820
Harding	Boston		1824
Wood	Washington	Miniature	1825
Sully	Do		1825
Stewart	Boston		1825
Browere	Washington		1826
Wheeler	Quincy		1827
Greenough	Washington	Bust	1825
Gimbrede	Washington		1827
Furst	Washington	Medal	1825
Harding	Washington		1829
Persico	Washington	Miniature	1829
John Cranch	Washington		1834
Chapman			1833
Durand	Washington		1835
Persico	Washington	Bust	1836
Rembrant Peale	Washington		1837
Powers	Washington	Bust	1837
Durand	Quincy		1836

Mr Towle	Washington		1837
Clevenger	Washington	Bust	1838
Englishman	Do	Mask	1838
S. M. Charles			1839
Page	Boston		1838

preserve for posterity the features of the old patriarch, the friend of Washington, of Jefferson, of Rush; a signer of the Declaration of Independence and one of the central figures attendant at the birth of the Great Republic. This historical sense of the value of a portrait likeness not only to one's descendants but as a permanent historical record and part of his country's heritage persisted throughout Adams' life. Nothing else can explain the hundreds of weary hours he gave to the scores of painters who besought them.

And so it was, in a moment of leisure in that busy day in the spring of 1839, that Adams looked back and recalled (and recorded), maybe with a touch of vanity, perhaps with some wistful pride as well as surprise, the many times he had sat for his portrait. First, long ago in Holland, when only sixteen, he was painted "in his best coat and powdered wig," then at the time of his marriage, later as Envoy, Ambassador, as Secretary of State, as President of the United States, and for almost a decade as Member of Congress from Massachusetts. These likenesses had been taken by the popular portraitists of the day—Copley, Stuart, C. W. Peale and his gifted son Rembrandt, Leslie, Cardelli, C. B. King, Harding, Sully, Browere, Greenough, Powers, and Durand—names that fill the pages of the history of portraiture in America during the early decades of the 19th century. At an age already beyond his biblical allotment, how could he know how much still lay ahead of him? Yet to be painted were the great and lasting likenesses of "the Old Man Eloquent," as he had been dubbed in the House in 1836: those to be done by Hudson, Marchant, Lambdin, G. C. Bingham, Eastman Johnson, G. P. A. Healy, J. C. King, and, inevitable as inventive ingenuity developed, those by the enterprising, talented followers of Daguerre: Brady of Washington, Southworth of Boston, and a host of other operators. By the time Daguerre's magic black box nudged its way firmly into the field of portraiture, Adams would have sat to artists for more than sixty likenesses, in every decade of his life except the first and third—one in his teens, four in his twenties, three in his forties, twelve in his fifties, fourteen in his sixties, and twenty-nine in his last decade.

The richness of the iconographic material available can perhaps be best appreciated by being considered in relation to several arbitrary divisions of Adams' life. Thus, this volume has six basic divisions reflected in its chapter titles: I, "Auspicious Beginnings," from Adams' youth to the end of his father's Presidency—during which period some seven portraits of Adams and his wife were taken; II, "The Diplomat," embracing the years 1801–1817, during which he was Senator, Professor, and Minister—approximately seven portraits in these years; III, "The Secretary of State," 1817–1825—fourteen portraits; IV, "The President," 1825–1829—nine portraits; V, "The Representative," 1830–1848—in excess of thirty, by far the largest number of portraits; and VI, "Old Man Eloquent in Daguerreotype," which includes a portion of the prior period but deals with photographic likenesses or painted or engraved copies of photographic likenesses. Each of the first five chapters commences with a brief chronology of Adams' life during the period, so that the likenesses dealt with and his changing appearance over those years may be seen in relation to his personal and political activity at the time. Within each chapter the likenesses are, to the extent practicable, dealt with chronologically, an obvious difficulty being that on occasions several portraits were in train at the same time, sometimes in the same studio.

With but few exceptions Adams had only the most disparaging remarks to make about the portraits of himself, a habit inherited from his father. This can be illustrated by a few of his comments taken from the chapters that follow, the artist's name in parenthesis following the comment on his work: "As a work of art, it rates too low to have any value elsewhere" (Schmidt); "Indifferent as a work of art" (Van Huffel); "We found that he had totally failed in the likeness" (Cardelli); "He has made a Caricature of my Portrait" (C. W. Peale); "It is *horribly* like" (Clevenger); "It has no pleasant aspect" (Page); "His likeness is already a failure" (Franquinet, after a first sitting); "The most hideous caricature that I have ever beheld" (Beard); "A hideous likeness" (Gibert); "All hideous"; "Too true to the original" (Daguerreotypes). In 1831 he wrote, "I have grown shy, and reluctant at exposing my infirmities to the men of the Palette and brush."[4] Yet he sat readily to all who asked, often at great personal inconvenience and at the expense of what must have been precious time.

Adams lived in the generation which benefited, or suffered, from the transition from painted portraits to photographs—the transition from a likeness which reflected the viewpoint and perhaps the philosophy of the artist, to the stark reality of the mechanical, photographic process. And we discover that the portraitists, with whatever imaginative means they used, produced likenesses that not only compared fairly with the photograph but also added the subtle nuances of gentleness or severity that reflected the mood in which they found the sitter at the time.

[4] JQA to Caroline Amelia de Windt, 20 Aug. 1831 (MHi:de Windt Coll.).

In 1833 Adams gave to a friend (and to us) a revealing self-characterization:

A warm heart I once had, and my manners were not then cold, nor had I then been sixty years cribbed in the thrilling regions of thick ribbed ice which encase a heartless world. A man might have a fund of caloric fresh from the lowest depth of Tartarus, to retain even a temperate portion of it after three score years of attrition with this best of all possible worlds as Candide calls it. My manners and my heart grew cold together, because I found that warmheartedness was a waste of good seed in thankless soil; and after less than one half your intercourse with mankind (and womankind) I brought myself to the conclusion that Justice, and Benevolence, and humanity, and kind-offices, were virtues due from man to man as a rational and responsible being, but that warmheartedness was not of the number—and that Temperance, Prudence and Fortitude selfish and cold hearted as they all are, stand quite upon a level with the others in the class of virtues or moral accomplishments. I did not, like Genl. Charles Lee, despise Prudence as a Rascally virtue. I did not, for here and there an injustice or a perfidy that I suffered from man or woman, suffer myself to fall into misanthropy—much less into *misoguny* (I suppose you do not know that this barbarous word means woman-hating). I took mankind as you must take your wife, for better for worse, and believed that the secret of dealing with my fellow creatures of my own times, was to keep my heart and my judgment always *cool*. I have not always succeeded, for

> Who can hold a fire brand in his hand
> By thinking of the frosty Caucasus,

but I did graduate the thermometer of my heart according to the climate in which I was to live, and my manners were but the scale upon which the graduation was marked.[5]

With certain notable exceptions, the likenesses of John Quincy Adams that have been preserved are not outstanding as works of art. We can, however, agree with him that in most instances they are "like." Too true to the original he found them, but it is this very fact which gives us the assurance that this extraordinary collection of likenesses does indeed reveal how the man appeared from the age of sixteen in 1783 until his death in 1848.

The record would not be complete without recording the known portraits of Adams' wife, Louisa Catherine, several of which were taken before her marriage. They are illustrated and described, as nearly as feasible, chronologically with those of her husband. Their number is not large, and they do not have the extraordinary variety

---

[5] JQA to Christopher Hughes, 26 Sept. 1833 (LbC, Adams Papers).

and progression shown in the likenesses of her husband; yet they do show the transition from a vivacious young girl, bright and happy, into her middle age, when she appears with a wistful, sad expression —what her son Charles termed "a sorrowful appearance too common to her."

Her youth had been gay and lived in a handsome style before her father's financial reverses. But her years as Adams' wife were fraught with difficulties—surmounted, to be sure, but which took their toll. She suffered in her travels and residence in Berlin and later in Russia. Her temperament and tastes were not at all those of her husband. Yet she played her part and was an accomplished hostess; her parties in Washington were always popular and gay occasions. "Mrs. Adams' Ball" for General Jackson in January 1824, on the anniversary of the Battle of New Orleans, was a good example and one long remembered. Her great grief of course was the tragic death in 1829 of her eldest and favorite son, George Washington Adams. She had scarcely recovered from this when she was thrown back again into another score of years of life in Washington during her husband's terms as Representative. She stood with him throughout these years, but with failing health and a desire to return to the ease of retirement. In the end, it was she who was left behind, to survive her husband for four years.

We could have wished for likenesses of Louisa in her later years to match the many fascinating ones of her husband, but none is known. We are nevertheless fortunate to have several pairs of portraits of them, taken at the same time, one before marriage, one when he was Ambassador at the Court of St. James's, one when he was Secretary of State, and silhouettes made during their White House years.

There are two themes that are repeated many times in the J. Q. Adams portraits, repeated so often as to make it clear that they appear at Adams' request and not at the instance of the artist. A book in hand, with a finger between the pages is not unknown as an artist's prop; Stuart, for example, used it in his handsome portrait of Horace Binney now hanging in the National Gallery in Washington. But in six of Adams' portraits he appears with a book in hand or on his lap, and in three instances, widely separated in date, he is shown with his finger between the pages of the book (Figs. 22, 48, 108 and its replicas). In addition, in many engravings or lithographs of portraits which showed only the head and shoulders of the sitter, the engraver

7

has added a book in hand and in several instances a finger between the pages (Figs. 128, 129). That this was a familiar and characteristic pose for the man rather than an artistic device may find support from Charles Bird King's portrait of Adams' son George in which the young man of twenty-two is portrayed holding a book with his finger between the pages, perhaps unconsciously imitating his father.[6]

A ready explanation of this theme is found in Adams' great love of books. He was a voracious reader and collector. His taste was catholic. The Bible was a daily staple; the classics, astronomy, poetry, and general literature absorbed what time he had free from his professional or social obligations. Numberless are the entries in his diary and the shelves holding the books he gathered over the years, now preserved in the two-storied Stone Library adjoining the Old House in Quincy—all attesting his consuming interest and occupation in reading and collecting. It is not surprising, then, to see him depicted so often as if he had been but momentarily interrupted by the artist and intended shortly to resume his reading.

The other and more significant theme that is repeated in several of the portraits is the device of the Lyre and Eagle Seal which Adams adopted and made both public and private use of. It meant so much to him that it is worthy of more than a passing word. His own explanation of the symbolism of the device is given in his diary entry for 7 September 1816:

In the Grecian Mythology, Orpheus is said to have charmed Lions and Tygers, the most ferocious wild Beasts, and to have drawn after him the very trees of the forest and the Rocks of the desart by the harmony of his Lyre. Its power was said to have triumphed even over the tremendous deities of the infernal regions, over the monster Cerberus, the Furies, and Pluto himself. The meaning of this Allegory is explained by Horace, De Arte Poetica, v. 390. Orpheus was a Legislator whose eloquence charmed the rude and savage men of his age to associate together in the State of civil Society, to submit to the salutary restraints of Law, and to unite together in the worship of their Creator. It was the Lyre of Orpheus that civilized Savage Man. It was only in Harmony that the first human political institutions could be founded. After the Death of Orpheus, his Lyre was placed among the Constellations, and there, according to the Astronomics of Manilius, still possesses its original charm, constituting by its concords the Music of the Spheres, and drawing by its attraction the whole orb of Heaven around with its own revolution. It is the Application of this Fable, and of this passage of Manilius, to the United States, the American political Constellation, that forms the device of the Seal.

[6] CFA, *Diary*, vol. 3, facing p. 314.

Adams then quotes the passage from Manilius (*Astronomicon*, i, 332 ff.) with a translation—perhaps his own[7]—and continues:

The modern Astronomers have connected a Vulture with the Constellation of the Lyre, and it is marked upon the Charts of Bode's Uranographia by the name of Vultur et Lyra [Fig. A].[8] Instead of that bird, by a slight poetical license, I have assumed the American Eagle as the bearer of the Lyre. The thirteen original Stars form a border round the Seal. The Stars marked upon the Lyre and on the wings of the Eagle are placed in the relative positions, as they may be seen by the naked eye in the Constellation of Lyra. The motto from Manilius [NUNC SIDERA DUCIT] is upon the Lyre itself. The moral application of the emblem is, that the same power of harmony which originally produced the institutions of civil government to regulate the Association of individual men, now presides in the federal association of the American States. That Harmony is the Soul of their combination. That their force consists in their Union; and that while thus United, it will be their destiny to revolve in harmony with the whole world by the attractive influence of their Union. It is the Lyre of Orpheus that now leads the Stars, as it originally drew after it rocks and trees. It is harmony that now binds in its influence the American States, as it originally drew individual men from the solitude of Nature to the assemblages which formed States and Nations. The Lesson of the emblem is *Union*.

Some few years later he noted in his diary that he was determined never to use his "seal-at-arms" to any public instrument, heraldic

---

[7] The passage and its translation read:

"At Lyra deductis per
 coelum cornibus inter
Sidera conspicitur, qua
 quondam ceperat Orpheus
Omne quod attigerat cantu,
 manesque per ipsos
Fecit iter, domuitque
 infernas carmine leges.
Hinc, coelestis honos,
 similisque potentia causae.
Tunc, silvas et saxa trahens,
 Nunc Sidera Ducit,
Et rapit immensum mundi
 revolubilis orbem."

"The Lyre of Orpheus,
 with erected horns,
Next in the Sky
 the starry world adorns;
That Lyre which once
 with fascinating spell
Tam'd the dread Lord,
 and tyrant Laws of Hell.
With soft compulsion
 won the Master's way
From Death's dire regions
 to the realms of day.
Nor yet, transferr'd
 in glory to the skies,
Has lost the power
 to draw, by kindred ties.
Then Rocks and Groves
 obey'd its magic force;
Now, of the Starry Orbs,
 it leads the course;
Extends its charm
 to Heaven's remotest bound,
And rolling, whirls
 the Universe around."

[8] Johann Elert Bode, *Uranographia sive astrorum descriptio*, Berlin, 1801, plate 8.

seals being "inconsistent with our republican institutions," adding, "I have substituted in their stead the Seal of my own device—The Constellation of Eagle and Lyra, with the motto from Manilius [Fig. C]. ... I first used it for the exchange of Ratifications of the Convention of 1802 with Mr. Onis [on 21 December 1818]."[9] The same device and motto were also used on United States passports (Fig. B), doubtless at his instance, from as early as 1822 to at least 1830. That this device was emblematic of Adams' whole public career is evidenced by a passage in his letter to Robert Walsh Jr. in 1829. The letter was con-

[9] Diary, 26 Jan. 1819.

cerned with the Hartford Convention and, after reciting some of the matters relating to that Convention, continued:

This, My dear Sir, is History—as much as the Newburgh letters or Aaron Burr's descent of the Mississippi. The federalism of Washington, Union, and Internal Improvement have been the three hinges upon which my political life and fortunes, good and bad have turned. Upon these I have risen, by these I fall,

> "Yet bate I not a jot of heart or hope."

My biographer if I have one must go to the Papers of Publicola in 1791, to those of Marcellus, Columbus, and Barneveld in 1793 and 4, to my Speech in November 1803 and my Resolutions in January 1804 on the Louisiana Cession. To my internal improvement Resolution in 1807. To my Embargo Letter, and my Report on the case of John Smith in 1808, and to my Commencement Oration of 1787, my 4th of July Orations of 1793 and 1821 and my Plymouth Discourse of 1802 for my principles. My inaugural Address, and my four Annual Messages to Congress are but Commentaries upon these—and the Seal which you will find upon this Letter is a Pythagorean Emblem of my whole political System.[10]

An impression of that device appears at the end of this Introduction;[11]

[10] 18 March 1829 (LbC, Adams Papers).
[11] Regrettably, the seal itself as fashioned by R. W. Silvester in 1816 has disappeared from view. It was last reported in 1938 in the estate of Brooks Adams (Boston Athenæum, *Catalogue of JQA's Books*, p. 146).

it or various elements of it were introduced by the artists in the portraits appearing as Figs. 22, 29, and 57; and it was presumably engraved on the watch fob so prominent in Figs. 32, 33, and 78.

Adams' popularity, if we can use that word, his hold on the affection of some and the admiration of most of the people increased with his age, until at the end he appeared a very monument to faithful, patriotic devotion. About a year before he died, as he entered the House, then in session, for the first time following a debilitating illness, the Speaker rose to his feet out of respect, and with him the entire membership of the House, friend and foe alike.

Small wonder that people were interested in his likeness. Who else could boast of sixty-three years of service to his country, who else with such a record could carry on to the bitter end, dying at his post? "The Old Man Eloquent," they called him; they may not all have agreed with his stand on the many issues of the day, but they knew his record for integrity, faith, courage, and constancy, and, because of the extraordinary variety and extent of his portraiture, we can now know, as did his contemporaries, what he looked like.

His career was eloquently epitomized by Senator Hoar at a banquet honoring Senator Henry L. Dawes of Massachusetts upon his retirement in 1893. Hoar began his memorial by listing in order Massachusetts' great Senators, and, after naming Benjamin Goodhue, continued:

Then comes John Quincy Adams, who left the Senate, after years of illustrious public service, in 1808, but to begin another public service of forty years, still more illustrious. He served his country in every department of public occupation. He was Minister to five great Powers in succession. . . . He negotiated and signed the Treaty of Ghent, the Commercial Treaty of 1815, the French Treaty of 1822, the Prussian Treaty, and the treaty which acquired Florida from Spain. He was Senator, Representative, Foreign Minister, Secretary of State and President. He breasted the stormy waves of the House of Representatives at the age of eighty, and when he died in the Capitol, he left no purer or loftier fame behind him.[12]

His is the likeness the following pages will disclose.

ANDREW OLIVER

---

[12] George F. Hoar, *Autobiography of Seventy Years*, N.Y., 1903, 1:229–230.

I

Auspicious Beginnings
1767–1801

"They should take him for my younger brother if they did not *know* him to be my son."

CHRONOLOGY OF JOHN QUINCY ADAMS' LIFE, 1767–1801

1767
July 11: Born in Braintree at the foot of Penn's Hill.

1775
June 17: Witnesses Battle of Bunker Hill with his mother (AA) from atop Penn's Hill.

1778
Feb.: Travels with father (JA) aboard the frigate *Boston* from Mount Wollaston to Bordeaux, thence to Paris, where JA serves as one of the American Commissioners; resides at Passy from 9 April and is enrolled in school there.

1779
March–June: Begins homeward journey with his father, moving from Paris to Nantes, Lorient, and St. Nazaire, awaiting passage to America.

June 17–Aug. 2: At sea, Lorient to Boston, aboard the frigate *La Sensible*.

Aug.–Nov.: In Braintree, among his family and friends.

Nov. 12: Begins to keep a diary, "A Journal by JQA/From America," not maintained with perfect regularity until 1795, whereafter there are virtually no gaps until his stroke in late 1845.

Nov. 13–Dec. 8: Accompanied by his brother Charles (CA), returns with JA to Europe aboard the frigate *La Sensible* from Boston to El Ferrol, Spain.

1780
Begins a program of translating from Latin and French into English.

Feb.: Arrives in Paris after an overland journey with his father from El Ferrol and resumes schooling there.

13

July–Aug.: Travels with his father and brother to the Netherlands, where JA endeavors to obtain a loan for the United States, and the boys are placed in a school in Amsterdam.

1781

Jan.: Is admitted to the University of Leyden.

July 7–Aug. 27: Travels with Francis Dana from Amsterdam to St. Petersburg. In St. Petersburg, serves as secretary and interpreter to Dana, appointed (but not formally received as) the American Minister.

1783

April: After travels through Finland to Stockholm, Copenhagen, and Hamburg, arrives at The Hague.

July: Is reunited with his father upon JA's arrival at The Hague. Painted in pastel by Schmidt (Fig. 1).

Aug.–Sept.: Father and son return to Paris where JA signs, with his fellow Commissioners, the Definitive Treaty with Great Britain.

Sept.–Oct.: Journeys with JA to London, where they take up residence, see the sights, and visit Bath.

1784

Jan.: Accompanies JA on a stormy crossing of the North Sea to The Hague.

July: Meets his mother and sister (AA2) in London, where they had arrived from Boston.

Aug.: The Adams family establishes residence at Auteuil, outside Paris, where JA serves with Franklin and Jefferson as a joint commissioner to negotiate treaties with European powers.

1785

May–July: Returns alone to the United States aboard the packet *Courrier de l'Amérique*, Lorient to New York. Resides at Haverhill with his aunt Elizabeth and her husband, the Reverend John Shaw, and prepares himself for admission with advanced standing to Harvard.

1786

March: Enters Harvard College as a member of the junior class; is elected to Phi Beta Kappa at the end of the academic year.

1787

July: Graduates from Harvard, delivering an oration at Commencement that is published in September in the *Columbian Magazine* of Philadelphia.

Sept. 7: Begins the study of law with Theophilus Parsons in Newburyport.

1788

June: Visits parents upon their return from Europe in their newly acquired residence in Braintree, the Vassall-Borland house.
July–Sept.: Attends commencement at Harvard and delivers oration to
the Phi Beta Kappa Society.

1789

Sept.: Following JA's installation as Vice-President, visits parents in New
York City.

1790

July: Concludes his three-year residence in Newburyport, during which
an affection for Mary Frazier becomes the first intense attachment
of his life and a source of lingering frustration.
Aug.: Opens a law office in Boston and resides there.

1791

June: Under the name "Publicola," begins to publish articles in the
Columbian Centinel attacking Thomas Paine's political theories and
defending JA's position as developed in his "Discourses on Davila"
and denounced by Jefferson.

1792

Protests Boston's anti-theater ordinances and defends the theater
in articles signed "Menander" in the *Columbian Centinel*; becomes
an original stockholder in the Boston Theatre, which opened in early
1794.

1793

As "Marcellus," opposes privateering and defends the policy of
neutrality; as "Columbus," denounces the Genêt mission in articles
in the *Columbian Centinel*. Delivers his first 4th of July Address at
Boston.

1794

May: Receives from President Washington appointment as Minister Resident to the Netherlands.
Sept. 17–Oct. 15: Sails from Boston to London on board the ship *Alfred,*
his brother Thomas (TBA) accompanying him as secretary.
Nov.: Establishes himself at The Hague as Minister.

1795

April: Painted in miniature by Parker (Fig. 6).

Oct.–Nov.: Proceeds to London following receipt of commission to exchange ratifications of Jay's Treaty with Great Britain.

1796

March–April: Sits to Copley (Fig. 11).

May 5: Becomes affianced to Louisa Catherine Johnson (LCA), daughter of American consul, Joshua Johnson, in London.

May 31: Returns to The Hague and to his duties as Minister Resident. Appointed Minister Plenipotentiary to Portugal, but remains at The Hague awaiting orders to proceed to Lisbon.

1797

June–July: Receives recall as Minister Resident and appointment by President JA as Minister Plenipotentiary to Prussia. At about this time LCA was painted by Barber (Fig. 9).

July–Oct.: In London where, on 26 July, he is married at the Church of All Hallows, Barking.

Nov.: Takes up duties as Minister in Berlin.

1799

Undertakes a verse translation of Wieland's *Oberon* and completes it in 1801.

July–Oct.: Travels with LCA in the German states.

1800

July–Oct.: Travels again with LCA in the German states, including Silesia. Begins to send literary contributions for publication in the *Port Folio*.

1801

Feb.: Receives word of the death of his brother CA and of the defeat of JA for reelection to the Presidency; determines to give up his diplomatic post and return to the United States.

April 12: His first child, a son, is born and christened George Washington (GWA).

July 8–Sept. 4: Aboard ship *America* from Hamburg to Philadelphia with wife and child.

Nov. 24: Arrives in Quincy after an absence of seven years.

ISAAK SCHMIDT (1740–1818)

In April 1783 John Quincy Adams, at age fifteen, returned to The Hague from St. Petersburg, where for the last twenty months he had lived as private secretary to Francis Dana, whose mission it was to negotiate on behalf of the United States a treaty of Armed Neutrality. Joined by his father in July, John Quincy returned with him the following month to Paris, in time for his father to take his part in signing the Definitive Treaty of Peace with England.

While at The Hague the young lad had resided with the family of Charles W. F. Dumas, a friend and adviser to the Americans and particularly to John Adams. As John Quincy later wrote in his diary: "It was the precise time of my change from boy to man, and has left indelible impressions upon my Memory."[1] He had apparently developed a *tendre* for Mademoiselle Dumas and whiled away the time by singing duets with her and playing the flute. His father is said to have written of him at the time, "He seems to be grown as a man; and the world says, they should take him for my younger brother if they did not *know* him to be my son."[2]

It was at some time during these few months at The Hague that the first surviving likeness of the younger Adams was taken (Fig. 1), "at the precise time" of his change from boy to man. Isaak Schmidt, the Amsterdam-born artist and one of the founders of the drawing academy at that city, drew in pastel or crayon this charming small portrait, scarcely 10 by 6½ inches in size, for which he received four ducats. We are told of Schmidt that, though he made several attempts at portrait painting, he did not live up to his own standards and so devoted his efforts to landscapes, painting in concert with his brother artist Juriaan Andriessen.

Adams gave the portrait to his sister Abigail, and she evidently kept it close by her. She wrote him that in her apartment in London "I have hung a picture intended for yourself, of which you have heretofore spoken to me. I would not mortify you by saying I think it a likeness nor Pay so Poor a compliment to my own judgment. However as it was intended for you I shall look upon it for you and derive some satisfaction from it, and at the same time wish it were better."[3]

---

[1] Entry of 22 June 1814.

[2] Undated note, apparently in the hand of Elizabeth Coombs Adams, after 1887 (Adams Papers). "There is in his [JQA's] manners, behavior, and countenance a strong resemblance to his papa," so Abigail Adams wrote to Elizabeth Cranch, 1 Aug. 1784, after her reunion with her husband and son in London (AA, *Letters,* ed. CFA, 1848, p. 186).

[3] AA2 to JQA, 4 July–11 Aug. 1785 (Adams Papers).

1. JOHN QUINCY ADAMS. PASTEL BY ISAAK SCHMIDT, 1783

The little portrait has dropped from sight, but was described in an article in *The Studio* when still at hand. "The head is powdered, but a lock of the dark hair is indistinctly seen falling down the boy's back in a queue, and tied with a black riband. The complexion is a fine blond, charmingly accented by the dark eyes and irregular arched eye-brows, while a slight cast in the left eye, with the faint roguish smile that plays about the mouth, add a certain piquancy, making the face very pleasant to look at. The coat is of pale blue silk, with a jabot of lace." [4]

When he was almost half a hundred years older, Adams wrote in his diary: "I received a letter from Mrs. DeWint today which I answered.... Mrs. DeWint gave to Lieut. T. B. Adams, on his last visit to Cedar Grove, a Portrait of me in Crayons, done by a German named Schmidt at the Hague in 1783 when I was 16 years old. I gave it afterwards to my sister from whom it descended to her daughter. Mrs. DeWint seems now to regret that she has given it away and she asks me for a Portrait of myself." [5] In his reply to his niece he remarked that he was "glad for the Picture's sake as well as for that of the original that it remains in the family." Then, like his father, derogatory of portraits of himself, he continued:

As a work of art, it rates too low to have any value elsewhere—And they who look at the bald head, the watery eye, and the wrinkled brow of this day, would search in vain for the strong likeness which it was said to exhibit when it was taken.... When I go to Washington next Winter, I will look up and send you an engraved Print from a Portrait of me by King [Fig. 41]. [6]

Adams' plan to send an engraving of his portrait by King to Mrs. de Windt in lieu of the pastel by Schmidt seems to have been changed, for the pastel did return at some date to the de Windt family. In 1887, when the article in *The Studio* appeared, it was said to belong to a granddaughter of Mrs. de Windt. [7]

To illustrate the article, an etching of the portrait was made by Sidney L. Smith (Fig. 2), an example of which has long hung in the Old House in Quincy. Smith, born in 1845, entered the engraving establishment of Joseph Andrews in Boston after the Civil War, and

[4] *The Studio*, New York, new series, 2:154 (March 1887).
[5] Entry of 20 Aug. 1831. The Lieutenant referred to was Thomas Boylston Adams Jr., son of John Quincy's brother. In the Army and stationed at West Point, N.Y., he was a frequent visitor at Cedar Grove, the Fishkill Landing home of his cousin Caroline A. de Windt, who gave him the portrait in the summer of 1830.
[6] JQA to Caroline Amelia de Windt, 20 Aug. 1831 (MHi:de Windt Coll.).
[7] The early history of the ownership of the portrait, as given in the text, was written on a paper label and pasted on the back of the painting. What remained in 1887 of the writing on the label is quoted in *The Studio* at p. 154.

some years later assisted John La Farge in decorating Boston's Trinity Church. He also designed stained glass windows, his work "always marked by taste and discretion." This etching certainly captures the charm and spirit of Schmidt's original and evidences marked ability. The etching was again reproduced, without acknowledgment to Smith or to *The Studio*, in Dorothie Bobbé, *Mr. and Mrs. John Quincy Adams* (New York, 1930), facing page 34.

The history of the original since 1887 is obscure. It was shown in, though not listed in the catalogue of, an exhibition entitled "Parade of Patriots" held at the Grand Central Art Galleries in New York from 21 March to 5 June 1942. It is believed to have been owned at that time by Mrs. George Seaman of Beacon-on-Hudson, New York, and was then photographed by Peter A. Juley and Sons, from which our illustration is derived. Whispers of its present existence in Westchester County have been heard, but it has so far eluded discovery.

At some period before 1825, the original was copied in gouache, approximately the same size, and the copy (Fig. 3) given by John Quincy Adams to his wife. Written on the back of the paper on which the copy is painted, in Adams' hand, appears the following somewhat ambiguous inscription:

> To my Dear Companion, —
> My portrait copied at
> the age of 16 with my best
> coat and powdered hair while
> in Holland with my Father, 1785
>
> 1825   J. Q. Adams

The word "copied" must have meant "painted." The date 1785 is but the result of a lapse of memory excusable after the passage of forty-two years. The identity of the copyist is unknown and there are gaps in the provenance of the copy itself. No record of it has been found from 1825 until 1926, when it turned up in the hands of Simon J. Schwartz of New Orleans. In 1934 it belonged to Erskine Hewitt and was then lent by him to an exhibition at The New-York Historical Society. At the Hewitt sale at Parke-Bernet Galleries on 18 October 1938, as item 1086, it fetched $105. Its next appearance was in 1955 in the hands of the late Forest H. Sweet of Boston. At his death it passed to Annie I. Grant of the New England Sanitarium, Stoneham, Massachusetts, who had taken care of Mr. Sweet in his last years, as part payment for her services to him. It was acquired by the present writer from her, through Goodspeed's Bookshop, in 1963.

The coloring of the copy conforms to the description of the origi-

3. JOHN QUINCY ADAMS.
GOUACHE BY AN UNKNOWN ARTIST, BEFORE 1825

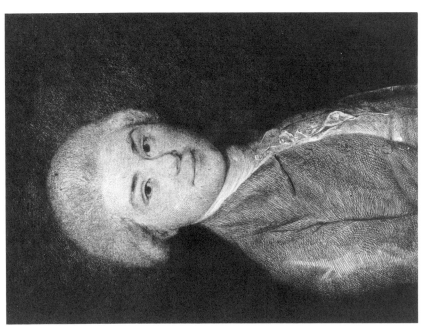

2. JOHN QUINCY ADAMS.
ENGRAVING BY SIDNEY L. SMITH, 1887

nal given above; the wavy powdered hair and pink cheeks, the "best" blue coat, and the lace jabot all combine to present a picture of the young lad full of warmth and charm.

EARLY MINIATURES

During the last decade of the 18th century several miniature likenesses were taken of John Quincy Adams and of Louisa Catherine Johnson, both before and after their marriage. Some have survived, others are known only through the records of diary entries or correspondence. Although in date of production they straddle Copley's portrait of John Quincy Adams (Fig. 11) and Savage's likeness of Louisa (Fig. 13), these miniatures may not inappropriately be dealt with as a group.

Unknown Artist

The first in order of date (and its exact date is only conjecture) is a likeness presumed to be of Louisa Catherine Johnson, daughter of Joshua Johnson, brother of the Revolutionary Governor of Maryland, Thomas Johnson. On 7 August 1790 Secretary of State Jefferson wrote to Johnson, to tell him that Washington had nominated him to be the American Consul at London, where he had lived all his mature years except during the war. The Johnsons had eight children, one son and seven daughters, and shortly after Johnson's appointment the whole family, except, apparently, for the son, had their portraits painted "in small." In 1920 a group of nine small oval oil portraits, measuring approximately 6 by 4½ inches in size, was deposited with the Massachusetts Historical Society by Mr. E. E. Sparhawk in an envelope marked "9 small paintings on canvas, said to be connected with the Adams Family." With them is an earlier letter, dated 15 July 1909, from Mr. Sparhawk to Worthington C. Ford, Editor of the Society, stating that these paintings had been in his family for "over 100 years" and had been "known as the Johnson pictures." This is all that is positively known of the group. Two of them, undoubtedly Joshua and his wife Catherine, bear a marked resemblance to larger paintings of the Johnsons in the Smithsonian Institution, thought in 1951 to have been by Trumbull but now suspected to be by Edward Savage. The miniature presumed to be of Joshua Johnson also corresponds closely to a miniature of him by Thomas H. Hull, also in the Smithsonian Institution.[1] These nine likenesses are reproduced

[1] *The Opening of the Adams-Clement Collection ... April 18, 1951,* Washington: Smithsonian Institution, p. 9, 13.

here as Figs. 4a to 4i, not only as an unusually attractive group of 18th-century portraits of a single family, but so that independent conclusions may be formed as to which of the daughters is Louisa and as to the date of painting of the group. As can be readily seen, the paintings are oil on old worn canvas, unframed, and with the paint flaked off in many places. Included here, to aid in the inquiry, is a table giving the dates, so far as known, of birth, marriage, and death for each member of the Johnson family.

The Johnson Family

JOSHUA JOHNSON (1742–1802) m. 1772? CATHERINE NUTH (ca. 1757–1811)

their children:

NANCY (or ANN) (1773–1810)
m. 1798, WALTER HELLEN (d. 1815), whose second wife was ADELAIDE (see below)

LOUISA CATHERINE (1775–1852)
m. 1797, JOHN QUINCY ADAMS (1767–1848)

CAROLINA VIRGINIA MARYLANDA (1776?–1862)
m. 1st, 1807, ANDREW BUCHANAN (1766–1811)
m. 2nd, 1817, NATHANIEL FRYE (d. 1855?)

THOMAS BAKER (1779–1843)
unmarried

HARRIET (1781–1850)
m. 1805, GEORGE BOYD (1781–1846)

CATHERINE MARIA FRANCES (d. 1869)
m. 1813, WILLIAM STEUBEN SMITH (1787–1850)

ELIZA JENNET DORCAS (d. 1818)
m. 1810, JOHN POPE (1770–1845)

ADELAIDE (d. 1877)
m. 1813, WALTER HELLEN (d. 1815), whose first wife was NANCY (see above)

I suggest, although there can be no certainty, that Fig. 4c represents the eldest child, therefore Nancy, and that Fig. 4d may safely be considered a likeness of Louisa. All presumably were painted at the same time, and the best clue to the date of painting is the relative ages of the children in the light of what is known of their birth

4a. JOSHUA JOHNSON.
OIL BY AN UNKNOWN ARTIST, CA. 1792

4b. CATHERINE NUTH JOHNSON.
OIL BY AN UNKNOWN ARTIST, CA. 1792

4c. NANCY JOHNSON(?).
OIL BY AN UNKNOWN ARTIST, CA. 1792

4e. CAROLINA VIRGINIA
MARYLANDA JOHNSON(?). OIL BY AN
UNKNOWN ARTIST, CA. 1792

24

4d. LOUISA CATHERINE JOHNSON(?).
OIL BY AN UNKNOWN ARTIST, CA. 1792

4f. HARRIET JOHNSON(?).
OIL BY AN UNKNOWN ARTIST, CA. 1792

4g. CATHERINE MARIA
FRANCES JOHNSON(?). OIL BY AN
UNKNOWN ARTIST, CA. 1792

4h. ELIZA JENNET DORCAS JOHNSON(?).
OIL BY AN UNKNOWN ARTIST, CA. 1792

4i. ADELAIDE JOHNSON(?).
OIL BY AN UNKNOWN ARTIST,
CA. 1792

dates. My best guess is approximately 1792,[2] which would make Louisa seventeen years old, three years before Adams began to court her. In 1825 Louisa wrote: "It was at this time [the early 1790's] that the family portraits were painted or rather began. Most of them were thought good likenesses but mine never gave satisfaction to my friend, nor indeed any one that was painted in those days. The one George has was thought the best and that squints." [3] This statement may help to date these portraits but it is at best ambiguous. It would seem to mean that the early portraits of Louisa (Figs. 4d?, 7, and 9 perhaps) did not win her husband's approval, and that the one at that time in possession of her son George, squinted. Which one that was, however, is not apparent.

But whatever Louisa's exact age at the time her little portrait was painted, those were gay and happy days for the many lovely, lively Johnson daughters. Their father, at the time a successful businessman, commercial agent of Maryland, lived in a style enjoyed and appreciated by his daughters. Louisa was later to write of their life in France during the Revolution, of the "handsome style" in which they lived, "enough to turn the head of a beautiful and much admired young Woman like my Mother." [4] And on their removal to England, her father maintained a large, well-staffed house, with eleven servants (if we can today let our imagination run away with us); sufficient, at any rate, to cope with the social activity fired by the fashionable, attractive, and almost numberless Johnson girls. With such an establishment, it is not surprising to discover that many family portraits were painted, some by well-known artists. The height of their social activity can, perhaps, be measured by the depth of their depression when Johnson's business venture collapsed. This family disaster, coming as it did simultaneously with Louisa's marriage, was long to haunt her with the suggestion that she had been married off in the nick of time.

The likeness (Fig. 4d) which I have assumed to be Louisa seems to correspond favorably with the miniature by Shelley (Fig. 7) and that by Barber (Fig. 9) painted four or five years later. If I am correct in attributing this little portrait to Louisa, it is her earliest known likeness.

[2] There are what appear to be stamps or marks on the back of several of these miniatures. They may be duty or bounty marks of the sort required on exported British or Irish linen and painter's canvas in the 18th century, but in this instance they are inconclusive as to date and have so far evaded satisfactory interpretation.

[3] LCA, "Record of a Life, or My Story," p. 42 (Adams Papers, Microfilms, Reel No. 265). The Adamses customarily used "friend" in addressing or speaking of a spouse.

[4] LCA to ABA, 2 March 1834 (Adams Papers).

Parker, "SS," and an Unknown Artist

In 1794, President Washington, who had a high regard for young John Quincy Adams, appointed him Minister to The Hague. He set sail from Boston for his new post in mid-September of that year, his fifth crossing of the Atlantic, accompanied by his brother Thomas. Their mother, Abigail Adams, well aware from her personal experience years before that diplomatic appointments abroad meant absence from home for many long years, sought to obtain keepsake likenesses of her sons before they departed. John wrote to her from Philadelphia: "I received your favour of the 20th inst. and my brother is now prepared to go with me. We should be very happy to comply with your request respecting the bracelets, but we shall certainly not have time for the miniatures to be taken here; and indeed our miniature painters are so indifferent workmen, that it will be best to have them done in Europe."[5] Adams remembered his mother's request and wrote to her from London: "But our immediate departure [for The Hague] obliges us further to postpone the fulfilment of our promise of the Miniatures in Bracelets; We have been so much employed every moment of our time, that it has been altogether impossible for us to get the likenesses taken; we shall however, if we can find an artist in Holland, of proper skill, have them taken there, and the setting, we can have done here at any time."[6] Abigail continued to correspond on the subject:

I thank you for your attention to this and my other commission, but there was one of more importance to me, of which I fear both your Brother and you were unmindfull, and I have no fancy for a stiff dutchman. I mean the Miniatures for Bracelets which I wish to have taken and executed in England. The expense of them I should request the Willinks to reimburse. The setting of them in gold with the Hair in cypher I would have executed by an old acquaintance of mine in cheepside, Savory by Name, a Quaker a very honest and honorable Silver Smith and Jeweler from whom I used to procure all articles which I had occasion for in that way.[7]

But by the time this letter was received, the project was in train.

Late in February 1795 Thomas, while skating, met a young Englishman and "took the liberty to ask his name." His name was Parker and he was a native of Birmingham, desirious of going to Hamburg but prevented by the French from doing so. He and Thomas struck up a

<hr/>

[5] JQA to AA, 29 July 1794 (Adams Papers).
[6] 25 Oct. 1794 (Adams Papers).
[7] AA to TBA, 11 Feb. 1795 (Adams Papers).

friendship (though his first name is never revealed), and he persuaded the young American to sit to him for his portrait in miniature. His pronunciation of English, Thomas observed, "is conformable to the practice of many of his Countrymen I have met with before. They drop the aspiration of the letter H where it begins a word or syllable, and place it before words beginning with a vowel. The accent reads thus; 'h-I find the language h-of this Country -orridly -arsh h-and h-un-armonius.'"[8] Brother John evidenced a diplomat's circumspection about the association with Parker but apparently approved of it, his brother recording that "JQA thinks well of my acquaintance Mr. P[arker] though it is an accidental one, and therefore requires caution, perhaps reserve as to conversation upon political subjects."[9]

During March and April, Thomas was frequently with Parker, and before long the miniature (Fig. 5) was finished, a "tolerable like-

5. THOMAS BOYLSTON ADAMS.
OIL ON IVORY BY PARKER, 1795

ness, though there is something about the mouth that strikes me as wanting exactitude." An earlier comment had been that the likeness was "a little *geflatteerd* as the Dutch say." Of Parker's ability, Thomas noted: "Miss B[oetslaer] observed that Mr. P[arker] has the talent of making handsome portraits when the original is not so. There is justice in the remark, but it is a circumstance which offends no body, and is sure to please the person flattered."[10]

The miniature of Thomas must have pleased his brother because he commenced to sit to Parker for his own portrait (Fig. 6) in May. "Sat this afternoon," John wrote, "to Mr. Parker, an English Painter

[8] TBA, Diary, 21 Feb. 1795 (Adams Papers, Microfilms, Reel No. 282).
[9] Same, 27 March 1795.
[10] Same, 31 March, 11 April, 28 Aug. 1795.

for a miniature I have promised to my mother." At the same time he wrote to reassure her: "Your miniatures are not forgotten. We were so short a Time in England, and our Time there was so busily employed, that we did not find a moment we could spare for the painter. We have however accidentally met an Englishman here, who is now about the work, and we believe it will be executed to your satisfaction." [11] From that day into August the brothers met Parker frequently, discussing painting with him, viewed his pictures, and even indulged in some musical activity together. [12] Thomas records two payments for miniatures: on 25 April, "P[arker] was with me. Paid him for my picture," and on 4 August, "Miniature picture G53–S6–D6." [13]

John wrote again to his mother:

> In my last letter I mentioned that we should send you the miniatures by that opportunity. They were not finished however in Season to go by that vessel, and we have now recommended them to the care of Captain Gardner of the Lydia, about to sail from Rotterdam to Boston, and by whose conveyance you will receive this Letter. The pictures are both in one small case, addressed to the care of Mr. Smith.
>
> The likenesses we think will be satisfactory to you, and the execution will convince you of the talents of the artist. The only part of your directions which we have been unable to perform is with respect to the hair. To have it introduced on the reverse of the bracelet is beyond the skill of a Dutch Jeweler and we were obliged therefore to supersede that part of your orders. [14]

The implication in the latter part of this letter that the bracelets were already finished is borne out by a note made by Thomas in July 1795: "Beck brought the bracelets—paid him for them." [15]

It is not hard to appreciate how Abigail longed to receive her sons' portraits, and we can rejoice with her when they finally arrived, after two false alarms. She wrote that Captain Trevett had arrived from Rotterdam with the books and letters, but not the bracelets. Later: "The Miniatures oh the Miniatures, a Blundering Captain forgot that he had such a precious Charge. After waiting a reasonable Time to receive them, I wrote to request Mr. Smith to inquire for them. The Captain recollected that for better security he had put them in to the bottom of his Trunk, which Trunk he had sent to Nantucket, and there they still are to my no small mortification." But the tale has a

[11] JQA, Diary, 12 May; to AA, 16 May 1795 (Adams Papers).
[12] JQA, Diary, 19, 30 May, 2 June, 18 July, 14, 19 Aug. 1795.
[13] TBA, Diary, 25 April; Account Book, 4 Aug. 1795 (Adams Papers, Microfilms, Reel Nos. 282, 283).
[14] 30 July 1795 (Adams Papers).
[15] TBA, Diary, 25 July 1795 (Adams Papers, Microfilms, Reel No. 282).

happy ending: "Last Evening I received the Miniatures," she at last could write, "and they were next to personally seeing you; for the likenesses are very good. The Painter however, it is said has given a more flattering Likeness of you than of Thomas. I am perfectly Satisfied with them and want to be constantly looking at them."[16] She shared her joy with her husband, writing: "I received the miniatures . . . and feasted myself upon them for they are most admirable Likenesses." He responded from Philadelphia, "I congratulate you upon the Receipt of your Miniatures, and am very glad you find them Likenesses. I shall have my feast in looking at them next summer."[17] Two more letters to her sons and the subject is done. "The Miniatures are my delight. No present could have been so acceptable to me, and they are pronounced good likenesses by every one who sees them." And lastly, "The last Letters received from you prior to this came by Captain Gardner; and brought me the Miniatures and I can say with as much truth as the Lady of old, Here are my Jewells. The likenesses are so strong, the Execution so admirable, that they are invaluable to me."[18]

In November 1795 John was sent from The Hague to London to exchange ratifications of Jay's Treaty with Great Britain, though by the time he arrived the exchange had taken place. While in London he took the opportunity to renew his acquaintance with Joshua Johnson, whom he had known when John Adams was Minister to Great Britain. Soon his diary reveals daily visits to the Johnson home. With two Johnson daughters of marriageable age the inevitable happened, and before Adams returned to the Netherlands he and Louisa Catherine Johnson were betrothed. When this significant bit of family news reached Abigail Adams she wrote at once, eager to obtain a miniature of her future daughter-in-law and a lock of her hair. In due course she received the miniature (Fig. 7), presumably painted in 1796 but by an artist whose name was not mentioned. Upon close examination there can be seen just over the sitter's left shoulder the initials "SS" which, it is believed, are those of Samuel Shelley (1750–1808), the well-known, fashionable English miniaturist.

For a long time the family record of these three miniatures is silent. In 1888 an article on the Adams family by Mrs. Harriet Taylor Upton appeared in *Wide Awake* magazine. It is illustrated by many portraits of the family, including one (Fig. 5) identified as "Thomas Boylston

[16] AA to JQA, 8 Oct.; to TBA, 30 Nov.; to JQA, 5 Dec. 1795 (Adams Papers).
[17] AA to JA, 10 Dec.; JA to AA, 17 Dec. 1795 (Adams Papers).
[18] AA to JQA, 23 Jan.; to TBA, 10 March 1796 (Adams Papers).

Adams at 23" (which was his age in 1795), with the following legend beneath the picture:

From the miniature worn by his mother, Mrs. Abigail Adams, as a bracelet-clasp; the original shows the gay colors affected by the young gentlemen of the day; a scarlet waistcoat enhances the soft richness of T.B.A.'s complexion. Owned by his daughter, Miss E. C. Adams.[19]

At the death of his parents this miniature apparently passed to T. B. Adams himself or to his wife; on the widow's death in 1845 it was bequeathed to her son Joseph Harrod Adams, from whom it passed to his sister Elizabeth C. Adams, who died in 1903. It was later owned by the late John Adams of South Lincoln, Massachusetts and, after his death, by his son, Thomas Boylston Adams of South Lincoln, who presented it to the Massachusetts Historical Society in 1966.

Also illustrated in the *Wide Awake* article are two miniatures identified as John Quincy Adams and Mrs. John Quincy Adams, with the following legend running beneath them both:

Miniatures made about the time of their marriage, and now in possession of W. C. Johnson, Esq., Newburyport, Mass. That of John Quincy was worn by his mother, Mrs. Abigail Adams, as a clasp on a bracelet of black velvet ribbon; the clasp on the companion bracelet was a miniature of her son, Thomas Boylston Adams.[20]

In 1843, listing the best portraits of himself, Adams singled out, among others, "A miniature, in a bracelet for my mother, painted at the Hague in 1795 by an Englishman named Parker, now in the possession of my Son John's widow." [21] When John's widow died in 1870, she bequeathed to her granddaughter Mary Adams Johnson (daughter of William Clarkson Johnson of Newburyport, and later Mrs. Charles Andrews Doolittle), a "Bracelet of J. Q. Adams portrait." This was undoubtedly Parker's miniature of J. Q. Adams, and the only query is why Louisa's companion miniature was not also mentioned.

This pair is illustrated here as Figs. 6 and 7 in their actual size, which corresponds almost exactly to the illustrations in *Wide Awake*. The pair descended from Mrs. Charles Andrews Doolittle to her son Ebenezer Brown Sherman Doolittle, whose daughter Lois (Mrs. Carter Inches) sold them to the State Department, their present owner. They now hang in the John Quincy Adams Drawing Room at the top of the new State Department building in Washington.

[19] Harriet Taylor Upton, "The Household of John Quincy Adams," *Wide Awake, An Illustrated Magazine*, 27:376 (Nov. 1888).
[20] Same, p. 363.
[21] JQA, Diary, 15 Aug. 1843.

6. JOHN QUINCY ADAMS.
OIL ON IVORY BY PARKER, 1795

7. LOUISA CATHERINE JOHNSON.
OIL ON IVORY BY "S.S.,"
PERHAPS SAMUEL SHELLEY,
1796 OR 1797

The likeness of John Quincy Adams (Fig. 6) is striking and re-markably like Copley's larger portrait taken a year later (Fig. 11). If we did not know the facts we could readily believe that one is a copy of the other. That of Louisa (Fig. 7) is in no way as attractive, but there is perhaps some resemblance to Barber's likeness (Fig. 9).

The roster of Adams miniatures would not be complete without that of Charles Adams, second of the three brothers. Although he had gone abroad with his father and his brother John in 1778, when only a lad of eight, he was in America when his brothers were painted by Parker. Yet Charles, too, had his likeness taken in miniature (Fig. 8)

8. CHARLES ADAMS.
OIL ON IVORY(?)
BY AN UNKNOWN ARTIST, CA. 1795

33

at about the same time, by an artist whose identity has not been discovered. This miniature of Charles, only 1 1/8 inches tall, reveals a good family resemblance when compared with those of his brothers by Parker. It was reproduced at page 377 in the *Wide Awake* article, and there stated to be owned by Mrs. D. C. Woods of Baltimore, Maryland, Charles' great-granddaughter. Its present whereabouts is unknown.

Thomas H. Hull and Mr. Birch

By the time Adams returned to The Hague from London in May 1796, he was betrothed to Louisa. One of the first things the young couple did was exchange miniatures to lend solace during the separation until their marriage. John Quincy Adams' likeness was taken, presumably in England, by Thomas H. Hull, who had painted the miniature of his prospective father-in-law that is now in the Smithsonian Institution's Adams-Clement Collection. Louisa's miniature was taken by an artist named Birch, also presumably in England. All that we know of either is from the following correspondence between the young couple. Adams described to Louisa his departure from London for Holland:

As I had however one very good reason to believe my Dutch *Skipper* would not willingly come away and leave me behind, I set myself about performing my indispensables in the morning so as to step into a Chaise the instant that my order from the Duke of Portland's office should be delivered me. Among my indispensables I will own to you, was about an hour devoted to a last sitting to Mr. Hull. He has I think as good a likeness as has yet been taken of *that* original, and you, I think, will like it better than the large portrait [Copley's portrait (Fig. 11) painted earlier in the year] because it is *not so much flattered.* As soon as it is finished, he will send or carry it to your Pappa, who will doubtless know that it is destined for you. Accept it as a token of an affection which will cease only with the last pulse of the heart of him whose image it is, and may it often meet your eye with one half the delight which at this instant *he* derives from a look at the precious corresponding pledge of your regard, which now lays on the table before him.

Two weeks later he wrote her:

Mr. Hull told me that he would deliver the miniature, in a fortnight at the latest after the time when I came away. If he has been as good as his word you have it ere now. I have a curiosity to know whether it meets your approbation. The likeness cannot I think be mistaken. Mr. Hull in his Execution wants a little assistance from The Graces, but in this instance that deficiency became a capital qualification.

I am at this moment looking at Mr. Birch's young lady, and using all my little eloquence to sollicit a smile from her countenance. It has indeed become one of my favourite occupations. Hitherto she continues inexorable, and seems to tell me, that she knows her power and is sure to please me let her look how she will. So I shall resign the hope of a perpetual smile from the image, and comfort myself with the hope of an occasional one from the original.[22]

Shortly afterward Louisa received Hull's miniature and wrote:

I yesterday received yours of the 17 instant in which you desire my opinion of your Picture. I approve the likeness tho' the complexion is much too dark and the figure altogether too large. I have lately been introduced to a Mrs. and Mr. Gore of Boston who say they should never have known it but I cannot allow them to be such competent judges as myself who finds the original too deeply engraven on my heart to admit of a mistake in the likeness.[23]

John Quincy continued to allude to the subject:

You were afraid of looking at my picture lest you should meet with a frown. As I was obliged to leave it unfinished, I can hardly tell how it looks, but Mr. Hull promised me that it should be very pleasant; which I strongly recommended. If it partakes of the feelings of the original, I am sure it will be ashamed to frown upon you, or upon your sister Nancy. If it were to undertake to express my affection for you, or my regard for her, I readily believe indeed that in that case, it would find the sentiments altogether *unspeakable*. They are beyond the reach of any expression that can be given to the pencil, the pen, or the tongue.

Still later he wrote in the same vein:

After reading your letter of the 30th of last month which I received this morning, I looked at your picture, and methought it looked unusually *cool*. I read the letter a second time, and upon again turning to the picture, it seemed to look *severe*. Upon a third reading, I dared not again consult the portrait; I feared to find it disdainful. Between us two, my lovely friend let there be Peace. In the intercourse of friends, of lovers, but more especially in the [ten]der and inseparable connection which I hope is destined for us, nothing bears so hard upon the ties of mutual kindness and affection as suspicion and distrust. Between you and me may it never rise.[24]

The last contemporaneous mention of the picture was made by Adams in the following month: "The picture resumes whatever it can express of that mild and gentle disposition which is one of the

[22] 2, 17 June 1796 (Adams Papers).
[23] To JQA, 4 July 1796 (Adams Papers).
[24] To LCA, 9 July, 12 Oct. 1796 (Adams Papers).

greatest ornaments of the original, and which in my eyes is of more worth than graces or beauty, riches or honours."[25]

From this correspondence and from other likenesses of the young lovers taken at the same period we can only speculate on what Hull and Birch produced. The fate of the pair of miniatures is noted in Adams' diary thirty-four years later:

> In November [1830] we had shipped at Boston in the schooner Caledonia for this place [Washington] a large Trunk . . . and other baggage. The vessel stranded near the mouth of the River . . . the Trunk and boxes were transshipped and then frozen up in the River. After the ice broke up they finally reached Alexandria, and this day were our effects brought to us. . . . The lock of the Trunk had been picked. My wife's miniature and mine, given to each other before marriage, those of her father and mother, relics of their parental affection . . . all stolen. The loss is more than money can repair.[26]

James Thomas Barber (1774–1841)

At or about the time of her marriage to John Quincy Adams, Louisa sat again for her portrait, this time to the English miniaturist James Thomas Barber. Here again records reveal but little. On a paper backing of her miniature (Fig. 9) appears the legend "J. T. Barber, Pinxt. 1797." On the face of the painting can be seen at the lower right edge the initials "JTB." It was reproduced opposite the first page of an article entitled "Mrs. John Quincy Adams's Narrative of a Journey From St. Petersburg to Paris in February, 1815," in *Scribner's Magazine,* 34:448 (October 1903), and described as being in the possession of Mrs. Henry Parker Quincy, that is, Mary, youngest daughter of the first Charles Francis Adams. This locket-sized likeness came to light again at a sale at Parke-Bernet Galleries on 12 January 1946, where it was illustrated and catalogued as item 18 and stated to be "From the Heritage of Mary Adams Quincy (1846–1929) granddaughter of President John Quincy Adams, Belonging to Mrs. Dorothy Quincy Nourse Pope and Mrs. Margaret D. Nourse." It subsequently belonged to the late Mark Bortman, of Boston, and is now a part of the Bortman-Larus Americana Collection. It was on display at the Old South Church in Boston in 1965–1966.

A copy of the miniature (Fig. 10) was owned by Mrs. Robert Homans and is now in the Old House (Adams National Historic Site) in Quincy; it is reproduced in Bemis, *JQA,* vol. 1, facing p. 82. It bears the initials "JTB" on the face, but is also inscribed "copy JMW 1810,"

[25] To LCA, 21 Nov. 1796 (Adams Papers).
[26] Entry of 11 March 1831.

9. LOUISA CATHERINE JOHNSON.
MINIATURE IN OIL
BY JAMES THOMAS BARBER, 1797

10. LOUISA CATHERINE JOHNSON.
MINIATURE IN OIL
BY "J.M.W.," 1810

and is almost an exact copy of Barber's original. The identity of JMW is unknown and the provenance of the copy is obscure.

We can however accept the pair as likenesses of Louisa at the time of her marriage. They correspond recognizably with Figs. 7 and 4d taken a short time before, though the subject does not appear so mature as in what is believed to be Savage's small portrait (Fig. 13).

JOHN SINGLETON COPLEY (1738–1815)

Late in 1783, after the signing in Paris of the definitive Treaty of Peace with Great Britain, John Adams' portrait was painted by Copley. It was a striking representation, almost 8 feet tall, showing the elder Adams the size of life in Court dress and aristocratic bearing. Although the portrait was finished before the end of the year, Copley retained possession of it for the customary purpose of having engravings made from it, of which there were many. It was not until 1817, after Copley's death, that the Adams family obtained possession of the portrait.[1] Mrs. Copley was an admirer of Abigail Adams; they had seen much of each other in London. So, when John Quincy Adams, treading almost in his father's steps, came to London from The Hague during the winter of 1795–1796, Mrs. Copley took advantage of his presence in the city to persuade him to sit for his portrait which she wished to present to his mother.

Adams' line-a-day diary lists seven sittings during February, March, and April 1796, the first on 11 February, the last on 4 April. The finished portrait (Fig. 11) was sent to Mrs. Adams early in 1797. She wrote enthusiastically to her son telling of its receipt and her delighted surprise:

In March last I received a very polite Letter from Mrs. Copley desiring to introduce to me a Friend of ours.[2] One only expression led me to suppose it was a portrait. I sent to the Captain of the vessel. He knew not of anything for me. Mr. Smith went to the custom House and found a case with DDR upon it. He inquired of Mr. Rogers if any thing had been sent him for me. He had not received any advice of anything. Mr. Smith ordered the case to his House. Upon opening it, we were not any of us at a moments hessitation. I recognized the striking resemblance of my dear absent Son. It is allowed to be as fine a portrait as ever was taken, and what renders it peculiarly valuable to me is the expression, the animation, the true Character which gives it so pleasing a likeness, and I have been not a little flattered by strangers saying, they can trace the resemblance of my features in it. I cannot do that myself, but I have those of Thomases, who I never before thought, looked like you. Mrs. Copleys Letter was designedly enigmatical, and I know not to this Hour whether the picture was sent me by your direction or whether it comes unknown to you, as a present from her. It is most elegantly Framed, and is painted in a masterly manner. No present could have been more acceptable.[3]

There was an undoubted resemblance between Abigail Adams and her son John Quincy. Eighteen years later, when writing to her son about Stuart's portrait of her commenced in 1800, she said: "It has however a strong resemblance of you."[4]

The circumstances under which the portrait was painted are told in a letter from Adams to his mother following her enthusiastic report of its arrival:

[1] Oliver, *Portraits of JA and AA*, p. 33–35 (Fig. 9).
[2] This letter has not been found.
[3] 23 June 1797 (Adams Papers).
[4] 8 June 1815 (Adams Papers).

II. JOHN QUINCY ADAMS. OIL BY JOHN SINGLETON COPLEY, 1796

The history of the Portrait which you received last March was this. While I was here, the last time, Mr. Copley told me that Mrs. Copley had long been wishing to send you some token of her remembrance and regard, and thinking that a likeness of your Son, would answer the purpose, requested me to sit to him; which I did accordingly and he produced a very excellent picture, as you see. I had it framed in a manner which might correspond to the merit of the painting, and after I left this Country it was sent out by Mr. Copley in the manner in which you received it. I never mentioned it to you in any of my former Letters, because I knew not exactly when it would be sent out, and I wished to reserve to you what I thought would be the pleasure of an agreeable surprise; it seems that Mrs. Copley's letter to you by its enigmatical style was written in the same Spirit, and the Portrait served really as its own introduction. It is therefore to the delicate politeness of Mr. and Mrs. Copley, that we are indebted for a present so flattering to me, and in your maternal kindness so acceptable to you. They are well, with all their family and continue to remember you with affection.[5]

The portrait (Fig. 11) is in Copley's English style and lacks the brilliance of his American portraits, but it was always a family favorite. It descended to Charles Francis Adams; from him it passed to his son Charles, at whose death in 1915 it was bequeathed to the Museum of Fine Arts, Boston, where it now hangs.

The only engraving of it that has come to light is shown here as Fig. 12 and bears the initials "H R," presumably those of the engraver, whose identity is not known.

Flexner commented on the painting: "In the background ... Copley sketched in, very rapidly, a little landscape about a foot square. Sky, hills and meadow are not drawn but indicated with sweeps of color.... Should we frame this landscape for itself, it would seem to be a mid-nineteenth century work, so completely is form subordinated to color.... We see a young man more handsome than interesting."[6] Adams himself always included it among the few likenesses of himself that he approved. Shortly after Adams' death, his son Charles had a reproduction (now lost) made for his distant cousin the Hon. Josiah Quincy, writing:

In thinking of some little memorial of my father which I could hope to make acceptable to his oldest friends, it occurred to me that you might be pleased with a transfer according to the new process, from the portrait taken of him by Copley which I have here. I have accordingly caused one to be made. It turns out less fortunate than I had expected, inasmuch as the artists find a difficulty in seizing the colours. But I trust nevertheless

[5] 29 July 1797 (Adams Papers).
[6] James T. Flexner, *The Light of Distant Skies*, N.Y., 1954, p. 55.

40

12. JOHN QUINCY ADAMS. ENGRAVING BY "H.R."

it may prove sufficiently good to remind you of the lineaments of one, who during his life entertained an affectionate regard for you, and who taught me when young the profound respect with which I am, Dear Sir, Your obedient servant.[7]

Years later Charles wrote: "I have in the room in which I am now writing a portrait of John Quincy Adams, painted by Mr. Copley. ... I cannot fix the date of it very certainly, but it must have been about 1796. It has never been engraved. I propose to have it done for insertion in the work I am about to publish, as soon as I get relieved from public duty."[8] An excellent photoreproduction appears as the frontispiece in the first volume of the *Memoirs of John Quincy Adams*, published in 1874.

[7] CFA to Josiah Quincy, 20 April 1848 (MHi: Quincy Papers).
[8] March 1872, quoted in Martha Babcock Amory, *The Domestic and Artistic Life of John Singleton Copley, R.A.*, Boston, 1882, p. 88.

II

The Diplomat
1801–1817

"He never looked so well or so handsome as he does now."

CHRONOLOGY OF JOHN QUINCY ADAMS' LIFE, 1801–1817

1801

Buys a house in Boston at 39 Hanover Street and resumes the practice of law at 23 Court Street.

1802

April: Elected as a Federalist to the Massachusetts State Senate.

Nov.: Defeated in his candidacy for election to the House of Representatives from the Boston district.

Dec.: Delivers oration at Plymouth "on the first landing of our ancestors, at that place"; published in the same year as a pamphlet.

1803

Suffers serious financial reverses through the failure of the London banking house of Messrs. Bird, Savage & Bird.

April: Appointed United States Senator from Massachusetts to fill an unexpired term lasting until 1808, throughout which he adheres to policies expressive of national strength and growth.

July 4: Second son (JA2) is born and named for his grandfather.

1804

Breaks with Senator Timothy Pickering and the Essex faction of the Massachusetts Federalists in giving support to the Louisiana Purchase in the Senate and in a series of articles in *The Repertory* under the pseudonym "Publius Valerius."

1805

Appointed Boylston Professor of Rhetoric and Oratory at Harvard, and thereupon undertakes preparation for the lectures to be delivered from 1806 to 1809 and published in 1810 in 2 volumes as *Lectures on Rhetoric and Oratory*.

1806

Purchases a house in Boston at the corner of what are now Boylston and Tremont streets. Receives LL.D. from the College of New Jersey. In the Senate frames resolutions of protest against British commandeering on the high seas and urges economic coercion in retaliation.

1807

Begins in the Senate his championship of an "American System"—a plan of internal improvements buttressed by a protective tariff and the rational disposal of public lands. Again using the name "Publius Valerius," he publishes a series of articles in *The Repertory* concerning the *Chesapeake-Leopard* affair and British impressment of American sailors.

Aug. 18: His third son is born and christened Charles Francis (CFA).

Dec.: Is the only Federalist to support Jefferson's Embargo Bill.

1808

Publishes *A Letter to the Hon. Harrison Gray Otis* justifying his support of the Embargo Bill.

Jan.: Attends the Republican caucus on the Presidential nomination.

May: Is denied Federalist renomination to the Senate; resigns to return to law practice in Boston.

1809

April–June: In a final break with Federalism, writes for the *Boston Patriot,* "American Principles: A Review of the Works of Fisher Ames." A searing critique of Ames' political philosophy, it appears later the same year in pamphlet form.

June: Commissioned Minister Plenipotentiary to Russia, a post he held until 1814.

Aug.: Silhouettes cut by Williams (Figs. 15–18).

Aug. 5–Oct. 23: With LCA and CFA, sails from Boston to St. Petersburg on the ship *Horace,* with a stop at Copenhagen in the interest of American shipping.

1811

Begins systematic studies of astronomy, numismatics, cartography, and metrics; continues to collect books in many fields.

Feb. 22: Appointed by President Madison as Associate Justice of the United States Supreme Court; declines on account of LCA's pregnancy, which made travel inadvisable.

Aug. 12: Birth of a daughter, Louisa Catherine, who dies 15 Sept. 1812.

1812

With the outbreak of war between America and England, he experiences an increase in responsibilities as Minister.

1813

Spring: Together with Albert Gallatin and James A. Bayard is commissioned Envoy Extraordinary and Minister Plenipotentiary to negotiate peace with Great Britain under the mediation of Emperor Alexander I at St. Petersburg—a negotiation never concluded because declined by Great Britain. These envoys also hold a commission to negotiate a treaty of commerce with Russia.

1814

Jan. 18: Commissioned with Bayard, Gallatin, Henry Clay, and Jonathan Russell to negotiate peace with Great Britain, this time at Ghent; serves as chairman of the American delegation.

April 28–June 24: Travels alone from St. Petersburg to Ghent with stops at Stockholm and Gothenburg (where it was at first thought that negotiations would take place).

Aug. 8: Meetings with British Commissioners at Ghent begin.

Dec. 24: Signs Treaty of Ghent with Great Britain.

1815

Is sketched and painted by Van Huffel (Figs. 19 and 20).

Jan. 26–Feb. 4: Travels from Ghent to Paris.

Feb. 4–May 16: Remains in Paris; renews absorption in the theater; visits Lafayette at his ancestral home, La Grange.

Feb. 12–March 23: LCA and CFA journey overland from St. Petersburg to Paris; her recollections of this trip ultimately edited by Brooks Adams (BA) and published in *Scribner's Magazine* in 1903.

Feb. 28: Commissioned Envoy Extraordinary and Minister Plenipotentiary to Great Britain; receives this news early in April at Paris.

May 16–25: Travels to London with LCA and CFA, where they are met by GWA and JA2, newly arrived from Boston.

July 3: With Clay and Gallatin signs Commercial Convention with Great Britain and establishes the principle of "diplomatic equality" in the use of the *alternat* in signing.

Aug. 1: Resides at Little Ealing with family until 28 April 1817.

1816

Sept.: Painted by Leslie (Figs. 22 and 23).

1817

March 5: Commissioned by the newly inaugurated President, James Monroe, as Secretary of State; receives news of this appointment in London in mid-April.

June 10–Aug. 6: Sails with family on the ship *Washington* from London to New York.

Aug. 18: Arrives in Quincy after an absence of eight years.

EDWARD SAVAGE (1761–1817)

A charming and at the same time frustrating problem presents itself in the likeness of Louisa (before or after her marriage) reproduced here as Fig. 13. By tradition this delightful young lady has always been identified as Louisa Catherine Johnson "at or about the time of her marriage" to John Quincy Adams. Two possible claimants to authorship of this likeness have presented themselves over the years. The older tradition has been that the artist was Mather Brown. As a claimant on the basis of proximity and association with the family he rates high. He painted two portraits of John Adams and one of Abigail,[1] as well as one of their daughter Abigail and her husband William Stephens Smith. Brown's portrait of the younger Abigail (Fig. 14) was painted in 1785 and was described by the subject, in a letter to her brother John Quincy Adams, as being "an admirable likeness of my Ladyship, the Honble. Miss Adams you know. It is a very tasty picture I can assure you, whether a likeness or not."[2] For some years it hung in the Old House and belonged to Louisa Catherine Adams. It descended to Mrs. Robert Homans and now belongs to George C. Homans, her son.

Brown, therefore, is clearly eligible for consideration as the painter of Fig. 13, and the portrait has long been attributed to him and dated at the time of Louisa's marriage in 1797. Except for the few miniatures mentioned above, this is the only remaining likeness of Louisa taken until after several years of married life.

An entry in John Quincy Adams' diary, written in Baltimore about half a century later, possibly throws some light on this problem:

My wife had charged me to procure for her two handsome picture frames for the portraits of her eldest sister, Nancy, the first Mrs. Hellen and of herself painted by Savage, before they were married. I went accord-

[1] Oliver, *Portraits of JA and AA*, p. 46–54 (Figs. 20 and 21, Cat. No. 39).
[2] 4 July–11 Aug. 1785 (Adams Papers).

45

13. LOUISA CATHERINE ADAMS. OIL ASCRIBED TO EDWARD SAVAGE, CA. 1801

14. ABIGAIL ADAMS (AA2). OIL BY MATHER BROWN, 1785

ingly to the shop of Mr. Fryer in Gay Street. My wife had named him
to me, and the bar-keeper at Barnum's had assured me that his shop was
the best shop for that Article in the city. I found and bespoke the two
frames for 20 dollars and directed them to be sent to the depot of the
rail-road cars, boxed up, this afternoon or tomorrow morning as I should
thereafter advise.[3]

It is perhaps a double surprise to discover that Adams in 1844 (aged
seventy-nine) patronized a "bar," and that barkeepers had already
become the sources of what could fairly be called miscellaneous information.

If Fig. 13 be the portrait of his wife to which Adams referred, then

[3] Entry of 28 Nov. 1844.

47

it would appear to have been painted by Savage. Furthermore, an acknowledged expert on Savage has, after comparison of Fig. 13 with Savage's portraits of Mary Brewton Alston and "The Washington Family," concluded that the likeness of Louisa can fairly be "ascribed to Edward Savage."[4] This attribution we would readily accept on technical, stylistic grounds, but the problem of dating the painting remains. Tradition, that is the tradition that ascribes the portrait to Brown, tells us the portrait was painted at the time of Louisa's marriage —1797. Savage left London for America in 1793 and was married in Boston in October 1794. Louisa was married in London on 26 July 1797 and was in Prussia with her husband the next three years, returning to Philadelphia from Hamburg in September 1801. If by Savage, the painting probably dates from after September 1801. Brown, however, lived in London from 1781 until his death in 1831. It is difficult to be certain of the age of a young lady simply on the evidence of an attractive, colorful portrait. However, Barber's miniature of Louisa, well documented as having been painted in 1796, is available for comparison. It appears to be of a much younger sitter.

It can be suggested then that Fig. 13 shows Louisa several years older than she appeared in 1796. The author is disposed to accept Miss Dresser's ascription of the portrait to Savage, whose works it more resembles than Brown's. That ascription, however, requires us to believe that Adams' memory played him false when in 1844 he said the portrait had been painted before Louisa's marriage, and that the portrait was in fact painted, not in London in 1797, but in America after 1801. The portrait, which has twice been reproduced,[5] now belongs to Mrs. Henry L. Mason of Boston.

HENRY WILLIAMS (1787–1830)

Upon succeeding Jefferson as President, Madison appointed John Quincy Adams as Minister to Russia, a post which would recall his early days there as Francis Dana's secretary. Once more he was obliged to leave his own country for a foreign land. On the eve of his departure for St. Petersburg in August 1809, he, with all his family, dined with Mr. Gray in Boston and after dinner, as Adams wrote, "I went to

---

[4] Louisa Dresser to L. H. Butterfield, 23 Jan. 1967 (Adams Papers Editorial Files).

[5] HA2, *Birthplaces*, p. 17; Wilson, *Where Amer. Independence Began*, following p. 108.

John Quincy Adams.
1. August 1809.
aged 42

15. JOHN QUINCY ADAMS.

Louisa Catherine Adams.
1. August 1809.
aged 34.

17. LOUISA CATHERINE ADAMS.

16. JOHN QUINCY ADAMS.

18. LOUISA CATHERINE ADAMS.

SILHOUETTES BY HENRY WILLIAMS, 1809

the Miniature Painter Williams's for my wife's pictures, and had two profile shades taken of myself." [1]

Henry Williams was a Bostonian, born in 1787, who not only cut silhouettes and painted miniatures, but also painted lifesized portraits and modeled in wax. Dunlap, the artist and diarist, described him frankly as "a small, short, self-sufficient man; very dirty, and very forward and patronizing in his manner." [2] But he was unquestionably a skillful silhouettist as the profiles of Adams (Figs. 15 and 16) and of his wife (Figs. 17 and 18) attest. Those of Adams are undoubted likenesses, well confirmed by later profiles, such as Cardelli's bust (Fig. 25) and Hubard's and Hanks' shades (Figs. 65 and 67), though these were taken a score of years later.

The legends over Figs. 15 and 16, as framed in a group, are in Adams' own hand, contemporary with the cutting. Each silhouette has embossed on it the word "Williams," which was the artist's customary method of marking his work. These, with their companion likenesses of John and Abigail Adams [3] and the two children, John and George, were for many years in one frame, in the possession of John Quincy Adams, "which," as he said, "I often look at with pleasure; all in one frame. It is a piece of family History." [4] The profiles of Adams, his wife and sons were at one time in the collection of Oliver Barrett of Chicago and, with six others cut by Hanks, were sold at auction at the Parke-Bernet Galleries in February 1959 for $225 to David M. Freudenthal of New York. Counterparts of some were made. Those of John Quincy and Louisa Catherine are in the Adams Papers.

It might be open to argument whether a silhouette is a work of art, but it cannot be denied that one well cut, as these are, is a good guide to the accuracy of likenesses taken in other mediums.

PIETER van HUFFEL (1769-1844)

The War of 1812, by almost any historical standard, was short-lived. With peace in the wind, President Madison appointed as his Peace Commissioners, John Quincy Adams, James A. Bayard, Henry Clay, Albert Gallatin, and Jonathan Russell, whose task it was to negotiate the terms of peace with Great Britain's Commissioners, Lord Gambier, Henry Goulburn, and William Adams. The site finally selected for the negotiations was the city of Ghent in Belgium.

[1] JQA, Diary, 2 Aug. 1809.
[2] Dunlap, *Arts of Design*, ed. Bayley and Goodspeed, 3:29-30.
[3] Oliver, *Portraits of JA and AA*, p. 129-131 (Figs. 62 and 63).
[4] JQA, Diary, 25 March 1829.

The issues over which the war was fought and the hopes of gain on each side, both political and commercial, accentuated the importance of the task of the negotiators. Yet Adams found some time for relaxation. Always interested in every branch of the arts, he visited the artists of the day then in Ghent. "I went ... to see the Pictures of Mr. Van Huffel, a Painter; and President of the Academy of fine arts. The principal curiosity that he possesses, is a Picture by John of Maubeuge a cotemporary of Albert Durer. It represents the day of Judgment, and resembles the Picture of Luke of Leyden. Mr. Van Huffel is a Painter not of the highest order, though he prides himself upon his colouring; the glory, as he thinks, of the Flemish School." [1]

Pieter or Pierre van Huffel, the Flemish artist, was born in East Flanders in 1769 and died in Ghent in 1844. He studied in Ghent and later in Paris, becoming Director of the Academy in Ghent and Keeper of the Municipal Museum. In the course of his career he painted many portraits as well as religious and historical pictures.

Adams found the Flemish artist eager to take his portrait. Arrangements for preliminary sketches are recorded in Adams' diary early in 1815: "Mr. Cornelissen called upon me, with a Letter from Mr. Van Huffel to Mr. Clay; containing copies of the likenesses of Messrs. Clay and Gallatin that he had taken. Mr. Van Huffel again requested that I would call upon him to sit, and I sent him word I would call at eleven O'Clock to-morrow Morning." The following day the diary reveals, "I had engaged to call at eleven O'Clock this morning upon Mr. Van Huffel the painter. He had taken likenesses in pencil of Mr. Gallatin, Mr. Bayard and Mr. Clay; and had asked me to give him an hour for the same purpose. While there, he urged me to let him take my Picture in Oil-Colours and on Canvass to which I finally consented. I sat an hour and a half." Sittings were repeated the next three days, Adams recording the third day: "At noon I called upon Mr. Van Huffel and sat until half past one. I asked him his price for the picture, but he prefers leaving it to my generosity. The painting is a good likeness, but indifferent as a work of art." Mr. Cornelissen, who saw it at the time, "thinks it a likeness pour le materiel." [2] Three more sittings were required to finish the picture. Adams' account book records his "generosity" to the artist: "Van Huffel, for a Picture 500 [francs]." Adams reviewed the whole proceeding relating to the portrait in a letter to his wife the following day, adding: "It was also understood that the picture was to be not for him, but for me; that

[1] JQA, Diary, 22 Nov. 1814.
[2] Entries of 17, 18, 21, 22 Jan. 1815.

19. JOHN QUINCY ADAMS. PENCIL SKETCH BY PIETER VAN HUFFEL, 1815

is to say, if you think it worth your acceptance, for you. The likeness is good, and the picture not a bad one. I leave it here to be finished, and then forwarded ... to England or to America as the circumstances shall require."[3] The pencil sketch (Fig. 19) was completed and, with

[3] JQA, Account Book, 23 Jan. (Adams Papers, Microfilms, Reel No. 210); to LCA, 24 Jan. 1815 (Adams Papers).

20. JOHN QUINCY ADAMS. OIL BY PIETER VAN HUFFEL, 1815

those of Bayard, Clay, and Gallatin, and of Christopher Hughes, secretary to the American Commissioners, turned up years later in Baltimore in the possession of a grandson of Hughes, having been given
to Hughes by Van Huffel in 1817.[4] This sketch is now in the William
L. Clements Library.

The disposition of the portrait in oil-colors (Fig. 20) was not so

[4] "Papers of James A. Bayard," *Annual Report of the American Historical Association for 1913*, 2:9–10.

simple as Adams had suggested to his wife. Early in January 1816 he wrote (in French) to Van Huffel from London asking him to deliver the portrait to John C. Gray, the bearer of his letter and "un de mes Concitoyens fils d'un de mes amis qui voyage pour son plaisir et son instruction."[5] But nothing seems to have come of this request. Later in the year he noted receiving "a Letter from P. Van Huffel, President of the Society of fine Arts, and of Literature, at Ghent, the Painter who took my Picture while I was there, enquiring how he shall send it to me." Van Huffel's letter said, among other things, that several copies of the portrait had been made. Adams replied asking that the portrait be delivered to "mon amie" Mr. Connell, having extracted a promise from Connell, who was going to Antwerp, to bring it back with him, and added: "Votre lettre parle de plusieurs copies comme en ayant été faites. Je vous serai obligé si vous voulez bien me faire savoir si c'est vous même qui les avez peints et à qui elles appartiennent."[6] No reply to this letter has been found and no copies of the portrait have come to light.

Mr. Connell carried out his commission to the letter but the portrait was taken from him at the Customs House at Dover, requiring Adams' intervention. "I requested Mr. Smith to write a Note on Monday to Mr. Hamilton of the foreign Department, asking an order to the Custom house for the delivery to me of the box addressed to me from St. Petersburg, and of the Portrait painted by Van Huffel at Ghent; which Connell, who has just returned brought over with him, but which was taken from him by the Custom House officers at Dover." By early December we learn that the portrait had been ordered to be sent to Adams at his own house, and after further delays we share his relief in reading, "The box containing my Portrait by Van Huffel was yesterday received from Dover."[7]

The portrait descended to John Quincy Adams Johnson, a great-grandson of Adams whose wife cleared out the Adamses' house in Washington after the death of Louisa Catherine in 1852 and came across the painting at that time.

At the time of its presentation to the Smithsonian Institution as part of the Adams-Clement Collection, Mrs. Katharine McCook Knox recalled Adams' toast to the City of Ghent in a farewell speech:

---

[5] 11 Jan. 1816 (LbC, Adams Papers).
[6] JQA, Diary, 2 July; Van Huffel to JQA, 12 June (Adams Papers); to Van Huffel, 21 Oct. 1816, printed in JQA, *Writings*, 6:110–111.
[7] JQA, Diary, 23 Nov., 5 Dec. 1816; 11 and 18 Jan. 1817.

"Ghent, the city of Peace; may the gates of the temple of Janus, here closed, not be opened again for a century."[8]

In his own diary entry made the day he left that city Adams summed up the significance of what he had been through: "At a quarter past eleven O'Clock I entered my Carriage, and left the Hotel des Pays Bas and the city of Ghent, probably never to see them again. My residence in the city has been of seven Months and two days, and it has been the most memorable period of my life."[9]

The painting, like the sketch, is an unquestioned and strong likeness of Adams the Peace Commissioner. He is shown in formal diplomatic dress (reminiscent of Copley's 1783 painting of John Adams after *his* success as a Peace Commissioner). His hand holds a scroll on which can be read "Pacification of Ghent, December 24, 1814." In the background over his left shoulder several tall Gothic towers can be seen. As Mrs. Knox pointed out, one has what might be a dragon on its pinnacle and if so it might represent the Belfry, near the Ghent Cathedral. On the reverse of the canvas is written "John Quincy Adams aet. 48. Painted at Ghent 1815 by van Huffel." Also on the reverse, pasted underneath one of the stretchers, appear six lines from Ben Jonson's play *Catiline* (1611). They describe Adams' plight during the peace conference, when tensions between him and his American colleagues had at times run higher than those between the Americans and their British counterparts:

> Great honours are great burdens, but on whom
> They are cast with envy, he doth bear two loads;
> His cares must still be double to his joys,
> In any dignity, where, if he do err
> He finds no pardon; and for doing well
> A most small praise, and that wrung out by force.

One hundred years after the signing of the Treaty of Ghent the occasion was commemorated by the painting of an historical picture (Fig. 21) depicting the event as it might have appeared that Christmas Eve 1814 in the old Carthusian Monastery at Ghent. The artist was Sir Amédée Forestier of London, well known as an historical artist and widely traveled. Many years before, he had been sent by Queen Victoria to Moscow, in 1896, to paint commemorative pictures of the Coronation of Czar Nicholas II. In 1922 his *Signing of the Treaty of*

---

[8] From a typewritten copy of "An Extension of the Remarks made by Katharine McCook Knox on the occasion of the Opening of the Adams-Clement Collection at the Smithsonian Institution on April 18, 1951" (Adams Papers Editorial Files).
[9] Entry of 26 Jan. 1815.

2 1. THE SIGNING OF THE TREATY OF GHENT.
OIL BY SIR AMÉDÉE FORESTIER, 1914

Ghent was presented to the American people as a token of good will by Mr. Barron Collier on behalf of the Sulgrave Institution of America and Great Britain. It was accepted on behalf of the United States by Chief Justice William Howard Taft and deposited in the National Collection of Fine Arts of the Smithsonian Institution.

Shown in the painting, from left to right, are the British delegates—Anthony St. John Baker, Secretary of the Delegation, Henry Goulburn and William Adams, Plenipotentiaries, and Admiral Lord Gambier, Chief Plenipotentiary; and, for the Americans: Adams as Chief, Gallatin, Hughes (Secretary), Bayard, Clay, Russell, and an unidentified figure. Adams' likeness is readily recognizable and, except for his costume, is clearly taken from Van Huffel's portrait.

Van Huffel's portrait of Adams is of particular interest in what it reveals of American diplomatic costume of the day. This was a matter that had long disturbed the American representatives abroad, for there had been no clear guidelines. The plain republican garb in which Franklin, John Adams, and others usually appeared now seemed hope

56

lessly out of place in the Courts of Europe. Jefferson had laid down some rules with regard to consuls and vice-consuls in 1790, and John Quincy Adams hoped similar authority could be established for the American diplomatic agents. But it was for Monroe, as Madison's Secretary of State in 1813, to prescribe a diplomatic costume for American Ministers. And it was in such a prescribed dress that the American Commissioners at Ghent were attired. Although Forestier's painting makes the American uniform seem simple when compared with the British representatives, Van Huffel's portrait displays considerable elegance and formality. "Straight standing cape, embroidered with gold, single-breasted ... buttonholes slightly embroidered.... Cuffs embroidered in the manner of the cape"—so read, in part, the State Department directive of 6 November 1817, using as its model the costume that had been authorized for the Ghent mission.[10]

CHARLES ROBERT LESLIE (1794–1859)

After signing the Peace of Ghent, Adams left Belgium for Paris for a few months and then crossed the Channel to London, where he arrived at the end of May 1815, and took up his duties as Minister to the Court of St. James's. As was his custom, he found time amid public obligations to pursue his interest in the arts by attending exhibitions whenever opportunity offered and by visiting the rooms of American painters in London. Diary entries for the month of June 1816 are a good example of this interest. On 11 June he notes: "I found at the Office Mr. Leslie, a young American Painter, who lives with Mr. Alston. He has painted a family picture of Mr. King's three Children. Has a picture of some reputation, at the present exhibition, at Somerset House; and is patronized by the President of the Academy Mr. West." On 17 June: "I had afterwards a visit from Mr. Allston and Mr. Leslie, the Painters."[1] Leslie dined with him a day or so later, and on 28 June he wrote: "I went, with all the family to see Earl Grosvenor's Collection of Pictures at his House in Upper Grosvenor Street N. 33. We were admitted by the Ticket procured for us by Mr. Leslie, as Mr. West's Friends." The entry continues with a detailed description of the collection.[2]

[10] For a discussion of this subject, see Robert Ralph Davis Jr., "Diplomatic Plumage: American Court Dress in the Early National Period," *American Quarterly*, 20:164–179 (Summer 1968); the State Department directive is given at p. 170.
[1] Entries of 11, 17 June 1816.
[2] Entry of 28 June 1816.

It is not surprising, then, that when Louisa's brother, Thomas Baker Johnson of New Orleans, wrote requesting his sister and brother-in-law to send him their portraits, they should choose Leslie as the artist. Leslie had been born in England in 1794 of American parents and was one of three talented children, both his sisters also being artists. His childhood was spent in Philadelphia until 1811, when he returned to England, where he studied under West and Allston. He had a successful career there, and after a trip back to America he settled permanently in England and devoted himself to painting and writing books related to his profession. He died in 1859.

A contemporary appraisal of Leslie and the other American artists in England at the time is preserved in a letter young Samuel Finley Breese Morse wrote from London in 1813: "The American character stands high in this country as to the production of artists.... Mr. West now stands at the head.... Mr. Copley next, then Colonel Trumbull. Stuart in America has no rival here. As these are now old men and going off the stage, Mr. Allston succeeds in the prime of life.... After him is a young man from Philadelphia by the name of Leslie, who is my room-mate."[3]

Louisa sat to Leslie for her picture on 5 September 1816, and a couple of days later Adams sat for two hours: "I took my Seal at the engraver Silvester's in the Strand and went to Leslie's where I sat two hours for my picture to send to T. B. Johnson. I asked Leslie if he could introduce the device of my Seal into the Picture; but he did not incline to it. We left the question, however, for future consideration."[4] On future consideration Adams succeeded in persuading Leslie, and the device of the Lyre and Eagle is plainly visible on the binding of the book in Adams' hand (Fig. 22). Also can be seen that other pose so prominent in many of Adams' portraits, his index finger marking his place in the book, as though his sitting for his portrait were but a momentary interruption in his reading.[5]

By 14 September some progress had been made: "Proceeded to Leslie's," Adams reported, "where I sat a couple of hours. He showed

[3] *Samuel F. B. Morse: His Letters and Journals*, ed. Edward L. Morse, Boston and N.Y., 1914, 1:102–103.

[4] JQA, Diary, 7 Sept. 1816. The making of this seal (Fig. C, tailpiece to Introduction) had been in train since the previous September with R. W. Silvester, Seal and Copper Plate Engraver of No. 27 Strand, near Charing Cross. It was not yet completed to Adams' fancy. Ten days later Adams stopped again at Silvester's and, as he noted in his diary, "Took Bode's Uranographia with me. I had left it there for him to consult the figure of the Constellation of Lyra, for the device of my Seal" (entry of 17 Sept. 1816). On Bode's *Uranographia*, see the Introduction and Fig. A there.

[5] See above, p. 7–12.

me my wife's portrait [Fig. 23], the likeness of which is not so good as mine." Louisa reported to her mother-in-law: "We are both at this time sitting for our pictures, (half length) for my brother Thomas. The Painter is a young American by the Name of Leslie who bids fair to become a very great Artist and whom Mr. West is very proud of. Mr. A. tells me his picture is likely to prove an excellent likeness at which I am much delighted as I think he never looked so well or so handsome as he does now." Adams himself also reported to his mother: "This is the second time that, according to a melancholy joke of poor Sheridan's, I have undergone the *operation* of sitting for my Picture within these two years. The first was at Ghent, where the President of the Academy of fine Arts of that place, Mr. Van Huffel, prevailed upon me to allow him to paint me, when I fancied it was much against my will; and so it is now. But there are cases in which one yields compliance as the least of two evils. Be that as it may, I went yesterday to town *to sit*."[6] From that day till the end of October, Adams and his wife sat some fourteen times for the completion of their portraits. Adams mentions each sitting in his diary, often adding running comments: "Allston is an older and more improved Painter than Leslie"; "Sat until five when it was so dark that he could no longer proceed. While riding in and out of Town, and while sitting at Leslie's I was employed incessantly upon my Ode of which I completed the first draft"; "My wife this day produced several stanzas addressed to Ellen [Nicholas]; and others to the Painter about my Portrait, which prove that with a little practice she would write very beautiful verses"; "The days have shortened so that Leslie was obliged to stop before five and I was home by half past six."

Finally the sittings were finished: "Went immediately to Leslie's and sat to him for the last time. He has asked our permission to send the Portraits to Philadelphia to the Public Exhibition there next May, before sending them to Mr. Johnson at New Orleans."[7] Permission was granted, as will appear later. Meanwhile, Louisa wrote again, en-

[6] JQA, Diary, 14 Sept.; LCA to AA, 11 Sept.; JQA to AA, 20 Sept. 1816 (Adams Papers).

[7] Entries of 23–25, 28 Sept., 8, 11, 15, 19, 23, 24, 26, 31 Oct. 1816. "My Ode," mentioned in the diary entry of 15 Oct., was to be in six stanzas–"To Fortitude, Written in the Manner of Gray – Stanzas of ten lines, like the Odes to Spring; and on the distant prospect of Eton School. My Ode will pass very well in the Class of Vers de Societé; and I think it no more like Gray than Allston thinks his Landscape like one of Claude's. But if ever my Ode should find a Critic, his first reproach will be that it looks like a Parody upon Gray. It might perhaps be taken for a Burlesque upon it. It has a few prosaic lines and some expressions not lofty enough for Lyric Poetry. I shall leave them for the sake of their energy." The MS is in the Adams Papers.

22. JOHN QUINCY ADAMS. OIL BY CHARLES ROBERT LESLIE, 1816

23. LOUISA CATHERINE ADAMS. OIL BY CHARLES ROBERT LESLIE, 1816

61

thusiastically, to her mother-in-law: "Our Portraits are most striking likenesses and should they reach America are to be exhibited at Philadelphia. You will keep the verses of Mr. Adams from the public as they are my own private property."[8] Whether she is referring to verses that Adams had written or to her own verses about his portrait is not clear. The latter, which met with encouragement from Adams, are typical of the age and were included in the letter to Abigail:

On the Portrait of my Husband

The Painter's art would vainly seize
That harmony of nature,
Where Sense and sweetness joined with ease
Shine forth in evr'y feature.
That open front where wisdom sits
That Eye which speaks the soul
That brow which study gently knits
That soft attemper'd whole—
That vast variety of Mind
Capacious, clear, and strong
Where brilliancy of wit refin'd
Enchants the list'ning throng
That sense of right by God impres't
That virtuous holy love
Of excellence whats'ere is best
Imparted from above
These Painter if thou canst impart
Shall fame immortal raise
And e'en the greatest in thy Art
Shall carol forth thy praise.

Louisa

In February, Leslie proposed sending the pictures by the *Electra* and asked Adams to call and see them. This he did, after first stopping on the way at "an auction of books and mathematical and philosophical instruments in Chancery Lane," and while at Leslie's he paid the balance due for the paintings. Another detail was disposed of not long afterward: "Masser the Coachmaker called and Brock, the man of the Picture Frames, who had brought and left a letter of explanation about them from Leslie."[9]

Because the portraits had been ordered for T. B. Johnson, a word of explanation was owed him to explain the delay he was to be subjected to. Adams wrote:

[8] To AA, 11 Nov. 1816 (Adams Papers).
[9] JQA, Diary, 10, 13 Feb., 8 March 1817.

In conformity to the request contained in your favour of 25 June last and to that in one of your Letters about the same time to your Sister, we have had our Portraits painted by Mr. Leslie an Artist of very handsome talents, from our own Country, whose performance will I hope give you satisfaction. As there has been no vessel bound from London directly to New Orleans; and as Mr. Leslie was desirous of having the Pictures exhibited at Philadelphia, the ensuing Season they have been lately shipped for that City, with directions that they should be forwarded by water, after the exhibition is closed, to you. I trust you will receive them before the expiration of the next Summer.[10]

The two portraits are indeed a handsome, if perhaps a slightly pompous, pair and have been coveted possessions of the family. We learn of the first change of ownership from Louisa herself: "He [T. B. Johnson] has presented to Charles much to Mary's [Mrs. JA2] sorrow, poor thing, the two Portraits of Mr. Adams and myself painted by Leslie. Thus C. is overburthened with likenesses while the other branches have not one." A month later Charles wrote that he had been "superintending the opening of the pictures by Leslie of my father and mother which Mr. Johnson has sent me."[11]

By 1921 the pair were owned by Brooks Adams, at which time that of John Quincy Adams was thought to have been painted by Sully. Biddle and Fielding included it in their list of his paintings: "No. 8 Portrait painted by Sully when Adams was Secretary of State. Head three-quarter to right, left hand on a book on his knee, size 28″ x 36″. Owned by Brooks Adams Esq., Boston, Mass."[12] The foreword to the catalogue in the Sully volume contains a paragraph that gives some amusement at this date, when we have the benefit of hindsight: "Sully for some unexplainable reason failed to note a number of his portraits in his register, and these omissions have taken away to some extent the value of the original list as an authority, or as a means of identification of his work; therefore a more complete catalogue of his work has been required by the student of American painting."[13] So "complete" as to include a portrait by Leslie! Yet the error is quite understandable, for at the time the new catalogue was prepared the Leslie portrait was on loan to the Museum of Fine Arts in Boston and described as being by Sully.

From Brooks Adams the two portraits descended to his niece, Mrs. Robert Homans, and are now owned by her son Robert Homans, of

[10] To Thomas Baker Johnson, 28 Feb. 1817 (Adams Papers).
[11] To ABA, [11?] April (Adams Papers); CFA, Diary, 12 May 1836.
[12] Edward Biddle and Mantle Fielding, *The Life and Works of Thomas Sully,* Phila., 1921, p. 84.
[13] Same, p. 81.

Louisa Catherine Adams

24. LOUISA CATHERINE ADAMS.
ENGRAVING BY G. F. STORM, BEFORE 1840

Hillsborough, California. Recently when the State Department was furnishing the John Quincy Adams State Drawing Room in the new State Department building in Washington, it procured through the generosity of Mr. and Mrs. Myron Cowen a copy of Leslie's portrait of Adams, painted in 1962 by Gregory Stapko.

No engraving of Leslie's portrait of John Quincy Adams has come to light. That of Louisa was engraved in 1874 by Forbes & Co. as the frontispiece to the third volume of *Memoirs of John Quincy Adams*, and earlier, as shown in Fig. 24, by G. F. Storm, the English stipple engraver, lately come to Philadelphia, for Longacre and Herring's *National Portrait Gallery of Distinguished Americans*, 1834–1839. Storm had also engraved Stuart's portrait of Abigail Adams for the same work.

WILLIAM SHIELS (1785-1857)

Upon being recalled from England by President Monroe to become his Secretary of State, Adams left for America, sailing on 14 June 1817 from the Isle of Wight on the ship *Washington*. Among his fellow passengers whom Adams listed in his diary was "Mr. Shiel a Scotchman and a Painter." [1] This was undoubtedly the William Shiels (or Shields) who became a member of the Royal Scottish Academy, and painted and exhibited portraits in New York, Charleston, South Carolina, and London. Although there were occasions to fish, be seasick, try out "one of Burt's patent sounding machines," (without success), converse with the crew, read a few passages in Bacon's *Novum Organum*, play chess with the Bostonian A. G. Otis, and write in his diary, nevertheless Adams early complained, "Our life on shipboard is as usual dull; and I fear my time will be much wasted in idleness." [2]

He and Shiels, in the confines of an 1817 transatlantic sailing vessel, must have soon struck up a friendly acquaintance. Landing in New York on 6 August, Adams stayed nine days before proceeding to Quincy. A dinner at Tammany Hall, a formal banquet at the Hotel Bellevue arranged in his honor by the Mayor of the City, visits to City Hall, the Academy of Art, The New-York Historical Society, and the like occupied his time. Yet during the period he records introducing Shiels at his request to Trumbull, and sitting to Shiels for his own portrait on three occasions for five or six hours in all. The portrait still unfinished, Shiels asked for another sitting on Adams' return to New York.

After a short visit to Quincy, Adams departed for Washington, stopping off in New York for a couple of days. From his diary we learn: "I went to Shiels at his painting room N. 20 Wall Street, and sat to him an hour to finish my picture. He says he has not been an hour disengaged since he arrived in New York; that he has more work than he can do, and has now more than fifty orders for Portraits upon hand." [3] The exhibition record of the American Academy of Fine Arts and American Art-Union discloses that in 1818 Shiels exhibited (under No. 161) a "Portrait of the honourable John Quincy Adams." [4] The portrait has not been located, and no further reference to it has come to light.

---

[1] Entry of 16 June 1817.   [2] Same.   [3] Entry of 14 Sept. 1817.
[4] Mary B. Cowdrey, *American Academy of Fine Arts and American Art-Union, Exhibition Record, 1816–1852* (NYHS, *Colls.*, 77 [1944]), p. 328.

III

The Secretary of State
1817–1825

"Everything in my head is difficult for a bust."

CHRONOLOGY OF JOHN QUINCY ADAMS' LIFE, 1817–1825

1817

Sept. 20: Arrives in Washington and assumes post; immediately begins work on a Report on Weights and Measures which the Fourteenth Congress had assigned to the Secretary of State on 3 March 1817.

1818

Concludes with Great Britain the Convention of 1818 on fisheries, boundaries, and transatlantic commerce.

July: Opposes in the Cabinet the censure of Andrew Jackson for invading the Spanish province of Florida without authorization. Sits to Cardelli the sculptor (Figs. 25–27).

Sept.: Painted by Stuart for the first time (Fig. 28).

Oct. 28: Death of his mother.

1819

Jan.: Painted by C. W. Peale (Fig. 36).

Feb. 22: Signs Transcontinental Treaty with Spain by which the United States acquires the territory of Florida and in the northwest extends her southern boundary to the Pacific.

April: Sits to C. B. King (Figs. 38–40).

1820

Takes up residence in Washington at 1333–1335 F Street NW.

1821

Feb. 22: Terminates, "blessed be God, two of the most memorable transactions of my life": the *Report on Weights and Measures*, an effort which anticipates the universal adoption of the metric system; and the definitive ratification of the Transcontinental Treaty with Spain by the Senate.

66

July 4: In an address given in the House of Representatives chamber, formulates anticolonial and antientanglement principles as touchstones of American foreign policy, particularly in relation to South American states.

1822

Publishes *The Duplicate Letters, the Fisheries and the Mississippi,* a pamphlet which exposed with devastating force the errors in Jonathan Russell's attack on JQA's diplomacy at Ghent.

1823

Acquires the Columbian Mills in Washington. Proposes a treaty to Great Britain outlawing privateering and defining a policy of maritime neutrality. As a prime participant in the formulation of the Monroe Doctrine (enunciated in President Monroe's Message to Congress, 2 Dec.), JQA enlarges his earlier position by extending the noncolonization principle to the whole of the Americas.

1824

Saves from extinction the Columbian College in Washington (now George Washington University) through personal loans.

Jan. 8: The Adamses give their famous ball for Andrew Jackson on the ninth anniversary of the Battle of New Orleans.

April: Concludes a Convention with Russia fixing latitude 54° 40′ as the boundary of the American sphere of influence and insuring the later incorporation of Oregon into the territory of the United States.

July: Painted by Wood (Fig. 48).

Nov.: In the national election no candidate receives a majority vote; JQA runs second to Jackson but ahead of William H. Crawford.

Dec.: Sully's first portrait painted (Fig. 49).

PIETRO CARDELLI (d. 1822)

The return of Adams from England in 1817 to serve as Secretary of State under President Monroe was the source of great satisfaction to his family. Jefferson wrote to the elder Adams, "I congratulate Mrs. Adams and yourself on the return of your excellent and distinguished son ... and I renew to both the assurance of my high and friendly respect and esteem." John Adams thanked his friend for his congratulations, adding, "If the Secretary of State can give Satisfaction to his fellow Citizens in his new Office it will be a Source of consolation to me while I live." [1]

The newly appointed Secretary of State had arrived in New York from London early in August, and after a short visit to his parents in Quincy departed for Washington, where he arrived in late September, having stopped briefly in New York and Philadelphia. He had been in Washington only a few days before the "starving Italian Sculptor Cardelli" presented himself with a letter of introduction from the artist Trumbull:

This Letter will be presented to you by Senr. Cardelli the Roman Sculptor, of whom I spoke to you, and Specimens of whose work you saw at my home. Having unfortunately failed to procure for him here, the employment which I hoped, I have advised him to go to Washington and if He should not meet encouragement there, to return to Europe as soon as possible.

He is desirous in particular, of being permitted to model a Head of the president in the persuasion, that, if Successful, many of the president's friends, not only in Congress, but in the Several States would be desirous of having Casts, which He could afford at 10 or 12 dollars ea.—and, if this should fail He still hopes there may be some opening for him in the works carrying on at the Capitol. On the latter subject I have given him a line to Mr. LaTrobe and on both I beg leave to recommend him to your protection as a worthy man, who appears to me to possess considerable talent in his profession, and to have been peculiarly unfortunate. [2]

Adams noted that "He draws in Crayons also, and asked my leave to take a portrait of my wife to give him something to do." Adams gave him permission to do his wife's picture at Mr. Nathaniel Frye's, where the Adamses lived, and a few days later remarked, "Cardelli brought me the Portrait of my wife that he has taken in Crayons, but as I was not satisfied with the likeness, he requested that she would sit again, which she did." He brought the drawing back a second time a week later, "not much improved," and later began a new one, "being dissatisfied with the first." [3] Whether the drawing was ever finished is not known. No trace of it has turned up.

Cardelli was an Italian sculptor from Rome who had been employed from 1806 to 1810 on the Vendôme Column in Paris, and came to Washington in 1817 in search of employment. It was obvious that the rebuilding of the Capitol, following its burning in August 1814, would require the services of architects and artisans, sculptors and

[1] Jefferson to JA, 8 Sept. (Adams Papers); JA to Jefferson, 10 Oct. 1817 (DLC: Jefferson Papers); both printed in Cappon, ed., *Adams-Jefferson Letters*, 2:519–522.
[2] John Trumbull to JQA, 25 Sept. (Adams Papers); JQA, Diary, 4 Oct. 1817.
[3] JQA, Diary; 4, 6, 18, 25 Oct., 1 Nov. 1817.

artists, and Cardelli, like many others, hoped for a prominent part in the task. Trumbull gave him letters of introduction to President Monroe, Benjamin H. Latrobe, and Sir Charles Bagot, then British Minister to the United States. In return for these favors Cardelli executed busts of Trumbull and his wife; the latter is now lost, the former is "a handsome affair."[4] Trumbull again wrote to Adams, this time in support of Cardelli's employment on the Capitol, but was told in reply: "I have this morning received your Letter of the 1st instant, which reached me too late, the office in question having previously been assigned to Charles Bulfinch, esq. Cardelli is now employed and has hitherto given satisfaction. There will probably be constant employment for him for a considerable time."[5] It is true that Cardelli was employed, but not to his liking. He was later described as "a Sculptor by profession, regularly educated, in the Schools where the Art is taught and practised in its highest perfection."[6] Bulfinch insisted upon his "working at the ornaments of the Capitol, instead of designing and executing Basso relievos, and the proper business of a Sculptor,"[7] but he was reduced by necessity to submit to it. As Adams quoted him as saying, he was working "upon leaves and ornaments; which gives him bread, but no reputation."[8]

Cardelli must have satisfied Adams of his ability, for we shortly find him sitting to the sculptor for his bust. Three times he sat in July, but Cardelli, he noted, found "everything in my head is difficult for a bust, which I well understand." Early in August the bust was finished but not, characteristically, to Adams' satisfaction. "We found," he wrote, "that he had totally failed in the likeness; so he asked for another sitting which I gave him; he altered it very much but will ultimately not get a likeness."[9]

The last step in the process was the casting, which Adams described: "Cardelli came, and cast the hollow mould, the creux perdu of the bust. I had never seen and had no idea of the manner of casting Statues in Plaster. There is nothing in the work that can properly be called Sculpture. The first mould is taken in soft red clay worked by the hand. The second is this Plaister Shell moulded over it in two

[4] *The Autobiography of Colonel John Trumbull, Patriot-Artist, 1756–1843,* ed. Theodore Sizer, New Haven, 1953, p. 269.
[5] Trumbull to JQA, 1 Dec. (Adams Papers); JQA to Trumbull, 4 Dec. 1817 (LbC, Adams Papers).
[6] Draft of Cardelli's petition to Congress to extend the copyright to works of sculpture, in JQA's hand, dated 28 Feb. 1820 (Adams Papers).
[7] JQA, Diary, 8 March 1818.
[8] Same, 6 April 1818.
[9] Same, 19 July, 9 Aug. 1818.

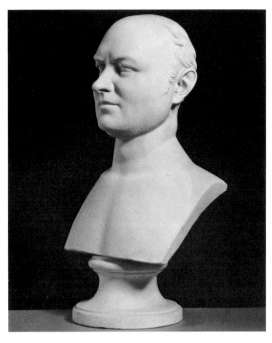

25. JOHN QUINCY ADAMS. PLASTER BUST BY PIETRO CARDELLI, 1818

halves. The Bust itself is cast in this, and must be done hereafter. Cardelli dined with us." [10] The bust was cast a week later, just before Adams returned to Quincy for a month. A later diary entry reports, "Cardelli was here and brought the bust, but I did not see him." [11]

We can judge the result ourselves by comparing the finished work (Fig. 25) with contemporary portraits of Adams, such as those by Leslie (Fig. 22), Stuart (Fig. 28), and Peale (Fig. 36), with all of which it compares favorably as a likeness. Adams' wife wrote her father-in-law that it was "a wonderful fine thing and the likeness speaking." [12]

Three examples of Cardelli's bust of Adams have survived. One (Fig. 25) was given to The New-York Historical Society on 11 April 1820 by Gulian C. Verplanck, who may have purchased it from the sculptor. A second (Fig. 26) was presented to the American Philosophical Society on 20 February 1829 by Dr. John Kearsley Mitchell. The third (Fig. 27) is now preserved in the Old House in Quincy, probably having been owned by the family since 1818. All three are

[10] Same, 16 Aug. 1818.
[11] Same, 25 Oct. 1818.
[12] LCA to JA, 8 March–3 April 1819 (Adams Papers).

27. JOHN QUINCY ADAMS.
MARBLE BUST BY PIETRO CARDELLI, 1818

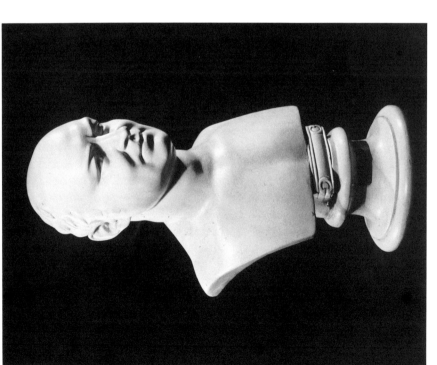

26. JOHN QUINCY ADAMS.
PLASTER BUST BY PIETRO CARDELLI, 1818

clearly from the same mold. The minutes of the meeting of the American Philosophical Society of 20 June 1832 record that "D. Harlan, on behalf of Mr. S. J. Wetherill, presented a bust of John Quincy Adams, cast in Iron at Keim & Jones's, Windsor Furnace, Bucks County, Pennsylvania."[13] The iron cast has disappeared, though the Society has a photograph of it. No other copies or reproductions have come to light.

Described in an exchange of correspondence between Judge Joseph Hopkinson of Philadelphia and Louisa Catherine Adams in 1823 is what was in all probability a fourth example. Hopkinson wrote:

A few days ago there arrived at this port of Philadelphia, in a packet from Alexandria, a certain box, directed to me; which, when opened, was found to contain a *very fine head*, in *excellent order*. As no letter accompanied the box, or was received by any other conveyance, the head was left to speak for itself; and inform from whence it came, and to what it was destined. The recollection of a conversation with you on the subject of a certain head had left me no doubt as to whom I should address myself to acknowledge the receipt of this valuable acquisition to the Penna. Academy of the Fine Arts. It is duly and honourably deposited in the Hall of Great men; and I shall give a special caution to its companions to be civil, and make no unprovoked attacks upon it, as it has a marvellous faculty of breaking any head that comes too roughly against it.

To this Mrs. Adams replied from Washington: "The safe arrival of the Bust has given me much pleasure, and its installation in the Academy of Arts and Sciences, which the *head* was formed to grace, assures to me its permanent security."[14]

Adams must have become reconciled to his bust; at least he went out of his way to aid the sculptor. He helped Cardelli obtain the consent of President Monroe and of Jefferson and Madison to take their busts.[15] The sculptor thought so well of his own work and was so anxious for public recognition that he told Adams he planned to give up working on ornaments at the Capitol and to rely upon the income from the sales of his busts for his support, quoting the Italian proverb, "the egg of to-day is better than the hen of to-morrow." Adams advised against the move but gave some advice on the problem of copyright,

[13] American Philosophical Society, Curator's Record, 20 June 1832.
[14] Hopkinson to LCA, 1 Jan.; LCA to Hopkinson, 5 Jan. 1823 (both in Adams Papers). The annual catalogues of the Pennsylvania Academy of the Fine Arts for the years 1824–1830, 1849, 1852, and 1853 list a bust or cast of John Quincy Adams. The 1852 entry gives the name of J. H. King as the owner, but no entry names the sculptor (Louise Wallman, Registrar of the Academy, to the Author, 24 March 1969).
[15] JQA, Diary, 7 March, 17 April; LCA to JA, 8 March–3 April; Cardelli to JQA, 15 June 1819 (both in Adams Papers).

72

remarking in his diary, "I cannot but admire the sentiment of honour and love of fame, displayed by this man, in his deep distress."[16]

A few months later Adams again displayed his confidence in Cardelli—or at least his desire to help him—by engaging him to give "lessons of Drawing, three times a week, to my Son Charles and Mary Hellen—Tuesdays, Thursdays and Saturdays, at seven in the Evening."[17] Entries in Charles' diary during January and February 1820 show that this plan was carried out.[18]

GILBERT STUART (1755–1828)

No sooner was Adams through with the ordeal of having his bust taken by Cardelli, with its attendant, though perhaps temporary, disappointment, than he was engaged in a similar project with Stuart. Adams left Washington 28 August 1818 for a month's visit to Quincy. As usual he lay over in Philadelphia and New York for a few days and did not reach home until 4 September. He was to set out again on 1 October.

On 16 September he and his wife visited Stuart's studio in Boston: "After breakfast we called at the house of Mr. Stewart the Painters and saw several Portraits upon which he is now engaged. As we came home my wife persuaded me to sit to Stewart for my own Picture, for my children. I returned to him and engaged to sit at seven O'Clock to-morrow Morning."[1] He made this engagement despite the fact that only a few years before he had despaired of ever getting from Stuart his father's portrait, withheld by the artist, unfinished, for seventeen years![2] Adams had then written from St. Petersburg to his brother, "I never think of this subject without feeling against Stewart an indignation, which I wish I could change into contempt";[3] but he had also said, "There is in America no other Painter capable of executing a Work, which I should wish to see preserved."[4] What he and Louisa had just seen in Stuart's studio must have fortified this opinion, and so the following day he sat to Stuart from seven to nine in the morning and similarly the day after, with an interval of half an hour.

On 19 September his diary reports:

[16] Entry of 17 April 1819.
[17] Entry of 19 Oct. 1819.
[18] CFA, *Diary*, 1:3–7.
[1] JQA, Diary, 16 Sept. 1818.
[2] Oliver, *Portraits of JA and AA*, p. 133–135 (Fig. 64).
[3] To TBA, 13 May 1811 (Adams Papers); printed in JQA, *Writings*, 4:70–71.
[4] To John Singleton Copley, 29 April 1811 (LbC, Adams Papers).

A continual storm of rain. . . . I sat to Stewart before and after breakfast; and found his conversation, as it has been at every sitting, very entertaining. His own figure is highly picturesque, with his dress always disordered, and taking snuff from a large round tin wafer box, holding perhaps half a pound which he must use up in a day. He considers himself beyond all question the first portrait painter of the age, and tells numbers of anecdotes concerning himself to prove it, with the utmost simplicity, and unconsciousness of ridicule. His conclusion is not very wide from the truth.[5]

Adams was not alone in enjoying Stuart's conversation; a few years later his father was to comment: "I should like to sit to Stuart from the first of January to the last of December, for he lets me do just what I please and keeps me constantly amused by his conversation."[6] Though all admired Stuart's portraits, all were anxious to point out his peculiarities: "We saw Stuart," Adams' kinswoman Eliza Susan Quincy wrote, "and many of his pictures. He is one of, if not the most frightful looking man I ever saw, but his small grey eye is sharp and so acute that his glance seems to cut into the individual before him."[7]

After an abortive visit on 22 September, Adams sat the following day, noting: "He told me at first that he should want only four sittings from an hour and a half to two hours each. He has had four sittings of more than two hours each, and has not half finished the head. He says he is much satisfied with what he has done but I cannot exactly say the same."[8] But 1 October, the day marked for Adams' return to Washington, proved the day of the seventh and last sitting: "I sat this Morning before Breakfast and he finished the head."[9]

The portrait (Fig. 28) is next heard of in a letter to Adams from Michael H. Bowyer:

My motives for addressing your Excellency will I hope plaid my appology for the freedom. I beg leave to bring to your recollection that last April, when I had the Honor of presenting you my engraved Portraits of Comes. McDonough and Perry, I apprized you of my intention of bringing forward one of yr. Excellency. Agreeable to your wish I call'd on your friend Mr. Cruft, to view that in his Possession by Stuart. I find it to correspond with my expectation, from that inimitable Artist, possessing

---

[5] Entry of 19 Sept. 1818; see also William T. Whitley, *Gilbert Stuart*, Cambridge, 1932, p. 157.

[6] Quincy, *Figures of the Past*, p. 71.

[7] Eliza Susan Quincy, MS Journal, 13 March 1816 (MHi: Quincy Papers).

[8] Diary, 22 Sept. 1818. Fifteen years later Adams said of this portrait, "This . . . is a very indifferent picture and no likeness." JQA to George F. Morris, 20 Sept. 1833 (LbC, Adams Papers).

[9] Diary, 1 Oct. 1818.

28. JOHN QUINCY ADAMS. OIL ON PANEL BY GILBERT STUART, 1818

Charactor, and a strong *likeness* which will enable me to Hand to posterity a correct likeness of a Statesman revered by the friends of literature and science. As it is indispensable that I should have the Painting to copy from, you'll Please to write to Mr. Cruft to that effect, as he'll be guided by yr. instructions. You may rely on it being returned in safety, as soon as the engraving will be completed, which, will I hope be finished next year (God willing). I should be glad to hear from your Excellency before I return to New York as my personal care in bringing the picture along would be agreeable. If more eligible to yr. Ex., to communicate with Cruft he will apprize me of it.[10]

Adams complied with the request, advising Bowyer he could have the portrait for a period, "not to exceed two years," and wrote Cruft approving its delivery.[11]

As could be expected, the project took much longer than anticipated. Joseph Delaplaine, the Philadelphia bookseller, sought to borrow the portrait for the same purpose in 1823, but it was still in Bowyer's hands, and Adams urged Delaplaine "not to incur the risk and cost of having another engraving made which could not but result in loss both to you and to him." [12] Bowyer must have returned the portrait when, a year and a half later, Charles Francis Adams mentions visitors arriving in Quincy "to look at the portraits [by Stuart] of my grandfather and my father." [13]

Time passed, Adams was inaugurated as President, and at length heard again from Bowyer:

Allow me the pleasure of congratulating you on receiving the highest honor, the gift of a free People can bestow by placing you to preside over their destinies and I hope the happiness of the nation.

I rejoice in your elivation particularly as I spoke with confidence on that event, more than two years back. I beg leave to refer your Excellency to a communication I had the honor of making in a former letter on business where I adverted to that event as certain.

My motive for this address will I hope plead some appology, as its to inform your Excellency, that I have persevered in bringing forward and I hope to have shortly compleated an Engraved Portrait, taken, from the Portrait in the Possession of Mr. Crufts, that you favoured me with. It is engraveing by Gimbrede and I anticipate its being superior, to any that has been or will be executed; under this coviction I rely on the liberality of my fellow Citizens to reward, by at least, purchasing. A little pecuniary

[10] 24 Oct. 1821 (Adams Papers).
[11] JQA to Bowyer, 31 Oct. 1821; to Edward Cruft, same (both LbCs, Adams Papers).
[12] 19 March 1823 (LbC, Adams Papers).
[13] CFA, *Diary*, 1:318 (9 Sept. 1824).

aid would at this time come most opportunely, it would enable me to make good some unavoidable engagements enter'd into in bringing it forward. I beg leave to offer you my most respectful wishes for your Happiness, both temporal and eternal.[14]

Thomas Gimbrede was a competent stipple engraver who was born in England in 1781 and had come to America in 1802. He was first known in New York as a dancing master, but later became a teacher of drawing at West Point. He took up the correspondence with Adams in June 1825, signing himself "Thos. Gimbrede professor of Drawing USMA." He wrote: "I had the pleasure six months ago to commence an Engraving of yourself which I composed and made use of a fine Head painted by Stuart. Nevertheless if I could be so fortunate to be informed by you of the probable time you'l be in Newyork I would go there with my plate and design to see you and to consult you on somme of the deatails of the composition. I expect to finish the plate after the examination is over in july." [15]

Adams was not soon to be in New York; but, anxious as always to oblige artists seeking to take his likeness, he arranged a meeting in Washington, noting in his diary:

Macomb, General, with Gimbrede, teacher of drawing at the Academy at West Point. Gimbrede brought several specimens of drawing by the Cadets, and an unfinished drawing for a plate which he has begun from Stewart's Portrait of me. He requested of me a sitting; for which I fixed Monday at ten O'Clock. He had a good likeness of Genl. Scott of which he intends to publish a Plate. Gimbrede is discontented with his Establishment at West Point because his art is not on a level of rank with the other subjects of instruction.

He recorded in an entry two days later: "Sitting to Gimbrede—gave him my device of Lyra." [16]

Gimbrede took the "device of Lyra" and made good use of it. The lyre can be seen repeated many times in the border of the drapery behind Adams, the eagle and shield surmount the chair back, and thirteen arrows and as many stars (two of which are concealed) decorate the column at which he stands. In the midst of the inscription beneath the engraving appears the device itself, eagle and lyre, bearing the motto NUNC SIDERA DUCIT and surrounded by twenty-four stars, representing the number of states then admitted into the

[14] 26 April 1825 (Adams Papers).
[15] 18 June 1825 (Adams Papers).
[16] Entries of 9, 11 July 1825.

Union. Except for the number of stars surrounding the eagle, Gimbrede's representation closely resembles the design in use on United States passports at about that time.[17]

A third and apparently last sitting took place three days later. The finished engraving (Fig. 29), which could be considered at least in part a portrait from life, is quite impressive. The pose and formal surroundings are reminiscent of Copley's portrait of John Adams. The engraving is inscribed, in part, "Respectfully Dedicated by the Author to Col: S. Thayer, Supdt. U.S. Mility. Academy."

Gimbrede's devotion to his profession and the frustration under which he had to exercise it at the Military Academy are evident from his letter to Adams from the Academy some years later:

> The responsibility devolving on me by the regulations as an instructor, the natural fondness I have for the fine Arts, and the extreme want of a Collection, have frequently obliged me to use my own and from time to time have added Engravings, or paintings, which have Enable me to teach with moore Sucess.
>
> The last board of Visitors could not satisfactorily account for the proficiency of my pupils in so short a time, deprived as we are of the necessary models to be seen in all other schools. I have satisfied them with these few words; with my mode of Teaching, my collection, and my zeal; I produce theese results since the beguining of this term. I have had ocasion to bring forward many of my prints, and twelve of my best pictures are also gracing the Walls of the Drawing Academy! They Enable me to answer to the Eager Enquiries of Somme by ocular Demonstration and to point out to them that the best principles of Drawing are derived from correct Forms, good composition, Aerial perspective, harmony, &c. &c. In fine their Eyes should becomme familliar with these settled principles if I do my duty as an instructor. I have purchassed somme good models during Eight years with my limited means; I hope the time is not far distant when the government will provide the means to purchase a good collection, and that I may be permitted to transfer mine for the use of my Dept.[18]

Shortly after Adams' sitting with Gimbrede, the stipple engraver James B. Longacre of Philadelphia made two engravings from Stuart's head, one published in *Le Souvenir, or Picturesque Pocket Dictionary for 1826*, and the other for *The Casket* in 1828. Longacre's diary describes the arrangements made to obtain access to the original. "Went later with Mr. I. P. Davis," he wrote on 23 July 1825, "to see the portraits of J. and J. Q. Adams at Mr. Cruft's. Mr. Cruft

[17] The Lyre and Eagle in Adams' iconography is discussed and illustrated in the Introduction.
[18] 12 Feb. 1827 (Adams Papers).

29. JOHN QUINCY ADAMS. ENGRAVING BY THOMAS GIMBREDE, 1826

30. JOHN QUINCY ADAMS. ENGRAVING BY JAMES BARTON LONGACRE, 1826

politely offered me an opportunity of copying the head of J. Q. Adams by Stuart." Again on 3 August: "Finished my drawing of Col. Pickering. Commenced at Mr. Cruft's my drawing of J. Q. Adams, from portrait painted by Stuart Aug. 1818." Finally on 6 August he recorded: "Finished my drawing of J. Q. Adams, to the satisfaction of Mr. Cruft who is to write to the President of the U.S. (whose property the picture is) for his permission for me to engrave it, which Mr. Cruft is anxious I should do. . . . I called in the afternoon to take leave of Mr. Stuart's family and in the evening on Mr. I. P. Davis who was pleased with my drawings of Pickering and J. Q. Adams; he said he had conversed with Stuart on the subject of my engraving the latter, who was desirous that I should do it."[19] Longacre's engraving (Fig. 30), typical of several he made, follows Stuart's portrait closely.

[19] *PMHB*, 29:140–142 (April 1905).

Later engravings were done, probably after Longacre's or Gimbrede's: by W. Ball, the lithographer who did a series of Presidential portraits about 1835 (Fig. 31); by Nathaniel Currier (Fig. 32); by D. W. Kellogg (Fig. 33); by the French engraver Vernier (Fig. 34); and many others. Ball, Currier, and Kellogg used the freedom practiced by current engravers in adding ancillary elements not in the original—a book in the hand, a chair, a table, stylized drapery, a column in the background. Each shows marked similarities to the others, along with minor variations such as in the column base, the watch fob with seal, the treatment of waistcoat and collar, and the like. It is not possible to say who conceived the form of the adaptation. Currier's acquires an added interest because he employed the body and background of his lithograph after Stuart in a lithograph (Fig. 78) adapted from Durand's portrait (Fig. 72). The efforts, after Stuart, of Ball, Currier, and Kellogg were all inferior to the likenesses produced by Gimbrede and Longacre.

At some time after Stuart painted Adams, he commenced, and later finished, a portrait of Louisa. Park's *Gilbert Stuart* (1:96) dates her portrait August 1818, which we now know cannot be correct because she was in Washington through most of August, reaching New York on 31 August on her way back to Quincy. A clue to the date of the commencement of the portrait may be Louisa's letter to her son Charles written in May 1821: "You reproach me without a cause and I dare say you got your Letter the very day after you wrote. My Time has however been very much occupied in sitting for a picture which is not quite finished and which it is probable will employ me the whole summer."[20] She does not mention Stuart in this letter, but no other portrait was to our knowledge *in limine* at the time.

Although there is no other evidence when Stuart's portrait of Louisa was commenced, in 1825 an unfinished portrait of her from Stuart's hand was nearing completion. Ward Nicholas Boylston, who had commissioned Stuart to paint the portrait of John Quincy Adams that was later finished by Sully (Fig. 57), wrote to Adams late in 1825 that he had seen the "two pictures that is as far as they have been compleated," and that Stuart had never "given a greater proof of his Talents, or done more justice to the precise likeness of those they were intended to represent."[21] Two months later he could only add that, "in defiance of every pursuasion of mine ... Mrs. Adams's and your portraits are as you last saw them."[22] It would not have

[20] 4 May 1821 (Adams Papers).
[21] 27 Oct. 1825 (Adams Papers).
[22] 22 Dec. 1825 (Adams Papers).

JOHN QUINCY ADAMS.
6th. President of the United States.

F. Currier's Lith & Et.

32. JOHN QUINCY ADAMS.
LITHOGRAPH BY NATHANIEL CURRIER

JOHN QUINCY ADAMS
6TH PRESIDENT OF THE UNITED STATES.

Published by G. ENDICOTT, 138 Broadway

31. JOHN QUINCY ADAMS.

34. JOHN QUINCY ADAMS.
ENGRAVING BY VERNIER, 1838

33. JOHN QUINCY ADAMS.
LITHOGRAPH BY D. W. KELLOGG & CO.

83

been at all unlike Stuart to have commenced Louisa's portrait in 1821, yet not to have finished it four years later.

Louisa herself wrote what could be called a typical mother's letter to her son George, enclosing verses relating to it:

> To my Sons with my Portrait by Stewart
> Go flatter'd image tell the tale
> Of years long past away;
> Of faded youth, of sorrows wail,
> Of times too sure decay—
> When Mem'ry ling'ring shall retrace
> Those days for ever flown;
> When in a Mother's fond embrace,
> Your purest joys were known. . . .
>
> When age maturer pleasures taught
> She listen'd to the tale,
> Of youthful games for ever sought,
> Mid school-boys rude assail—
> Of little sorrows, trifling cares,
> Of irritation strong;
> Of lessons missed, neglected prayers,
> Of College pranks; and wrong. . . .
>
> Oh! this the charm of life does prove
> And e'en in death shall cheer,
> The Spirit of maternal love
> In heaven's celestial sphere—
> When in the sleep of death those eyes,
> That heart shall cease to move,
> The Mother blest in yonder skies
> Shall guard thee from above.
>   L. C. Adams
>   To all together and individually
>   P.H.   Decb. 18, 1825 [23]

A year later Adams wrote of his first view of the portrait: "I stopped at Mr. Stuart, the Painter's, and there saw the Portrait of my wife for the first time. It is unfinished and he promised to finish it but asked that she would give him another sitting." [24] Stuart frequently

[23] The verses were enclosed in LCA to GWA, 18 Dec. 1825 (Adams Papers). "P.H." meant the President's House, not yet known as the White House.

[24] Entry of 9 Sept. 1826. Boylston had attributed the delay in completing the portraits not only to Stuart's desire for a further sitting but to his own sickness which had "prevented my personal and constant application to Mr. Stuart" to finish the portraits, adding: "he has nevertheless had my constant monitions, he pleads his own indisposition (gout) and a thousand impediments" (Boylston to JQA, 29 May and 15 Aug. 1826 [Adams Papers]).

did this when years elapsed before finishing a portrait. A little later Adams did write to his son George: "You have mentioned, I think in a letter to your mother that Mr. Stewart has finished the Portrait of your Mother," and instructed him to obtain the picture and pay Stuart for it.[25]

Mrs. Adams saw her own portrait (Fig. 35), when finally finished, at the Boston Athenæum the following year and wrote of it to her son John's future wife: "I saw my portrait at the exhibition. John and Jane were perfectly horrified. Nobody likes it and Stewart is quite vexed. It looks very much as I looked, like a woman who was just attacked by the first chill of death and the features stiffning into torpor. The hair is as white as the face and the fine lilac bows in the Cap seem to mock the general frigidity of the half Corps. It speaks too much of inward suffering and a half broken heart to be an agreeable remembrancer. Mais n'import—'tis but a speaking tell tale which may in time of need long after I am gone and I hope give a lesson both of feeling and wisdom."[26] Louisa's pessimism surely got the better of her in this judgment on her portrait. It is indeed a charming portrait, worthy of Boylston's comments; if a little solemn, it was because solemnity was a mood not unknown to her.

Shortly before his son Charles' marriage, Adams presented him with three portraits: "one of my Grandfather painted by Stuart and exceedingly valuable, and those of my father and Mother by the same artist but not so good."[27] A few days later they were delivered to him to his evident satisfaction:

I accomplished my purpose of having the pictures hung which belong to me. They now form quite a goodly collection. That of my Grandfather is invaluable both as a Painting and as a correct likeness of what he was in those times. My Mother is a likeness but not a good painting. Her face wears a sorrowful appearance too common to her, and also very fresh now in my recollection. But I shall value that picture as I do her Miniatures as presenting even something of her appearance in those days. For hereafter there will be nothing. And I love to think of her as she was, in the midst of her gaiety and her prosperity. My father's is not good being Stewart's first attempt, but I value it notwithstanding.[28]

In speaking of his mother's sorrowful appearance in Stuart's portrait as "very fresh now in my recollection," Charles was referring of course to the family tragedy which had occurred only four months

[25] 19 Nov. 1826 (Adams Papers).
[26] To Mary Hellen [Mrs. JA2], 13 July 1827 (Adams Papers).
[27] CFA, *Diary*, 2:426 (27 Aug. 1829).
[28] Same, p. 429–430 (31 Aug. 1829).

35. LOUISA CATHERINE ADAMS.
OIL ON PANEL BY GILBERT STUART, 1821

previously. His brother George, who was his mother's favorite son and was looked on as the most promising of the three boys, had not lived up to his parents' high hopes. He neglected the family business, fell into bad ways, sired an illegitimate child, and seemed to Charles on the verge of derangement. Summoned to Washington by his father, he took the steamer from Boston and, early in the morning of 30 April 1829, jumped or fell overboard to his death in Long Island Sound. Louisa's portrait, however, was finished prior to this tragic event and reflects her appearance as it must have been sometime between 1821 and 1825. If it appears sorrowful rather than merely wistful or contemplative, it reflects the state of mind to which she herself alluded. When she could speak of "inward suffering and a half broken heart," we can accept Stuart's likeness as indicative of her feelings. Charles' comments were simply intensified by the recent loss of his brother.

From Charles the portraits of his father and mother descended to his eldest son, John Quincy Adams 2d, whose widow in turn gave the oils to their son the late Arthur Adams. They are now owned by his son John Quincy Adams of Dover, Massachusetts.

CHARLES WILLSON PEALE (1741–1827)

Peale's activity at the age of seventy-seven was cause for astonishment and admiration. In the winter of 1818 he went to Washington to paint the portraits of such distinguished persons as he could, for his Museum, and he wished to try his hand on the new Secretary of State. In November he called on Adams with an introduction from Dr. Thornton, and Adams agreed to sit.[1] The sitter's diary and the artist's letters record the progress of the painting. Apparently the first sitting commenced on 2 December, and the following day Peale wrote his son Linnaeus that he had begun the portrait. A few days later he reported to his son Rembrandt that the portrait had "progressed toward the finishing."[2] At the same time Adams' diary recorded progress. "Mr. Peale was here this Morning to look at my Portrait painted at Ghent, upon which he made some small criticisms. He asked me to sit again, which I promised him I would if possible to-morrow."[3]

Important engagements made it impossible to keep that appoint-

[1] JQA, Diary, 1 Dec. 1818.
[2] Charles Coleman Sellers, *Portraits and Miniatures of Charles Willson Peale,* Phila., 1952, p. 23.
[3] Entry of 11 Dec. 1818.

36. JOHN QUINCY ADAMS. OIL BY CHARLES WILLSON PEALE, 1818

ment, however, and it was not for several days that Adams could report sitting, "I believe for the last time."[4] On 29 January 1819 we learn the result. "Mr. Peale had called upon me this morning to ask another sitting which I accordingly gave him, of about an hour. He has made a Caricature of my Portrait."

The painting (Fig. 36) is in Peale's usual warm colors and like so many of his likenesses, tends to give the sitter a long oval face like the artist's own. It is not as consistent a likeness as the other contemporary portraits, Leslie's (Fig. 22), Cardelli's (Fig. 25), or Stuart's (Fig. 28). Adams' usual complaint that his portraits were too "like" could scarcely apply here.

The portrait took its place in Peale's Museum in Philadelphia, where the artist's portrait of John Adams, painted in 1794 when he was Vice-President, also hung.[5] There they remained until the Museum collection was dispersed by auction in 1854. The portrait of John Quincy Adams was sold as item No. 142 for $12 to Charles S. Ogden; that of the elder Adams fetched $60.[6] Ogden was a distinguished merchant of Philadelphia, who evidently had an interest in the Historical Society of Pennsylvania, to which he presented the portrait of John Quincy Adams in 1896, accompanied by Peale's portraits of Joseph Bonaparte and Henry Clay.

B. BYRON

In 1958 the Smithsonian Institution commemorated the two hundredth anniversary of the birth of the fifth President of the United States with an exhibition in Washington entitled *Profiles of the Time of James Monroe (1758–1831)*, and issued a catalogue under that title. For the occasion a magnificent gathering of portraits was assembled, portraying many of the great Americans of Monroe's day by the hands of the foremost artists—all in profile. Monroe by Rembrandt Peale, John Adams by Stuart,[1] Jefferson by Sully, Washington by Marchant after Sharples, Madison by Vanderlyn were some of those

---

[4] Entry of 16 Dec. 1818.

[5] See Oliver, *Portraits of JA and AA*, p. 70–72 (Fig. 29).

[6] *Peale's Museum Gallery of Oil Paintings ... Catalogue of the National Portrait and Historical Gallery, Illustrative of American History ... Formerly Belonging to Peale's Museum*, Phila., 1854 (NHi, photostat copy formerly belonging to Mantle Fielding). The Supplement to the Catalogue contains the notation: "The prices paid and the names of buyers being copied from notes made by Mr. John MacAllister who attended the sale on Oct. 6th 1854."

[1] Oliver, *Portraits of JA and AA*, Fig. 94.

37. LOUISA CATHERINE ADAMS(?).
SILHOUETTE ON CARDBOARD BY B. BYRON, CA. 1819

represented. And included in this galaxy was a likeness said to be of
Louisa Catherine Adams (Fig. 37), described as "handpainted on
cardboard," 3¼ by 2¾ inches, by B. Byron "early 19th century."

Nothing else is known of the silhouette except that it belongs to
the Metropolitan Museum of Art, New York, as part of the bequest by
Mary Martin in 1938. It is not recognizable, but seems to disclose a
woman of about the age Louisa was not long before 1820. The Adamses
arrived in New York on 6 August 1817 and never again went abroad.
From 1809 to 1817 they had been in Denmark, Russia, the Low
Countries, France, and England. No record of a silhouettist by the
name of B. Byron has come to light, in England or in America, during
that period.

90

CHARLES BIRD KING (1785-1862)

During the early decades of the 19th century, one of the most active artists engaged in taking portraits in Washington was Charles Bird King. Born in Newport, Rhode Island, in 1785, King studied under Edward Savage at the turn of the century and later in London with Charles R. Leslie and Washington Allston. Although he is best known for his many likenesses of American Indians painted in Washington, he was also a prolific painter of portraits, both originals and copies.

William Dunlap, the diarist and artist, had something to say of King's painting methods: "He uses a slender rod of wire about a foot long, to ascertain the proportions of his picture, compared with the original. It is gauged with white paint, about an inch from the top, which is held upright at such distance from the subject as to effect one division—the face of a sitter for example.... But all mechanical aids are mischievous. The artist should depend alone on his eye." [1]

Most of King's summers were spent in Newport, where he was a generous benefactor of the Redwood Library and Athenaeum. In addition to a substantial amount of money, he gave the Redwood during his life some three hundred valuable books, fourteen bound volumes of engravings, and over two hundred paintings. At his death he allowed the library to choose other paintings from his estate.

Some of King's early commissions were arranged for him by Joseph Delaplaine, the Philadelphia bookseller, who was busily gathering likenesses of prominent Americans for his own "National Gallery." In November 1818, shortly before Adams was to sit to Peale, he received a letter from Delaplaine urging him to allow his portrait to be taken by King:

I am extremely desirous to obtain your portrait for my National Gallery.

Mr. King, a very respectable man, and an excellent portrait painter, of Baltimore, has arrived in Washington where he has gone to paint the portraits of several distinguished characters for me. . . .

Mr. King paints two sized portraits. Both large. One for Eighty Dollars, the other for One Hundred and twenty Dollars. In either case I shall pay for half the expence and I beg you to pay the other half. My wish is, that you will have the goodness to sit for the largest size. It is well known that in a public Gallery like mine, a large portrait embracing appropriate accompaniments, looks infinitely more interesting than one of the smaller size of merely the naked likeness. [2]

[1] Dunlap, *Arts of Design*, ed. Bayley and Goodspeed, 3:29-30.
[2] 2 Nov. 1818 (Adams Papers).

Adams at length agreed and records in his diary in the spring of 1819 his meeting with King:

> I had received a letter from Mr. Delaplaine, requesting me to sit for my Portrait, for his Gallery, to Mr. King's the Painter. King himself had spoken to me some weeks since, and told me that he expected very soon to leave the City. I called this morning at his rooms; but he told me he should be obliged to remain here two or three Months longer. He was now painting the foreign Ministers, who are all shortly going away. He proposes to call upon me afterwards. The Portraits that he has taken, are almost without exception very strong likenesses; and good Pictures. He had General Jackson, Genl. Parker, and Coll. Butler, Calhoun twice, Morrell of the Senate, Bagot, Onis, the Abbe Correa, John Graham Forsyth, Coll. R. M. Johnson, Alexr. Smyth of Virginia, Rhea of Tennessee, and several others. There were only three or four of the whole number that I did not immediately recognize at first sight.[3]

One of the portraits of Calhoun now hangs in the Redwood Library.

A few days after this visit Adams made an appointment for his sitting; thereafter until 7 August he sat some sixteen or seventeen times, sometimes with pleasure, often oppressed with the heat, and once finding the task "another noisome encroachment upon my time."[4] Following a sitting of more than two hours he wrote of King in his diary: "He is one of the best Portrait Painters in this Country; little inferior to Stewart. He is also an ingenious, thinking man, with a faculty of conversing upon almost every topic. He lead me this day into a long colloquy upon religion.... He has no faith in Christianity but professes to be a deist."[5] Years later Charles Francis Adams, an "art critic" after the manner of his father and grandfather, observed that "King is not a bad painter, and yet he can hardly be called a good one."[6]

Apparently King's religious views disturbed the Adamses. Louisa wrote on this subject to the elder Adams in 1819, saying that King "is amusing in conversation but is apt to introduce religious topics with so much levity and disrespect that I took the liberty of telling him he had better confine himself to subjects which he understood."[7]

Louisa saw King's portrait of her husband in its early stage and was not satisfied, and so King "changed its attitude," and later "began another."[8] Still later she visited King's studio and, seeking more

[3] Entry of 24 March 1819.
[4] Entry of 24 July 1819.
[5] Entry of 29 June 1819.
[6] CFA, Diary, 6 Dec. 1841.
[7] To JA, 13 or 14 Dec. 1822 (Adams Papers).
[8] JQA, Diary, 2, 14 July 1819.

warmth in the countenance than recent portraits had shown, with disappointment reported to her father-in-law that, although the portrait was a good likeness, it was "disagreeable as most of the last pictures are." [9]

Further sittings were given on three occasions in May 1820, after which no further mention of King or of this portrait comes to light until April 1821 when Adams again recorded: "I gave a sitting this morning to Mr. Charles King the Painter. It is nearly two years since he began my Portrait for Delaplaine's Gallery in Philadelphia, and he has not yet finished it." [10] It must have been completed shortly after this, however, for in February 1822 Delaplaine wrote from Philadelphia to John Adams: "I have the honour of informing you that I have received in my Gallery of the portraits of distinguished Americans within the last five months, a fine picture of your worthy and highly respected son, the honourable John Quincy Adams, painted by King in Washington." [11] Young Charles saw the finished painting (Fig. 38) in Washington in 1824: "I agreed to accompany Madame and the Girls to Mr. King's painting rooms. . . . The pictures, some of them are excellent, others only moderate and others bad. That of Cyr. King of Maine is said to be good, Mr. Wirt's is good. General Brown's and a number of others are remarkably fine. I think my father's a good one, but by no means so good as I think one could be made. His eyes are placed in such a way that one appears directly over his nose. . . . We went down into his painting room, he was copying his portrait of Mr. Webster, which is one of his best likenesses as it appears to me." [12] (The portraits of the Hon. William Wirt, General Jacob Brown, and Daniel Webster now hang in the Redwood Library.)

Adams himself was more than usually pleased with King's effort. Some years later he wrote to his niece, characteristically:

I have so often "submitted to the operation" of sitting for my picture, and so often have been caricatured, even by Painters of eminent reputation, that I have grown shy, and reluctant at exposing my infirmities to the men of the Palette and brush. When I go to Washington next Winter, I will look up and send you an engraved Print from a Portrait of me by King, as good as any that I know of except one by Copley, and one by Stuart, neither of which has been engraved. [13]

[9] 20 May–3 June 1820 (Adams Papers).
[10] Entry of 10 April 1821.
[11] 9 Feb. 1822 (Adams Papers).
[12] CFA, *Diary*, 1:47–48 (17 Jan. 1824).
[13] To Caroline Amelia de Windt, 20 Aug. 1831 (MHi:de Windt Coll.).

38. JOHN QUINCY ADAMS. OIL BY CHARLES BIRD KING, 1819

Yet, perhaps, the portrait bears out Adams' comment on himself written in 1819, the year the portrait was commenced: "I am a man of reserved, cold austere and forbidding manners; my political adversaries say a gloomy misanthropist, and my personal enemies, an unsocial savage. With a knowledge of the actual defect in my character, I have not the pliability to reform it." [14]

The portrait, though for a time part of Delaplaine's National Gallery, remained in King's possession until he died. Under the terms of his will the Redwood Library was given a choice of his paintings, and George Champlin Mason on behalf of the Library selected, among others, this one. It now hangs high on the wall of the reading room adjoining the rotunda of the Library. On the back of the painting is written in King's hand: "John Quincy Adams Sct. of State at the time this original picture was painted by C. B. King, Newport, Washington."

As early as 1824 it was engraved by Francis Kearney, a capable stipple engraver whose career included apprenticeship under Peter R. Maverick, study under Archibald Robertson, work on the Collins Quarto Bible, and partnership later with Tanner, Tiebout, and others in the banknote-engraving business. Adams records a visit from Benjamin O. Tyler, the Washington publisher of the engraving: "B. O. Tyler brought me an engraving of my Portrait painted in 1820 by King, and which is now in Delaplaine's Gallery. This engraving is by Kearney." [15] The engraver, with artistic license, reversed the pose and added details—hands, chair, and so forth; the likeness is recognizable but not good (Fig. 41). This engraving, "Price One Dollar," is probably the one Adams proposed to send to his niece Caroline A. de Windt in 1831.

In the course of my search for Adams' portraits, my attention was called to a portrait of John Quincy Adams owned by Lafayette College, Easton, Pennsylvania, said to have been painted by James Frothingham (Fig. 39). A photograph of the portrait was obtained from the College with the information that it had been presented to Lafayette College in 1946 by Allan P. Kirby and then hung in the Kirby Hall of Civil Rights. [16] I then wrote to Mr. Kirby asking about the source of the painting. Mr. Kirby replied that he was sending a copy of my letter to Mr. E. J. Rousuck of Wildenstein & Co., New York, who had been responsible for the painting's being hung at Lafayette College, and hoped that he would be able to help me with the information I wished to obtain. [17] With Mr. Kirby's letter came a little catalogue of an exhibition held at Storm King Art Center, Mountain-

[14] Diary, 4 June 1819.
[15] Same, 27 April 1824.
[16] A. E. Letts, Director of Physical Plant, Lafayette College, to the Author, 16 April 1963.
[17] A. P. Kirby to the Author, 6 May 1963.

39. JOHN QUINCY ADAMS. OIL BY CHARLES BIRD KING, CA. 1819

ville, New York, June–July 1961, entitled *Exhibition of Paintings of Famous Americans: a Portion of the Kirby Collection of Historical Paintings Owned by Lafayette College*. The introduction, written by Mr. Kirby, states that "The collection of which this exhibit is a part was assembled for Lafayette College by E. J. Rousuck, Executive Vice-president of the Wildenstein Gallery, New York City, N.Y." Fifteen "Famous Americans" are illustrated in the catalogue, No. 14 being John Quincy Adams by James Frothingham.

In answer to my letter, forwarded to him by Mr. Kirby, Mr. Rousuck wrote that he had always been keen about Frothingham's works and that a number of them had been confused with those by Stuart. He enclosed a copy of a short brochure he had prepared, which accom-

40. JOHN QUINCY ADAMS. PHOTOGRAPH OF FIGURE 39, 1946

panied the painting to Lafayette, and added that if there was anything further I wished, I could call on him.[18] Being struck by the close
similarity between the Redwood and the Lafayette portraits, I called
Mr. Rousuck's attention to the comparison and asked if his own records
contained any clue as to whether one was a copy or possibly a replica
of other.[19] In a prompt but uninformative response he wrote that he
had seen the King portraits at the Redwood Library but did not remember that of John Quincy Adams; it had always been his impression that most of King's paintings were after other painters, but he
had nothing to base this on but his own observation and he could well
be wrong.[20] Mr. Rousuck, to be sure, did not have ready access to

[18] E. J. Rousuck to the Author, 13 May 1963.
[19] Author to E. J. Rousuck, 24 May 1963.
[20] E. J. Rousuck to the Author, 27 May 1963.

Adams' diary and therefore would not, from that source, have known that King's Adams at Redwood was unquestionably the "original" and not a copy. Yet there was no suggestion as to when, or by whom, or for what reason the Lafayette version had been attributed to Frothingham.

Further research in the Frick Art Reference Library revealed a photograph of a portrait of Adams that had long been owned by Herbert Lee Pratt, who died in February 1945. The photograph was endorsed as having been taken by Peter A. Juley & Son, of New York City, and after some searching among its numberless glass photographic plates, the plate from which the Frick's copy had been made was found and is reproduced here as Fig. 40. The glass plate was upward of twenty years old when this reproduction was made from it, and much of the image had faded or rubbed off over the years. Yet enough remains to make it clear beyond a shadow of doubt that the Adams once owned by Herbert Lee Pratt is the portrait now at Lafayette, albeit "restored." But in the restoration many seemingly insignificant details are preserved. Notice the little lines or scratches on the top of the collar on Adams' left side, the wisps of hair behind his ear, and the highlights on parts of his shirt front. Bits of restoration are also clear, sideburns added, nose somewhat straightened, the sitter's right cheek made a little more full—all incidental to popular gallery restoration; and the frame now boasts the name of the alleged artist.

Some information about this portrait is typed on the reverse of the photograph at the Frick Art Reference Library. There it is stated, from correspondence with Mr. Pratt in 1937, that the painter was then thought to have been Jarvis; and that from later correspondence with Mr. Pratt's daughter in May 1946 it appears the portrait had been "sold at auction." It also appeared that in 1948 H. E. Dickson, an authority on Jarvis, had written that the portrait had formerly been said to have been by Jarvis but that it was "certainly not." No further information about the sale "at auction" has been discovered, nor anything justifying the attribution to Frothingham.

There can be little doubt that the portrait at Lafayette is by King, just as is that at the Redwood. They are of different sizes: Redwood's is 36 by 28 inches; Lafayette's, 23 by 19 inches. Delaplaine told Adams that King paints "two sized portraits," and urged him "to have the goodness to sit for the largest size" rather than "the smaller size of merely the naked likeness." Adams also records that King was not satisfied with the first attempt and began another. A likely explana-

41. JOHN QUINCY ADAMS.
ENGRAVING BY FRANCIS KEARNEY, CA. 1824

99

42. JOHN QUINCY ADAMS.
DRAWING BY GÉRARD, PERHAPS BARON
FRANÇOIS PASCAL SIMON GÉRARD, AFTER 1819

43. JOHN QUINCY ADAMS. ENGRAVING
BY FRANÇOIS LOUIS COUCHÉ,
1829 OR BEFORE

tion is that the first attempt was the smaller size and was not finished until after the completion of the larger one. This theory would seem to find support in an entry in Adams' diary in November 1823, almost two years after Delaplaine had written to the elder Adams that he had received the "fine picture" of John Quincy Adams by King. Adams wrote in his diary: "I sat to Charles B. King the Portrait Painter, to finish my portrait."[21] We know that the one that hung for a time in Delaplaine's Gallery and was used by Kearney in making his engraving in 1824 was the larger size and is that now at the Redwood. The smaller one must have found its way into Mr. Pratt's collection and was then transmogrified into an original by James Frothingham.

Several engravings after King's Redwood portrait have come to light, in addition to that by Kearney. I. W. Moore engraved a likeness, published by P. Price Jr. for the *Souvenir* in 1828. Though inscribed in part as "Drawn by King—Engd. by I. W. Moore," Moore undoubtedly copied Kearney and not King, the engraving exhibiting all the variations from the original that are noticeable in Kearney's.

At the Franklin D. Roosevelt National Historic Site, at Hyde Park,

[21] Entry of 10 Nov. 1823.

44. JOHN QUINCY ADAMS.
ENGRAVING BY AN UNKNOWN ARTIST

hanging over the President's bed is a lightly tinted drawing of the heads of John Adams and John Quincy Adams, facing each other; the latter illustrated here as Fig. 42. Each is clearly taken from a portrait of the subject by King hanging at Redwood. Both the drawing and portrait of John Adams are illustrated and discussed in *Portraits of John and Abigail Adams.*[22] The inscription under the drawing of John Quincy Adams is cryptic but reads, as far as can be ascertained, "J. Q. Adams, Teint-coloré, violet (Gérard)." The name in parentheses may be that of the artist. The drawing is not dated and nothing is known of its provenance. The fact that on one piece of paper both heads are depicted allows an inference that the drawing was not made until after 1882 when King's portrait of the younger Adams joined that of his father at Redwood, or that it was made at a much earlier date when both portraits were in King's possession. It is not impossible that Gérard may have been the Baron François Pascal Simon Gérard (1770–1837) who painted in 1814 the handsome portrait of Arthur Wellesley, first Duke of Wellington, which belongs to the Hermitage, Leningrad. Nor should we overlook the tiny engraving inscribed "Couché fils sc. Adams Jeune" (Fig. 43). Couché fils was François Louis Couché (1782–1849), son of Jacques Couché, best known for his *Galerie du Palais Royal.* The significance, and mystery, of Couché's engraving of Adams is that there is a matching one inscribed "Adams Père," [23] each probably taken either directly from the two Redwood portraits of the Adamses or from Gérard's drawings.

Also extant is a small French engraving (Fig. 44), only 1 15/16 by 1 5/16 inches in size, bearing the legend over the head, "J. Q. Adams Président Des États-Unis." It must therefore have been pro-

[22] P. 221–224 (Figs. 107 and 108).
[23] Oliver, *Portraits of JA and AA,* p. 224 (Fig. 109).

45. JOHN QUINCY ADAMS. LITHOGRAPH BY BÉRAUD LAURAS & CIE.

duced after Adams became President in March 1825. It bears little
or no resemblance to him, but the style of his hair, stock, ruff, waistcoat, and coat and lapel corresponds closely with Kearney's engraving
after King (Fig. 41). In this tiny French engraving, the model was
followed so carefully that the buttons on Adams' waistcoat end up on
the wrong side. Still another reproduction of French origin, the lithograph by Béraud Lauras & Cie. (Fig. 45), turns Adams into a Frenchman.

King was not satisfied with painting only John Quincy Adams, but
turned his attention to other members of the family. He painted George
and his brother John in 1823, young Charles Francis Adams in 1827,
executed a copy of Stuart's last portrait of old John Adams in 1827,
and ten years later portrayed little Fanny, daughter of John 2d.[24]
At or about the time King was painting Adams' sons he also painted
a large canvas of Louisa Catherine Adams (Fig. 46), probably about
1824. In size it is 51½ by 39¾ inches, brilliantly colored, and
thought by at least one of the family to be "overdressed."

Years after the portrait was finished and seven years after the tragic
death of her son George, Louisa wrote to King:

[24] Same, p. 192, 195, 221 (Fig. 95); CFA, *Diary*, 2:vii and 3:xv–xviii.

46. LOUISA CATHERINE ADAMS. OIL BY CHARLES BIRD KING, CA. 1824

Yesterday brought me your very polite and kind letter, which I hasten to answer. The kind and graceful manner in which you confer'd the obligation alluded to in that letter, stamped a value on that Portrait, which makes it impossible for me to relinquish it; more especially as it would have belonged to *one* whom it pleased the Almighty to take from me, at the moment that we were preparing to leave the City, probably forever. He appreciated the picture, and admired its execution. It is now intended for my Grand Children; but as their Mother [Mrs. JA2] has always disapproved of *my taste* in the Costume, it was my wish to please her, by having it new dressed which I had prepared to do seven years since, from the same motive. If therefore it will not put you to too great inconvenience, you would confer an added favour and I will defray the expence at whatever rate you may value it. At a former period of my life the *Portrait* might have possessed some intrinsic value even to you but now its possession can only be craved by the descendants of one who have learnt to pity and to love her for her misfortunes.

Among the friends long and abiding who have manifested on all occasions their flattering kindness and esteem, I am proud to rank you; and I trust that you are perfectly assured of the high regard and esteem of
Louisa Catherine Adams [25]

King's letter referred to by Louisa has not been found, but from what she says it would seem that he wanted to have the portrait for some reason. Whether it was ever "new dressed" is not known. The painting itself gives no external evidence of the fact. It is not hard to agree with Louisa's daughter-in-law about the "Costume" in this portrait.

The portrait descended in the family and was given to the Smithsonian Institution in 1951 by Mary Louisa Adams Clement in memory of her mother, Louisa Catherine Adams Clement. The occasion marked the opening of the Adams-Clement Collection, and we are fortunate to have had preserved the remarks (as later extended) made at the time about the various portraits and objects in the Collection, by Mrs. Katharine McCook Knox.[26] She pointed out that the portrait, when shown at the George Washington Bicentennial Exhibition at the Corcoran Gallery in 1932, had been catalogued as by an "Artist Unknown," and that in 1951 its authorship was still an open question. Mrs. Knox also remarked on the harp and the book of music opened at a song entitled, romantically, "Oh Say Not That Woman's Heart Can Be Bought," and noted that both were also part of the Adams-Clement Collection. Although Mrs. Knox was later herself to attribute the painting to King, the letter quoted above disposes of the question.

The subject of Mrs. Adams' "Costume" was revived again for a moment in an illustration to an article entitled "Mrs. John Quincy

[25] 16 July 1836 (PHi).
[26] 18 April 1951 ([typewritten], Adams Papers Editorial Files).

47. BALL GIVEN BY MRS. JOHN QUINCY ADAMS AT WASHINGTON,
JANUARY 8, 1824. PHOTOENGRAVING, 1871

Adams's Ball, 1824" published in 1871 in *Harper's Bazar*,[27] describing the famous Ball in the Adams house on F Street given in January 1824 in honor of General Andrew Jackson on the ninth anniversary of the Battle of New Orleans. This engraving (Fig. 47) is an anachronistic and imaginary but entertaining view of part of the throng in the Adams' ballroom on that occasion, said to have numbered some thousand persons. Mrs. Adams is seen at the extreme right, holding a fan and wearing a turban probably adapted from that in her portrait by King, and at the age she would have been in 1824. The likeness of her husband, however, who stands beside her, is after Healy's portrait (Fig. 108), painted in 1845. General Jackson himself, occupying the center of the scene, is depicted at an age reminiscent of Healy's likeness of him done in 1835. The ladies as always appear lovely and youthful, more like their escorts' daughters than their wives.

JOSEPH WOOD (ca. 1778–1830)

Adams' prominence as Secretary of State and as a candidate for the Presidency gave impetus to and almost compelled publishers to have new portraits of him on hand for display purposes and as a source of engravings for sale. It is not surprising therefore that he should have been approached on that subject, as he was by Joseph Wood during the election campaign of 1824. "I am a portrait painter," Wood wrote from Washington, "and have had applications from publishers and others for portraits of you. Should it suit your convenience to give me a few sittings, will you have the goodness to say by the bearer on what day and hour you will do me the favor to call at my painting room dwelling part of the house Prentiss' Store near the Patriotic Bank Penn: Avenue."[1] The request was later reinforced by a visit from the publisher Benjamin Owen Tyler: "B. O. Tyler came with a request that I would sit to Mr. Wood, the miniature painter; for a small engraving that he proposes to have made. I went and sat about a quarter of an hour."[2] After two more sittings the completion of the portrait is recorded. "Mr. Wood, the miniature Painter came, with B. O. Tyler, and finished the Portrait. Tyler is going off to-morrow for Albany with a budget of his Presidential pictures for sale."[3]

Wood was a well-known and, for a time, very successful miniaturist. He was born about 1778 in Clarkston, New York, the son of a farmer.

[27] Vol. 4, p. 166–168 (18 March 1871).
[1] 7 July 1824 (Adams Papers).
[2] JQA, Diary, 19 July 1824.
[3] Same, 2 Aug. 1824.

48. JOHN QUINCY ADAMS. OIL ON PORCELAIN BY JOSEPH WOOD, 1824

At the turn of the century he opened a studio with John Wesley Jarvis. After a few gay, convivial years they broke up and Wood continued alone, painting his miniatures on ivory in New York, Philadelphia, Baltimore, and Washington. In 1967 a pair of miniature portraits of President Monroe and his wife, painted by Wood in 1817 and bearing favorable testimony to his skill, were given to the Virginia Historical Society.[4] He also painted a curious likeness of Daniel Webster, signed and dated 1824, which very much resembles in style the miniature of Adams. It is now owned by the New Hampshire Historical Society. Although it is reported that at the time of his painting of Adams he was "more frequently found in his cups than in his workshop practising his craft," a year later, on 25 October 1825, the *National Intelligencer* carried a notice that "J. Wood continues to paint miniatures and small portraits and may be found at any hour at his dwelling on Pennsylvania Avenue, next door west of Way's Buildings."[5] But like so many artists of the period, Wood came on hard times and died in straitened circumstances in 1830 in Washington.

Nothing is known of the provenance of what I believe to be Wood's portrait of Adams (Fig. 48) except for the inscription it bears. Writ-

[4] Virginia Historical Society, *An Occasional Bulletin*, No. 15, p. 3–5 (Oct. 1967).
[5] George C. Groce Jr. and J. T. C. Willet, "Joseph Wood: A Brief Account of his Life and the First Catalogue of his Work," *Art Quarterly*, 3:153 (1940).

ten on the back of the picture appears: "Given to me by my brother Dr. Fordyce Foster when he resided in Cohasset Mass. Jane F. Porter, Quechee Vt. March 9, 1886." It was purchased in 1962 by the Boston Athenæum. Since it is not signed, there is no proof that Fig. 48 was painted by Wood, yet it shows a recognizable likeness of Adams of suitable age to have been painted in 1824, and no other candidate has appeared for the miniature the record shows was painted that year by Wood. It does not measure up to Wood's early portraits, and it is by no means a pleasing likeness of Adams.

THOMAS SULLY (1783–1872)

As President Monroe's second term drew to a close, the race for succession was hotly contested, the principal contenders being Adams, Calhoun, Clay, Crawford, and Jackson. Calhoun withdrew from the race and became the Vice-Presidential candidate on both the Adams and the Jackson tickets. On 1 December 1824 the Electoral College cast its votes: Jackson, 99; Adams, 84; Crawford, 41; and Clay, 37. No candidate having received a majority, the election was to be decided by the House of Representatives, whose choice, under the rules, was limited to the three candidates having the largest number of votes from the Electoral College. The Jackson forces, hostile to Clay and believing that if Adams were elected he would appoint Clay as his Secretary of State, began to whisper "corruption and bargain" and published accusations to that effect, though to no immediate avail. The House of Representatives met on 9 February 1825, and at half-past three o'clock Adams was elected President, by a slim majority. When shortly afterward Adams did offer Clay the position as his Secretary of State, he accepted. The revival of charges of bargain and corruption were to embitter permanently relations between Adams and Jackson.

We are fortunate in having a record both in words and in a painted likeness of Adams' appearance at the period just before his elevation to the Presidency. The lady journalist Anne Royall described him in her own style:

I called upon Mr. Adams, Secretary of State. It being his hour of business, I found him in the State department. Mr. A. received me with that ease of manner, which bespeaks him what he really is, the profound scholar, and the consummate gentleman: he saluted me in softest accents, and bid me be seated. I had heard much of Mr. Adams. I had admired him as a writer, and applauded him as a statesman. I was now in his presence. While beholding this truly great man, I was at a loss how to reconcile such rare endowments with the meek condescension of the being before me. He neither smiled nor frowned, but regarding me with a calmness peculiar to him, awaited my business. Mr. A. appears to be about fifty years of age, middling stature, robust make, and every indication of a vigorous constitution. His complexion is fair, his face round and full, but what most distinguishes his features, is his eye, which is black; it is not a sparkling eye, nor yet dull, but one of such keenness that it pierces the beholder. Every feature in his face shows genius, every gesture is that of a great man, his countenance is serene and dignified, he has the steadiest look I ever witnessed, he never smiled whilst I was in his company, it is a question with me whether he ever laughed in his life, and of all men I ever saw, he has the least of what is called pride, both in his manners and dress.[1]

It was in the interim between the Electoral College's indecisive vote and Adams' election that he began to sit to Thomas Sully for the first of the portraits and sketches that the painter would do of him during the next several years. Sully, who was born in England in 1783, had come to America as a child and later settled in Philadelphia, where before long he became that city's leading portrait painter. Adams seems to have become acquainted with his work first in 1819 and was not impressed: "Mr. John E. Hall the present Editor of the Port Folio ... took me also into an adjoining chamber, where Sully the Painter is engaged upon a large picture of the passage of the Delaware by General Washington, in December 1776. I think it will not be more successful than Trumbull's picture of the Declaration of Independence.[2] The principal figure is not even a likeness of Washington, and there is no character in the whole composition. The large picture is however as yet barely in chalk."[3]

An effort was made to get Adams to sit to Sully in 1822, but at the time it was apparently unsuccessful. His wife wrote: "Mr. Hopkinson is very desirous that you should come on and sit to Mr. Sully and was so polite as to beg me to do the same which I declined."[4] Two years later, however, Adams' diary discloses: "Sat to Sully for my picture;

---

[1] *Sketches of History, Life, and Manners, in the United States.* By a Traveller [Anne Royall], New Haven, 1826, p. 166.

[2] Adams was probably referring to Trumbull's large replica of his *Declaration of Independence*, which, though not hung in the Rotunda of the Capitol until 1826, was at the point of completion in 1819. When finally hung, the picture seemed to Adams much improved.

[3] JQA, Diary, 14 Oct. 1819. The Legislature of North Carolina had asked Sully to paint two full-length portraits of Washington, but he countered with an offer of an historical painting, selecting Washington crossing the Delaware, and his choice was accepted. The painting, on canvas, 17 feet 4 inches by 12 feet 5 inches, was found to be too large to be of use and was rejected. Sully finally sold it to a framemaker in Boston for $500. Ultimately the painting passed to Boston's Museum of Fine Arts.

[4] To JQA, 28 June 1822 (Adams Papers).

49. JOHN QUINCY ADAMS. OIL BY THOMAS SULLY, 1824

at King's house." A second sitting was given on 28 December, and on the eve of the New Year he noted: "Third and last sitting to Sully. He and King have both taken likenesses of La Fayette, of which I think King's the best." [5]

This portrait is listed as No. 7 in Biddle and Fielding, where it is stated that there was inscribed on the back of the canvas "Painted from life in Washington City 1824." The assistant Chief Curator of the National Gallery advised me that the inscription reads "T.S. [monogram] from Life/Washington D.C./1824." [6]

This likeness (Fig. 49) was first owned by Henry Clay, Speaker

[5] Entries of 23, 31 Dec. 1824. Adams' failure to comment on the portrait may be attributed to the fact that for the period 7–31 Dec. we have only brief notes which he intended to expand into full diary entries but apparently did not.

[6] Edward Biddle and Mantle Fielding, *The Life and Works of Thomas Sully* (*1783–1872*), Phila., 1921, p. 83; William T. Campbell to the Author, 16 April 1963.

50. JOHN QUINCY ADAMS. OIL BY THOMAS SULLY, 1825

of the House of Representatives and later Adams' Secretary of State. The record does not reveal whether Clay commissioned the painting or received it as a gift from Adams, nor exactly when it came into Clay's possession. If it had been known to have been owned by Clay before the February election of Adams as President, Jackson's forces presumably would have tried to make political capital of the fact. From Clay the portrait descended to his grandson George H. Clay of Lexington, Kentucky. It was later owned by the collector Thomas B. Clarke, and in 1921 by C. Harris of New York City. In 1942 it was part of the Mellon Collection and now hangs in the National Gallery.

Both Charles Henry Hart, in 1908, and Biddle and Fielding, in 1921, list as in Sully's Register of Portraits a small whole length, 33 by 25 inches, of John Quincy Adams, painted in 1825. Hart's description states that it was painted for W. H. Morgan, a printseller of Philadelphia and that the "head in this picture was after Stuart." Biddle and Fielding state that it was begun 28 February 1825 and finished 7 May 1825, and that "it was painted from life," adding that Sully's price was $250.[7] Adams' diary is silent on the subject during the period February to May 1825, and we conclude that both Hart and Biddle and Fielding were wrong. The head and shoulders of the 1825 portrait (Fig. 50) were clearly taken from the 1824 portrait (Fig. 49). At least two preliminary sketches were made for the whole length (Figs. 51 and 52). The former (Fig. 51), at one time part of the Erskine Hewitt Collection, was listed as item No. 220 in a *Catalogue of a Loan Exhibition of Portraits of the Signers ... 150th Anniversary of the Constitution, 1937–1938*, published by the United States Constitution Sesquicentennial Commission and described as being of John Adams. It was acquired by the Metropolitan Museum of Art and for a long time similarly described. Its likeness to the other sketch leaves no doubt that the sitter was John Quincy Adams and not his father. The other sketch (Fig. 52) was the one followed in the final oil painting. It remained in the possession of the painter's family and belonged to Mrs. A. W. Sully of Brooklyn, New York, who died in 1947.

The full-length portrait (Fig. 50) is now owned by the American Scenic and Historic Preservation Society at Philipse Manor, Yonkers, New York, having been part of the collection of Alexander Smith Cochrane left to that Society at his death in 1929. Like its prototype

---

[7] "Thomas Sully's Register of Portraits 1801–1871," arranged and edited by Charles Henry Hart, *PMHB*, 32:395–396 (1908); Biddle and Fielding, *Sully*, p. 83 (item No. 4).

52. JOHN QUINCY ADAMS.
DRAWING BY
THOMAS SULLY, CA. 1824–1825

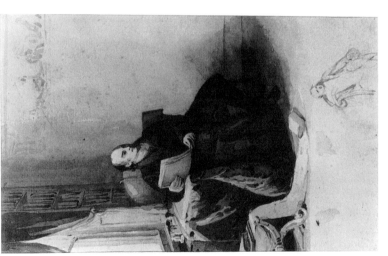

51. JOHN QUINCY ADAMS.
WASH DRAWING, SEPIA, BY
THOMAS SULLY, CA. 1824–1825

(Fig. 49) it is an excellent likeness of Adams at the time he became President. Morgan, the printseller, recognized this and employed Asher B. Durand to engrave it, which he did in his usual and thoroughly competent manner (Fig. 53). Durand's reputation as an engraver had been made only a few years before by his magnificent engraving of Trumbull's small *Declaration of Independence*. His oil portraits of John Quincy Adams (Figs. 72 and 74) were still to be painted. His engraving after Sully's portrait is inscribed as being "Published Oct. 6, 1826," and appears in two states, the later one eliminating the names of the publisher and printer and the description of Adams as "President of the United States." For his work Durand is said to have received seven hundred dollars, almost three times what Sully was paid for the painting itself. The engraving was exhibited at the National Academy of Design in New York in 1827 as item No. 106. Years later Adams said of Durand's engraving that it was the best that had been published but could not "be called a good likeness"; that the "principal defect is a failure in the expression of character."[8] Other engravings derived from Sully's head of Adams, or Durand's engraving, have appeared both in this country and abroad, but none approaches the excellence of Durand's.

We must not overlook in Sully's painting (Fig. 50) and Durand's engraving of it (Fig. 53) the significant surroundings and "props" that each introduced. In the painting Adams appears, as often is the case, with a book in his lap, but also with maps strewn about him. He was at the height of his success in negotiations with Spain, Russia, and England relating to the American Northwest. We can recognize Adams' hand in the choice of these appurtenances. And our presumption is even more forcibly borne out by Durand's engraving. The engraver, with a finer tool than the painter's brush, could give details Sully necessarily glossed over. In Durand's engraving there can be read on the map that lies beside Adams' chair fragments of a few words: "CH," and beneath it the letters "CAN" clearly implying the word Canada, and below that, "Profile of" and "Topographica." Here, then, is a map of the very territory contended for. This painting was not so designed by chance, but is a well-planned contemporary view of the new President, who as the late Secretary of State had forever changed the map of America; and it is a likeness well disposed to keep alive that fact.

[8] JQA to George F. Morris, 6 Nov. 1833 (LbC, Adams Papers).

Painted by T.Sully.   Published Oct.6.1826, by W.H.Morgan. 114 Chesnut st.Philad?   Eng. by A.B.Durand.
Printed by S.Gug, no Philad?

JOHN QUINCY ADAMS,
President of the United States.

53. JOHN QUINCY ADAMS.
ENGRAVING BY ASHER BROWN DURAND, 1826

IV

The President
1825–1829

"The lineaments of my face, in the simplicity of nature, and the perfection of art."

CHRONOLOGY OF JOHN QUINCY ADAMS' LIFE, 1825–1829

1825

Feb. 9: Elected President of the United States by the House of Representatives; inaugurated, 4 March; appoints JA2 his private secretary.

May: Likeness taken for Indian peace medal (Figs. 54a–54c).

Oct.: Second portrait by Stuart commenced (Fig. 57); Browere's life mask taken (Fig. 59).

Dec. 5: Sends first annual Message to Congress recommending establishment of a Department of the Interior; a national university, naval academy, and astronomical observatory; uniform laws governing bankruptcy, militia, weights and measures; a more effective patent law; and a nation-wide system of internal improvements.

1826

His efforts with Secretary of State Henry Clay to establish an enlightened and energetic Latin-American policy through participation in the Inter-American Congress in Panama are frustrated by opposition in Congress and a series of mischances.

July 4: JA dies in Quincy on the fiftieth anniversary of the Declaration of Independence.

1827

Settlement of the Oregon question is postponed indefinitely by extension of free-and-open occupation agreement of 1818 with Great Britain.

Feb. 5: His Message to Congress takes up the cause of the Creek Indians by asserting the authority of the national Government over the state of Georgia.

1828

Sponsors the establishment of a live-oak plantation in Florida, a pioneering effort in government forestry and conservation. Sits to Harding (Fig. 61); and to Greenough (Figs. 68–70).

Feb. 25: JA2 marries Mary Catherine Hellen in the White House, and is installed as manager of the Columbian Mills.

May–June: Succeeds in winning congressional approval for policy of internal improvements, exemplified in authorization of construction of the Chesapeake and Ohio Canal, and passage of a tariff for protection of American manufactures.

Nov.: Defeated for reelection by Andrew Jackson; engages the New England Federalists in a controversy over secessionist policies in their ruling group from 1803 to the Hartford Convention, 1814.

1829

Feb.: Composes "A Reply to the Appeal of the Massachusetts Federalists," and additional papers in support of the principle of federal union.

March: Moves to the Commodore Porter House on Meridian Hill.

April 30: GWA dies by jumping or falling from a steamer in Long Island Sound.

June 11–18: Travels alone from Washington to Quincy.

June–Dec.: Begins reassembling his library in Quincy from its various storage places and undertakes the ordering of JA's papers and the writing of a life of JA.

Sept. 3: Attends CFA's marriage to Abigail Brown Brooks (ABA) in Medford.

Oct.–Nov.: In Quincy dedicates memorial to JA and AA in the Stone Temple; reburies the remains of GWA; surveys lands inherited from JA.

Dec.: Returns to LCA in Washington.

MEDALS

Moritz Furst (b. 1782)

The practice of giving peace medals to the chiefs and leaders of the Indian tribes "as marks of friendship" was, as Jefferson said, "an ancient custom from time immemorial."[1] Originating in America with the Spanish, French, and British, the custom was continued after the Revolution by striking a medal in honor of each new President for presentation to Indian chiefs on important occasions, visits to the capital, or the signing of treaties. With Jefferson's Presidency the type of Indian peace medals was stylized and thereafter followed by succeeding Presidents. The medals were made in three sizes: 76 mm., 62 mm., and 51 mm. The obverse bore the likeness of the President

[1] To Messrs. Carmichael and Short, 30 June 1793, printed in Jefferson, *Writings,* ed. Lipscomb and Bergh, 9:157–158.

117

in profile with his name and title and the year he took office. The reverse showed two hands clasped, a crossed calumet and tomahawk, and the words "Peace and Friendship."

When Adams became President, the medalist employed by Thomas L. McKenney, the new head of the Bureau of Indian Affairs, was Moritz Furst, the Viennese die-sinker who had designed the Monroe medals with success. The usual three sizes were requested, the largest to be given to chiefs of the highest rank and distinction and the smaller to less influential leaders. Time was of the essence, as McKenney wrote to the Secretary of War in 1825: "The sooner the work is done the better, as it is not the custom to distribute medals except they bear, at the time of presentation, the likeness of the then President— whom the Indians claim for their 'Great Father.'"[2]

A likeness taken from life rather than from a portrait was desired, and Adams was approached for permission: "Mr. Furst is the medalist employed by the War Department to make the dies for the medals to be distributed to the Indian Chiefs. He came to enquire when I could sit to him to take my profile. I fixed upon Monday Morning at eight O'Clock." A few days later: "Mr. Furst the Medalist came this morning and I sat to him about half an hour to take a profile of my face, with a pencil on paper from which he is to engrave it on the die for the medals to be distributed to the Indians. In about ten days the die will be so far advanced that he will ask two or three sittings more, and he is engraving a separate medal for himself, the head of which he intends to engrave in the antique costume. In the medals for the Indians the bust is in the modern dress."[3]

Adams sat again on 6 June; on the following day the drawing was finished and Furst left for New York. Work on the three sizes of dies was completed, and impressions sent to McKenney early in September, and the dies to the chief coiner of the Mint. At the same time Furst wrote to Adams sending him similar impressions:

Your Excellency please to excuse me, that I take the Liberty to foreward you some Impretions from the Dies which I had the Honor to Engrave with your Likeness for the Indian Office.

I am about Engraving your Likeness for the Medal which I intend to publish on my own Account, and as you was so kinde to tell me, that you would send me the impretion of your Private Seal for the reverse, for which, I shall be obliged to your Excellency.[4]

[2] T. L. McKenney to Secretary of War, 5 May 1825 (DNA:Department of the Interior, Office of Indian Affairs, Letters Sent, 2:2–3); quoted in Francis Paul Prucha, S.J., "Early Indian Peace Medals," *Wisconsin Magazine of History*, 45:286 (Summer 1962).
[3] JQA, Diary, 27, 30 May 1825.
[4] 6 Sept. 1825 (Adams Papers).

To Furst's distress, McKenney told him that only the middle-sized impression was acceptable, the largest and smallest not so. Bitter correspondence between the two men ensued, each taking a firm stand. The head of Indian Affairs affirmed laudably: "These medals should be as perfect in their resemblance of the original, as the artist can make them. They are intended, not for the Indians, only, but for posterity."[5] Furst backed down, some modifications were made in an effort to appease, or satisfy, McKenney, and the medals were struck.

In November, Furst pursued Adams further:

I beg leave to inform your Excellency, that your Italian Vallet called on me and told me that it is your wish, to have ten silver Medals from those Dies of which I took the liberty to send your Excellency the Impressions, while in the City of New York. I have oppen'd a subscribtion paper, for the purpose to collect subscribers, and as soon as I have obtained a suffitient number of subscribers, I shall get the Medallions Coined, and among Them, your 10 silver Medalls, shall be the best collected out. About two weeks, I tooke the liberty to write to the Secretary of War, and requested him to send me a letter of Credit, so, that I may be able to proceed with my Business, but I received no Answer.

I beg your Excellency will be so Condesending to interfere in this business; as I am Convinced of your good will.[6]

Furst presumably was referring to the medal "in the antique costume," which he was publishing on his "own Account" and for which he needed "a suffitient number of subscribers." Whether Adams "interfered" cannot be discovered, but his criticism of Furst's work could readily be foretold: "McKenney T. L. brought me the casts of three medals executed by Furst. Afterwards sent me others of Mr. Monroe, Mr. Madison, and the second Presidency of G. Washington 1796 all badly executed."[7] Adams continued in this opinion of Furst's work, though he lived up to his undertaking as a subscriber for the "private" medal: "Mr. Furst came at last with his bill for the ten silver Medals, which I bespoke of him. They are intrinsically worth about one dollar each, but he charged me, and I paid him without asking any questions ten. That is one hundred dollars for the ten medals."[8]

For the next several years Adams was plagued by Furst in his effort to obtain patronage and employment, and at the mention of each such occasion in his diary Adams adds his familiar strictures: "The man is pinchingly poor, both in purse, and as an Artist." "This person is a wretched Medalist, and a half-witted man; but an untiring peti-

[5] McKenney to Samuel Moore, Director of the Mint, 17 Sept. and 13 Oct. 1825; quoted in Prucha, "Early Indian Peace Medals," p. 287.
[6] 5 Nov. 1825 (Adams Papers).
[7] Diary, 14 Nov. 1825.
[8] Same, 22 Dec. 1826.

54a

54b

54c

JOHN QUINCY ADAMS. MEDALLIC PORTRAITS BY MORITZ FURST, 1825

55. JOHN QUINCY ADAMS. MEDALLIC PORTRAIT BY MORITZ FURST, 1825

tioner, and an unrelenting facheux. He came to me the other day with a subscription paper for a Medal of Alexander Hamilton, which he wants me to subscribe for, and to patronize. That I declined." [9]

The medal illustrated as Fig. 54a, in modern dress, is the largest size, 76 mm., and shows some of the features McKenney found so objectionable, the long pointed nose and the heavy shoulders suggesting a fat man, which Adams was not; yet it is a recognizable likeness. Fig. 54c, the smallest medal, 51 mm., though essentially similar, shows a somewhat less pointed nose, which may reflect Furst's efforts to modify the die. Fig. 54b shows the middle-sized medal, acceptable from the beginning; a finer work and a better likeness.

The example "in the antique costume" (Fig. 55) which Furst engraved and published as a private venture is scarcely a likeness. Whether Adams ever sent Furst "the impretion" of his private seal or at what stage a new idea for the reverse evolved is not known, but the representation of the seal was abandoned. Instead, the reverse shows Science personified as Minerva offering an olive branch to America in the person of an Indian seated on a cornucopia. On the left of these figures the design is completed by a tree trunk and eagle. The inscription at top and bottom reads: "Science gives Peace / and America Plenty." The inclination toward mythology and allegory shown in the figures, together with the sentiment of the inscription, suggest that the iconographic concept was Adams'. This notion is confirmed by his son's unqualified attribution in 1876: "This design

[9] Same, 14 Feb. 1831, 27 Nov. 1833.

121

56. JOHN QUINCY ADAMS. MEDALLIC PORTRAIT
BY GEORGE HENRY LEONARD, AFTER 1848

was his own." [10] Furst's signature appears on the ground-line as well as in smaller letters on the obverse where it is placed on Adams' shoulder just beneath the toga knot.

All forms of these medals are rare today, the last discussed especially so. Most of the Indian medals, like Fig. 54a, have had a hole bored near the edge so as to be hung around the neck. Adams' peace medal has been once engraved, by Jules Jacquemart. [11]

George Henry Leonard

Another medallic likeness of Adams (Fig. 56) was issued with a companion of John Adams, showing on the reverse the Old House in Quincy. It is signed "G.H.L." and made by George Henry Leonard sometime after 1848. Leonard probably used a contemporary daguerreotype for his model.

GILBERT STUART AND THOMAS SULLY

Ward Nicholas Boylston, a relative of the Adamses and a man of very substantial means, was so favorably impressed by Sully's bust portrait of John Quincy Adams that he commissioned from Stuart a full-length portrait, with the same likeness, which he intended to present to Harvard. It was to be as much as possible like Copley's portrait of John Adams done in 1783 and since 1811 in Boylston's possession. [1]

[10] CFA to George W. Ware Jr., 13 Sept. 1876 (DLC:The George Hay Stuart Collection).
[11] Joseph F. Loubat, *The Medallic History of the United States of America, 1776–1876*, N.Y., 1878, vol. 2, plate 54.
[1] Oliver, *Portraits of JA and AA*, p. 23–25, 33, 35, 38 (Fig. 9).

Boylston wrote from Roxbury to Adams shortly after his inauguration as President, expressing felicitations and asking his consent:

I felt as if [I] partook of the sentiments of Simeon of old: "Letest now thy servant depart in peace for mine eyes have seen the Salvation of my Country."

There is however one thing which I crave as a favour and heretofore repeatedly express'd the warmest wishes of my heart to see accomplished, and thought, or fancied had your assent, namely, that you would sit for your Portraiture to be the companion to that of my Dearly beloved and venerated Friend your Father, which you bestowed on me. The period has now arrived when of all others is the fittest to commence the design without the additional reason, that I am too far in advance of years to speculate on time. You will therefore my Dear Friend permit me to indulge the hope that when you revisit Boston you will allow as much time as your leisure will admit to the completion of my wishes. In anticipation I invited Mr. Stuart to view the portrait of your Father as to size, leaving the attitude and costume to your direction.[2]

Adams replied from Washington in May, after apologizing for the delay:

Your familiarity with the Holy scriptures suggested to you on this occasion a text, which I hope will long be inapplicable to your condition. There is one which has very frequently and earnestly presented itself to my remembrance. "Let not him that girdeth on his harness boast himself as he that putteth it off." . . .

On my next visit to Boston I shall very cheerfully comply with your request of sitting to Mr. Stuart, but am uncertain whether I shall find it practicable the present year.[3]

Driving in to Boston from Quincy later this same year, Adams sat to Stuart a half dozen times in early October, to the great satisfaction of Boylston, who wrote:

A Letter I rec'd yesterday from Mr. I. P. Davis informed me he had had an opportunity of seeing you at Mr. Quincys in company with Mr. Stuart, and that you had consented to sit to him for your full Length portrait four days this week, for which you cannot conceave half the pleasure it convey'd to me, or the obligations I owe you for this condescension to my long and fervent petitions for this object of my wishes, and do hope that Mr. S will go on with diligent and unremitting labour to finish it before the end of the year. I shall haunt him as the evil spirit did Saul and employ the energies of Mr. I. P. Davis who has great influence with him to get it out of his hands into mine with as few put offs as possible.

[2] 15 March 1825 (Adams Papers).
[3] 10 May 1825 (LbC, Adams Papers).

In the future disposition of it with that of my beloved Friend your Fathers,
I shall consult you if I live to see yours compleated.[4]

There was, however, some disagreement about the dress in which
Adams was to be portrayed; Boylston, having lived for years with the
pompous portrait of the elder Adams by Copley, favored the formal
costume John Quincy Adams had worn at the Court of St. James's.
Adams, on the other hand, preferred "the plain American dress."
Their exchanges, at this distance, are cause for some amusement.
Boylston wrote, later in October:

> The two pictures [Adams' and his wife's] that is as far as they have been
> compleated I visited as the first object on returning to Boston. I think
> Mr. Stuart has not at any period of his Life given a greater proof of his
> talents, or done more justice to the precise likenesses of those they were
> intended to represent. But, But, the intention of the *Pantaloon's* I shud-
> der at. What? to convey the Idea of the very first character in the nation
> as a Sailor or Hornpipe Dancer is too intolerable to be admitted.[5]

Adams, nothing daunted, replied: "I have confirmed myself in the
opinion that the portrait should be painted in plain black pantaloons
and boots under them. A round hat should be also introduced whether
in one hand or on a table is immaterial. I enclose herewith an engraved print of the device which I mentioned to you at Princeton
and an explanation of its emblematical purport."[6] Boylston continued:

> I am honored with your Letter of 8th of Novr. with the device and
> explanation, which is truely beautiful and interesting. I show'd [it] to
> Mr. Stuart with your wishes. He express'd great pleasure in complying
> with them, but I regret to add, that in defiance of every persuasion of
> mine, and many of his Friends, Mrs. Adams's and your portraits are as
> you last saw them. . . . Alas I have an uphill labour to induce him to go
> on. He says his Room is not large enough to finish yours, but that he has
> an expectation Mr. Alston will oblige him by giving up his large Room
> for that purpose; when that will be obtained is impossible for me to say:
> —I have however some hopes, that in these hard and money pressing
> times, I shall starve him into action. I set out with informing him through
> his F[rien]d Davis, that not a Dollar should be paid in advance, but the
> whole sum had 3 months before been deposited to be paid the hour he
> should say it was ready for delivery. In the meantime I have beset him
> with other tongues, and surely he will not be proof against such a com-
> bination.
> *The Pantaloons*, however, appear to meet universal Dissapprobation in
> Boston, and likewise in the Circle at Quincy, particularly by my ever

[4] 4 Oct. 1825 (Adams Papers).
[5] To JQA, 27 [Oct.] 1825 (Adams Papers).
[6] 8 Nov. 1825 (LbC, Adams Papers).

beloved Friend your Father, who declares War against them in so much
he says, if he can procure a painters brush, and he lives to see it finished
in the manner you have directed, he will deface them, and desires me
to give you his opinion.[7]

There was a stalemate on the question of costume, compounded
by Stuart's procrastination. In August the following year Boylston
wrote Adams that he was going to ask Mr. Davis to offer Stuart "one
Hundred Dollars in addition to the $600 which has lain idle a year
distinctly appropriated for that purpose and apart from any other
fund. If he should die before he finishes ... I see some difficulties
that may arise to prostrate all my hopes."[8] His worst fears were realized, though not in the order he had contemplated. Boylston died
first, survived for six months by Stuart, who died in July 1828, having
completed Adams' head only.

We are indebted to Dr. Benjamin Waterhouse for the preservation
of Stuart's head of Adams, as well as for an account of the faithfulness of Stuart's impoverished widow. Scarcely a fortnight after
Stuart's death, Dr. Waterhouse wrote to Adams:

My old friend Gilbert Stewart died about ten days past; and yesterday
I called upon the widow and children, one of whom, a son of about
30 years of age, is insane, and has been several years. In the course of the
visit we talked about the fine head he had painted of yourself, and that
is my special reason for writing to you at this time. I took pains to ascertain Mrs. Stewart's ideas and feelings about it, knowing she had been
assailed by some "speculators" on that head.

She seemed resolved that no artist should paint a body to it if she
could prevent it; for I perceived she had imbibed to the full all those high
notions of her husband's superiority to all other painters; and she spoke
as if determined not to swerve from what she knew was Mr. Stewart's
sentiments.

The estate will doubtless be rendered insolvent; and the unpaid pictures inventoried with the other articles of his property. Your's, begun by
direction of Mr. Boylstone, is, I presume in the same condition with the
rest. Mrs. Stewart told me that she was fixed in her wish that none but
yourself should possess the head in question; but I drew from her this
idea, that she was not willing that anyone should have the whole canvas,
lest they should paint a body to it; and it is this which induces me to
write at this time, to obtain your ideas and directions on the subject; in
the interim, keeping my own a profound secret. I confided them only to
Mr. Alston, and Mr. Isaac P. Davis; for, as I have already hinted, speculation is awake, with a view, I suspect, of obtaining a popular picture for
exhibition.

[7] 22 Dec. 1825 (Adams Papers).
[8] 15 Aug. 1826 (Adams Papers).

If in the regular course of probate business this picture should be exposed to sale by auction, how much above *two hundred dollars* would you wish any friend of yours to bid for yourself? Or rather, and with more propriety, will you express your ideas and wishes to me on the subject; for the widow and the two gentlemen already mentioned have wished me to write to you on the subject.

The widow expresses a reliance on my judgment and friendship: she shall have it, provided you obtain that head, and the canvas entire *as it now is*: for I fear if any one should make a bargain with her for *the head,* she would cut the canvas to a kit-kat size. I find she is disposed to adhere pertinaciously to the extravagant whims of her heteroclite husband. Neither solicitation nor argument,—nor honour, nor justice could move, at times, that strange man, Gilbert Stewart, who was about as ⟨strange⟩ selfish a man as ever lived. An obstinate, ungovernable, self sufficiency marked and marred his character through life.

There is and has been a pretty general wish that I should give a biographical sketch of the man I knew so thoroughly: But the widow entreated me with tears, not to do it. The *poetry* of Richard Savage, and the *heads* of Gilbert Stewart, are all that ought to be preserved of them.

I considered him only six months younger than myself, but it appears, by a family memorandum, that he was two years younger, making him 72. Yet on the last portrait he painted, he inscribed æt 75; exhibiting his character "strong in death." What a hard task does *genius* impose on the vigilance of reason and conscience!

From your steady friend,

Benjamin Waterhouse [9]

Adams replied promptly:

I have received your kind letter of the 21st and thank you for the interest you have taken in the subject to which it relates. I understood from Mr. Boylston that the portrait to which you refer was his property, paid for as far as it was finished, and that he had a written acknowledgment to that effect. He has disposed of it by his will.

But should this prove to be a mistake, and the Portrait is to be sold as part of Mr. Stewart's Estate, I presume that his widow has no more control over it than a Stranger. It must be sold in the condition in which it was at his decease, and I suppose sold at Auction. In its unfinished state I suppose it would not sell for much, and as it has been once paid for by Mr. Boylston, I should certainly not be inclined to pay for it again. In no event would I take it in any other condition than that in which it was left by Mr. Stewart, or with any condition other than that I should dispose of it as I might think proper.

I hope to see you at Quincy or at Cambridge within a month and will then discourse further with you of the picture and the Painter.[10]

[9] 21 July 1828 (Adams Papers).
[10] 26 July 1828 (LbC, Adams Papers).

126

Dr. Waterhouse wrote back saying:

I have seen Mr. Isaac P. Davis, and the two Miss Stewarts who confirm what was told me by the widow, that Mr. Boylston never paid a dollar towards the picture; that Mr. Stewart signed an agreement or conditional obligation written by Mr. Davis, being a modification of a paper first drawn by Mr. Boylston.

Mrs. S is administratrix: and Mr. Davis who is the efficient friend of the family, authorises me to say, that nothing will be done with the unfinished picture till after your arrival in this quarter. He thinks with me that it must not be exposed to auction because "speculation" will bid high for it. Such a *Lion* will not be found very soon in the market.

They are making a collection of Stewart's portraits to exhibit them for the benefit of his family, who are left in poverty.[11]

It might seem captious at this late date to suggest that Stuart's creditors were entitled to the benefit of the highest bid such a "Lion" might bring.

A month later Adams the art critic commented on that exhibition, which was held at the Boston Athenæum. "The collection of Stewart's Portraits at the Athenaeum has not answered to the reputation of the Artist, nor to the expectation of profit to his family which had been formed. It has brought into strong relief the fact already known; of the extreme inequality of his works, but it has proved what was not before generally believed—the marked inferiority, with two or three exceptions, of all the pictures painted by him in the last ten years of his life. They look like the works of another man."[12] Stuart's portraits of old John Adams and the head of John Quincy Adams, though not shown at that exhibition, were certainly among the exceptions!

Just when the unfinished portrait was acquired from Stuart's estate is uncertain, but the subject appears in Adams' diary a year later. "Davis spoke to me of a half-pipe of Madeira Wine, that he has received for me from Mr. March at New York; and also of the unfinished portrait of me, commenced in 1826 by Stewart, for Mr. Boylston, and which he bequeathed to Harvard University. It has been proposed to Mr. Sully of Philadelphia to finish it; to which he has consented, and Mr. Davis promises to write to him, to come as soon as he can to Boston for that purpose."[13]

Two months later Davis called on Adams in Quincy with Sully: "There was some conversation," Adams reported in his diary, "about the costume of dress suitable for the picture, and upon which there

[11] 4 Aug. 1828 (Adams Papers).
[12] To LCA, 24 Aug. 1828 (Adams Papers).
[13] Entry of 29 June 1829.

had been a difference of opinion between Stuart and me. Sully will agree with me." A few days later, as promised, Adams "went into Boston and stood, for Mr. Sully. . . . He was at the House at the corner of Hamilton Place, owned by Mr. Quincy; and where he resided when he was Mayor of Boston. I was with him about two hours. He took only a miniature pencil drawing upon paper, but is to take the canvass with him to Philadelphia, and to finish it there." We have to rub our eyes periodically and remember that all this time Adams was President of the United States! Two days later he stood again for an hour and Sully finished his sketch, at the same time giving Adams a lecture on "the preservation of Pictures on Canvass." [14] Sully's own journal confirms the President's account: "On the 13th removed my baggage to Robinson's opposite the Common in Hamilton Place. . . . Visited Stuart's family. Rode out to Quincy and made arrangements with Mr. Adams to sit for the purpose of finishing Stuart's picture of him. 17th Finished the study of Adams. 21st Removed Stuart's whole length of Adams [from the stretcher] and had it cased up and shipped to Philadelphia." [15] For this chalk sketch of Adams to complete Stuart's portrait Sully's Register indicates that he received $5.00.

Not a word more appears about Mrs. Stuart's sentiments as to a completion of her husband's unfinished work.

Three months later Adams encountered Mr. Davis in Boston, recently returned from Washington: "He said also," Adams wrote, "that he had seen Sully in Philadelphia who had as yet only a miniature sketch of his finishing part of Stuart's last Portrait of me. And he thought I should do well in going through Philadelphia to ask judge Hopkinson to see to Sully's finishing the work." At the same time Davis asked Adams to sit for Stuart's daughter Jane, who had painted a copy of Stuart's unfinished portrait. Adams promised to do so and a couple of days later called on Stuart's widow in Boston. The subject of Jane's copy of her father's painting came up and Adams noted that "she merely chalked out my dress intending to finish it as a work of her own." [16]

Adams took Davis' advice, and while passing through Philadelphia on the way to Washington on 4 December, Judge Hopkinson called on him but does not appear to have mentioned the portrait. But the following day Adams' diary discloses: "I gave Mr. Sully the engraving of the device of the Eagle and Lyre with the explanation of it in prose and verse which I wrote for Mr. Boylston in 1825, and which I was

[14] Entries of 13, 15, 17 Aug. 1829.
[15] Quoted in Park, *Gilbert Stuart*, 1:95–96.
[16] JQA, Diary, 25, 27 Nov. 1829.

desirous of having introduced in the full length Portrait which Sully is finishing."[17] Sully finally finished the painting a few months later and was paid $350 for his work.[18] The large painting (Fig. 57), 95⅜ by 60¼ inches in size, is signed

Stuart

1825

T.S.

1830.

The first half of the new year saw much attention paid to the purchase of a suitable frame for the finished portrait. Davis asked Adams' son to consult his father on the problem. The picture having been acquired with funds provided by Boylston, his executors, Nathaniel Curtis, Mrs. Boylston, and Adams, had to approve any expenditure for the frame. Charles, who had been entrusted with helping his father in this matter, wrote to him from Boston in January 1830:

I had a Letter from Mr. Sully, to Mr. Isaac P. Davis with patterns for the frame of the Picture. You will please to return it to Mr. Sully. I submitted the matter to Mr. Curtis this morning, who is willing to assent to any arrangement. The Will of Mr. Boylston directs that this should be as much as possible like the picture of my Grandfather presented by him and Mr. C. thinks it might be proper to consider that point, as relating also to the Frame. But he does not precisely recollect what that of the other picture is.

Mr. Brimmer yesterday carried this plan to Mr. Doggett's here, who said he would agree to do it at the same price. Mr. B. thinks Doggett much the best framer in the Country. How this may be I do not know, it is merely inserted for you to consider of the whole question of expediency.[19]

In due course agreement was reached and the picture framed and delivered. Meanwhile it had been on view at Doggett's establishment on Cornhill, and Adams' dress was described in the *Boston Patriot*:

The Ex-president is represented in the plain costume, that best becomes a true republican, and in no other would we wish to see him apparelled. Our own simple dress, it seems to us, if not so becoming in a picture, is far more *appropriate*, than the flowing *toga* of the Roman Senator, or the laced and showy suit of the British nobleman. It is in this simple and unostentatious attire, free from all the vain foppery of foreign Courts, that we would wish to see the President of a Republican people attired;—and

[17] Same, 5 Dec. 1829; for the device and its significance for Adams, see the Introduction and Figs. A and C there.

[18] Edward Biddle and Mantle Fielding, *The Life and Works of Thomas Sully*, Phila., 1921, p. 83 (item No. 6).

[19] 29 Jan. 1830 (LbC, Adams Papers).

57. JOHN QUINCY ADAMS.
OIL BY GILBERT STUART, 1825, AND THOMAS SULLY, 1829–1830

why should we wish that his representation on the living canvass, which shall perpetuate him long after he shall have ceased to exist, should want that simplicity which characterized him both in public and private life.[20]

Adams' wishes to have the device of his seal introduced into the picture were carried out by Sully with considerable finesse. In the lower left-hand corner of the canvas, leaning against the table, a large folio volume can be seen in outline. Overpainting has obscured a substantial part of the emblem on its face, but enough is visible on close examination of the portrait itself to make certain that Sully had resolved the problem of introducing the Lyre and Eagle device by representing it on a book, much as Leslie had years before (Fig. 22). There is also a likelihood that Sully used for this purpose Bode's *Uranographia* (a folio of similar dimensions), in which Adams had first found "the figure of the Constellation of Lyra," the adaptation of which became the device for his seal. What is undoubtedly the seal itself can be seen suspended at Adams' waist.

Almost every detail of the painting and completion of the picture can be documented, but what of the result as a work of art? In the end there can be no doubt that Mrs. Stuart was right. No one should ever have been allowed to finish Stuart's work. The head is magnificent—a good example of the artist's incomparable art—but the body, however skillfully painted, is a bad fit and goes far toward destroying Stuart's work. Dunlap, the diarist and painter, made some telling comments on the subject: "If we judge by the portrait of the Hon. John Quincy Adams, the last head he [Stuart] painted, his powers of mind were undiminished to the last, and his eye free from the dimness of age. This picture was begun as a full length, but death arrested the hand of the artist after he had completed the likeness of the face; and proved that, at the age of seventy four, he painted better than in the meridian of life.... Sully ... would have thought it little less than sacrilege to have touched the head." [21]

Adams saw his own portrait at the Athenæum exhibition late in 1831, which he catalogued with some interest:

I then passed three hours at the Gallery of Pictures at the Athenaeum. The Fifth Annual exhibition—A Portrait of Sir Walter Scott by Leslie—Alston's Miriam—Greuze's Portrait of Franklin—Saul and the Witch of Endor by Allston—Chief Justice Marshall by Harding—Mr. West by Leslie—Governor Sullivan and S. Dexter by Stuart—West's Lear—King's boy reading a Newspaper—Dugald Stuart by Sir H. Raeburn, D. Webster by Stuart and also by Harding, and Patrick Lyon the Blacksmith in his shop,

---

[20] *Boston Patriot & Mercantile Advertiser*, 4 Aug. 1830, p. 2, col. 1.
[21] Dunlap, *Arts of Design*, ed. Bayley and Goodspeed, 1:245–246.

58. JOHN QUINCY ADAMS. WOODCUT BY OTTO H. PARKER, 1894

were the principal interesting pictures. A few very indifferent copies from celebrated Artists were there. Some maritime Landscapes by Vernet, but excepting Alston's no historical pictures worth anything, and his not the best. His Miriam the prophetess looks like a dutch washer woman, not like an inspired starveling in a wilderness. My own Portrait by Stuart and Sully was also there. Except the interest naturally felt in the Portraits by those to whom the Originals, many of them now deceased, were known, there was not much to attract notice in this exhibition.[22]

It was unlike Adams to have so little to say of his own likeness. Two years later, however, when asked for an acceptable likeness of himself to be used by the New York *Mirror* for a plate showing the first seven Presidents, he replied: "If you wish to have anything bearing a resemblance to me, the head of Stuart's Portrait at Cambridge is the

[22] Diary, 2 Sept. 1831.

132

only one that can serve as an original for it." "No engraving from any other Pictures will as a *likeness* be worth a five cent piece." [23]

Later still, the sculptor Horatio Greenough, whose bust of Adams (Fig. 68) had been modeled in 1828, gave Josiah Quincy (1802–1882) his candid opinion of the Stuart-Sully portrait, an artistic judgment with which it is hard to disagree: "I have been filled with grief at the news of Mr. Alston's death," he wrote:

I had intended to have written Mr. F. C. Gray to beg that he would use his influence to allow no *tampering whatever* with the unfinished works of Alston. From the chalk outline to the ultimate finish, they should remain as giving the best possible *history* of his *method* which is all that education can borrow from genius like his. What finished work would buy the sketches of Fra Bartolomeo and Lionardo da Vinci? None, though those sketches embody great errors they are part of the history of Art and shew what had yet to be learned when those masters flourished. I say this because I suffered grief at seeing Stuart's Head of Mr. Adams filled up by somebody else and were it mine so help me God I would give a thousand dollars to restore the blank canvas as Stuart left it. Not that I think the artist who *finished* that picture incapable of producing a masterpiece but because the 2 minds do not work well in double harness.[24]

That Greenough was not alone in his opinion is borne out by the fact that, of all the copies and engravings of the portrait that have come to light, it is principally the head or bust that has been reproduced—Stuart rather than Sully. A typical example is the miniature engraving by Otto H. Parker in 1894 for *Scribner's Magazine* (Fig. 58); Parker's model was a copy in oil of the bust only of the Stuart-Sully portrait.

As Boylston intended (and apparently having been paid for from his estate), the portrait went ultimately to Harvard and hangs today in Adams House.

JOHN HENRI ISAAC BROWERE (1790–1834)

Late in August 1825, after his first few months as President, Adams was visited by John H. I. Browere, the "Sculptor who has made at New-York a Bust of Genl. La Fayette, and proposes to take Busts of all the Presidents." [1] Browere's bust of Lafayette had met such a

[23] JQA to George F. Morris, 20 Sept. and 6 Nov. 1833 (LbC, Adams Papers).
[24] 13 July 1843 (MHi:Quincy Papers).
[1] JQA, Diary, 30 Aug. 1825.

favorable reception that he was able to approach the most prominent Americans of the day and be assured of an audience. His secret process of taking life masks produced likenesses so strikingly lifelike that almost anyone requested was willing to submit to the process, however disagreeable it occasionally turned out to be. Adams at the time was preparing to return to Quincy for a month and had no time to consider the matter, but on 28 October, shortly after his return to Washington, his son Charles wrote Browere: "The president requests me to state to Mr. Browere that he will be able to give him two hours tomorrow morning at seven o'clock at his (Mr. Browere's) rooms on Pennsylvania Avenue. He is so much engaged at present that this is the only time he can conveniently spare for the purpose of your executing his portrait bust from life."[2]

As the elder Adams noted, "Browere takes Busts from a plaistered mask."[3] Or, as Jefferson described the process, "successive coats of thin Grout [were] plaistered on the naked head."[4] Charles correctly observed, when he submitted to it on 17 September, that it was "disagreeable,"[5] and he tried to warn his grandfather against agreeing to the operation: "I regretted to hear that you was about to 'submit' to a bust maker. He was so severe upon Mr. Jefferson that I am apprehensive of much inconvenience to you. I hope that he will not have been suffered to proceed although it is now too late to make any representations from here. I mean the man who was here and took both my father and myself. I imagine it is the same. His method is disagreeable and dangerous."[6]

Browere disposed of John Quincy Adams in short order, as two diary entries laconically record. "At Browere's. He took my Bust," and "Browere. The Bust finished."[7]

Browere's secret process is lost but there is no doubt of its effectiveness. Despite controversies with Trumbull and others, who thought his process not an art but purely mechanical, the collection of the remaining examples of Browere's few years' production of busts of prominent Americans is one of our great historical treasures. During his life he was discouraged by criticism and fear of plagiarism, and on his deathbed urged his family to lay the collection

[2] 28 Oct. 1825, quoted in Charles Henry Hart, *Browere's Life Masks of Great Americans*, N.Y., 1899, p. 54.
[3] JQA, Diary, 16 Sept. 1825.
[4] Thomas Jefferson to James Madison, 18 Oct. 1825 (DLC).
[5] CFA, *Diary*, 2:12.
[6] CFA to JA, 27 Nov. 1825 (Adams Papers). See also Oliver, *Portraits of JA and AA*, p. 202–203 (Figs. 101–103).
[7] Entries of 29 Oct. and 5 Nov. 1825.

59. JOHN QUINCY ADAMS.
PLASTER BUST BY JOHN HENRI ISAAC BROWERE, 1825

aside for forty years. When the busts turned up in 1897, Charles
Henry Hart tried in vain to persuade the United States Government
to buy them. A generation later, in 1937, all but seven were purchased by the late Stephen C. Clark, reproduced in bronze, and at his
death bequeathed to the New York State Historical Association, with
the injunction that they never leave Cooperstown. Figs. 59 and 60
show respectively the plaster bust of John Quincy Adams and its
bronze reproduction, and compel acceptance as speaking lifelikenesses,
perhaps, as Hart observed, historical documents that "outweigh all
the portraits ever limned or modelled."

60. JOHN QUINCY ADAMS.
BRONZE BUST MADE FROM BROWERE'S PLASTER BUST, 1938

The few busts that were not acquired by Mr. Clark had been sold to the phrenologists Fowler and Wells and have dropped out of sight. Among them was that of Charles Francis Adams. Engravings of the busts of the three generations of Adamses were published in *Mc-Clure's Magazine*, October 1897.

During the mid-1850's Fowler and Wells had offered for sale a "set of forty choice plaster casts ... priced at twenty five dollars," which "ran the gamut from John Quincy Adams, Voltaire, Sir Walter Scott, and Senator Thomas Hart Benton ('conscientiousness and mirthfulness not sufficiently developed') to the lower depths with Aaron Burr ('secretiveness and destructiveness very large') and a select assortment of depravity."[8] It is not unlikely that the cast of Adams had been taken from Browere's bust.

[8] John D. Davies, *Phrenology, Fad and Science*, New Haven, 1955, p. 51.

136

In 1890 the Adams family had what would now seem the chance of a lifetime to acquire one or more busts from Browere's collection, but nothing came of it. The following letter to the second Charles Francis Adams from a New York dealer is among the Adams Papers. No answer has been discovered.

I have been advised to write you (by a gentleman connected with the New York Historical Society) regarding a portrait-bust of Charles Francis Adams—the Statesman, and your father,—a bust from the Cast taken from life in 1825, by the Sculptor and Painter—*John H. I. Browere*. . . . This bust belongs to a Collection of portrait-busts—(all by Browere) which is for sale, and seven of the number are in this city at present, among them the *Adams*, which is the most youthful of the distinguished Americans in the Collection. John Adams and John Quincy Adams are in the list (also taken in 1825). These busts have never been out of the Browere family, and have had good care, so are in excellent condition. I would send you a complete list, forty-four, including the masks—if you desire it.

Thinking that you would care more for the bust I mention of your father, than for the others, I write especially of that one—and will cheerfully send you any further particulars if you request it. Allow me to say that I am permitted to refer to the Hon. Chauncey M. Depew, who has once purchased from me a valuable *Stuart* (Gilbert) painting.

A postscript added, "Mr. Charles A. Dana thinks that the *Collection* ought to go to the Corcoran Gallery,—but it has not yet been offered there."[9]

A typewritten biography of Browere, written by his great-grandson Everett Lee Millard, came with the busts Mr. Clark acquired. From this account we learn that the seven of the original series sold to Fowler and Wells were busts of C. F. Adams, Dr. Valentine Mott, Frances Wright, Dr. Samuel Latham Mitchill, Richard Rush, Philip Barbour, and Samuel Southard. These are undoubtedly the seven that Miss Janes wrote Charles Francis Adams 2d about in 1890.

Whether art or mechanics, the bust of John Quincy Adams, like that of his father, is a veritable facsimile and affords a standard by which other contemporary likenesses may be judged.

NATHAN W. WHEELER

In his "Rubbish" list of portraits, Adams includes one by "Wheeler" painted in Quincy in 1827. Groce and Wallace in their *Dictionary* list two artists named Wheeler with the suggestion that they may be one and the same person. "N. Wheeler" is listed as a miniature painter

[9] Miss M. P. Janes to CFA2, 21 June 1890 (Adams Papers, Fourth Generation).

at Boston in 1809 and Portsmouth, New Hampshire, in April 1810. "Nathan W. Wheeler" is described as a portrait painter at Cincinnati in 1831, at New Orleans in 1844, and a veteran of the War of 1812. The entry concludes: "His work is known only through an engraving of his portrait of Sam Houston, President of Texas." [1]

Five short entries in Adams' diary supply all we have discovered of Wheeler's portrait.

7 August 1827: "Quincy. Mr. and Mrs. John B. Davis, and a Mr. Wheeler of Cincinnati, a painter, visited. Mr. Wheeler asked me to sit for him. I agreed."

9 August: "Wheeler arrived at 10 o'clock, and I sat for him until 2 o'clock, with various interruptions. He dined with us."

10 August: "Mr. Wheeler came at 10 and kept me sitting for him, with several interruptions for visitors, swimming, and dinner, until 5 P.M."

13 August: "Mr. Wheeler came out at 10, and I sat for him until 5 P.M. Interruptions were 10 or 12 visitors, and 1 hour for dinner."

14 August: "Elijah Deane, Jr., the basketmaker from Marshfield, was going into Boston. I asked him to take an easel which Wheeler had borrowed of Mr. Alston, and left here to be returned to Alston. Deane took the easel."

Entries in Charles Francis Adams' diary indicate that he was in and out of Quincy during this period but he makes no mention of Wheeler.[2] He does reveal, however, that one of the visitors on 10 August was Daniel Webster.

The portrait, for which Adams apparently sat for upward of fifteen hours, has not been discovered.

CHESTER HARDING (1792–1866)

Much of the time Adams was in Quincy during the summer of 1827, halfway through his single term as President, was spent sitting for his portrait. Chester Harding, the self-taught artist who, during his youth had been a sign painter in Pittsburgh, had returned from England with the reputation of having had a considerable fashionable success with his portraits, and was developing a Boston clientele. Of course he sought out the President, and Adams sat to him several times in September and October, finally noting in his diary: "I gave

[1] Groce and Wallace, *Dict. Amer. Artists*, p. 678.
[2] CFA, *Diary*, 2:150.

a sixth and last sitting to Mr. Harding; who finished my portrait."[1] Charles had seen his father at the first sitting and saw the finished work a month later, writing: "Went to Mrs. Frothingham's for Abby and walked with her to Harding's room to see the Pictures of my father and of Miss Dehon. They are likenesses but the former is not an agreeable one."[2] Not long afterward Adams as well as Harding left Boston for Washington.

Harding refers to his activities at this time in his autobiography: "During my stay in Washington ... I painted many of the distinguished men of the day, such as Mr. Adams, Mr. Wirt, all the judges of the Supreme Court, &c."[3]

He took Adams' portrait again early in 1828, as Adams recorded: "Mr. Harding, the Painter, from Boston; who told me he had disposed of my Portrait which he painted last Summer, to the Athenaeum, and had made a copy of it for himself, to finish which he wished me to give him a sitting to which I consented. He will take it to morrow, at the same time with Mr. Greenough, at Mr. King's."[4] Horatio Greenough, the sculptor, had engaged a studio in Charles Bird King's house, and had become acquainted with Harding. At one time they intended to produce each other's portraits, Harding to take Greenough in oil and Greenough to model Harding's bust.[5]

Adams sat to both artists for a couple of hours on 21 February, and to Harding alone on at least four other occasions; he recorded the finishing of the portrait early in April, noting that it was "a strong likeness."[6] Harding packed up Adams' portrait with the others he had taken to send to New York, but the President had an opportunity to show it to his son George, at the same time remarking that those of the judges of the Supreme Court were "good likenesses."[7]

The history of the two Harding portraits of Adams is not clear, in part because only one of them can now be found. Harding had told Adams that the 1827 example had been given to "the Athenaeum," but the Boston Athenæum has no record of the portrait whatsoever. One of the two was exhibited at the National Academy of Design in 1828, listed as item 92.[8]

[1] Entry of 5 Oct. 1827.
[2] CFA, *Diary*, 2:177 (26 Oct. 1827).
[3] Chester Harding, *My Egotistigraphy*, Cambridge, 1866, p. 142.
[4] Diary, 20 Feb. 1828.
[5] Nathalia Wright, *Horatio Greenough: The First American Sculptor*, Phila., 1963, p. 51.
[6] Diary, 5 April 1828.
[7] Same, 21 April 1828.
[8] *National Academy of Design Exhibition Record, 1826–1860* (NYHS, Colls., 74 [1941]), p. 209.

One of them (Fig. 61) became the property of the Redwood Library and Athenaeum, Newport, Rhode Island, under the circumstances described in the two following letters:

New Orleans, September 26, 1874

To the Redwood Library   Newport R.I.

By the will of the late William Newton Mercer, your Institution has been left two original portraits—of John Quincy Adams and Daniel Webster; both by Harding.

These portraits will be delivered to your accredited representative.

With great respect

For P. Butler and W. Shields   Executors of W. N. Mercer

G. G. Steever

Francis Brinley, vice-president of the Redwood, acknowledged this letter on 12 October 1874 by reporting a vote of the board of directors accepting the two portraits. He then added:

Governor William C. Cozzens of Newport was a friend of Dr. Mercer, and the Board of Directors have authorized him to obtain the portraits from their present custodian. Most of the Directors now in office were personally acquainted with Dr. Mercer, and held him in high esteem, as a gentleman and at one time co-director. The portraits have a threefold interest—the eminence of the originals, the distinguished character of the artist, a personal friend of Mr. Webster, and the honored source from which they are derived.

To me they have a special interest, for though much younger than either, circumstances made me well acquainted with them, particularly Mr. Webster.

In the Redwood Library, among the valuable works of art from the easel of the late Charles B. King, a native of Newport, and most liberal benefactor, there is a portrait of Mr. Webster when a young man. It will be an interesting study to contemplate and compare the features of the youthful lawyer with those of the mature counsellor and admitted head of the bar in the United States.[9]

Harding was probably following the practice of other artists of his period, in making duplicates of his own portraits. In 1831 Peter Chardon Brooks notes the purchase of "Hon. D. Webster's picture by Harding—$10."[10] This might have been a replica of Mercer's portrait, but it could also have been a contemporary engraving; the price suggests the latter.

Redwood's portrait of Adams is a sufficiently recognizable and con-

[9] Both letters printed in George C. Mason, *Annals of the Redwood Library and Athenaeum*, Newport, 1891, p. 337, 341–342.
[10] P. C. Brooks, Account or "Waste" Book, 31 March 1831 (MHi).

sistent representation of Adams to have been called by him "a strong likeness." At the same time we can appreciate Charles Francis Adams' sentiments when he attended an exhibition of Harding's portraits: "I was on the whole well pleased with the specimens I there saw of his painting, excepting in the resemblance of my father which I abominate." [11] Years later John Quincy Adams himself characterized Harding as "a third rate portrait painter." [12]

The earliest known copy of a Harding likeness of Adams is that by the Salem artist Charles Osgood, painted in oil on a panel and now owned by the Essex Institute. According to records in the possession of Miss Elizabeth S. Osgood, a descendant of the artist, in 1936, the Osgood copy was painted at the request of one C. A. Andrew[s], in 1828. He might at that time have had access to the 1827 original said to have been given to "the Athenaeum" or to the 1828 replica which was sent to New York in April of that year. Osgood's copy (Fig. 62) was presented to the Essex Institute in 1918 by another C. A. Andrews, presumably a descendant of the man for whom the copy was made.

A second copy (again, it is not known of which version) was made by Albert Gallatin Hoit when only twenty-two years old. Hoit was born in Sandwich, New Hampshire, in 1809, graduated from Dartmouth College in 1829, and for years exercised his art as a portrait and landscape painter in Maine, New Brunswick, and later in Boston. He died in 1856. His copy of Harding's portrait (Fig. 63) was made in 1831 and given to Dartmouth College that year. It now hangs in the Carpenter Gallery there.

Osgood's copy is a much better resemblance of the original than is Hoit's, which strangely elongates Adams' head and mouth. On the other hand, Hoit included the wrist of Adams' right hand, following the original, whereas Osgood chose to omit it.

Still a third copy (Fig. 64) in pastel and framed in oval belongs to the author. It had belonged to the late Mrs. J. Amory Haskell and had been at one time thought to have been painted by Sully, though it does not resemble Sully's work, and it would have been unlike Sully to have bothered to copy Harding. It is also hard to be certain whether Fig. 64 is after Harding's portrait, or Osgood's or Hoit's copy.

Harding's likeness of Adams is unpleasing and could not have been popular, but it was reproduced, reversed, in a lithograph by one of

[11] *Diary*, 3:411 (28 Jan. 1831).
[12] Diary, 15 Aug. 1843.

61. JOHN QUINCY ADAMS. OIL BY CHESTER HARDING, 1827

62. JOHN QUINCY ADAMS.
OIL ON WOOD PANEL BY CHARLES OSGOOD, 1828

64. JOHN QUINCY ADAMS.
PASTEL ON CANVAS BY AN UNKNOWN ARTIST

63. JOHN QUINCY ADAMS.
OIL BY ALBERT GALLATIN HOIT, 1831

65. JOHN QUINCY ADAMS.
SILHOUETTE BY WILLIAM JAMES HUBARD, 1828

the Pendleton brothers (John B. or William S.) from a drawing by David Claypoole Johnston. The lithograph was undated but probably done in the 1830's. It is inscribed, "Drawn on stone by D. C. Johnston from a picture by C. Harding / Lith by Pendleton,"[13] but more clearly resembles Hoit's copy (Fig. 63) than Harding's original (Fig. 61).

WILLIAM JAMES HUBARD (1807–1862)

Among the most charming of the likenesses of Adams and his wife are the shades cut by Hubard at the end of Adams' residence in the President's House. Hubard had come to America in 1824 from England, where he had been thought a sort of child prodigy because of his talent for cutting silhouettes. As is revealed in *A Catalogue of ... the Hubard Gallery*, published in New York in 1825 and of which

[13] An example is at the American Antiquarian Society, Worcester.

144

Silhouette of Mrs. John Quincy Adams

66. LOUISA CATHERINE ADAMS.
SILHOUETTE BY WILLIAM JAMES HUBARD, 1828

a copy is at the Massachusetts Historical Society, almost immediately upon his arrival in New York City he successfully opened a gallery at 208 Broadway, where he exhibited the large collection of silhouettes he had brought with him, and where, "merely by a glance at the Profile, and with a pair of common scissors," he produced "a striking and spirited likeness."

It was Stuart who persuaded him to give up silhouettes for oil painting. He later became interested in sculpture, and developed a foundry in Richmond for casting bronzes; from casting bronzes it was an easy transition to becoming a munitions manufacturer when the Civil War broke out. In 1862 he was fatally injured in the service of the Southern Confederacy in an explosion at his foundry.

It must have been late in 1828 when he visited the President's House and cut these portraits of the President and his wife (Figs.

145

65 and 66). These have descended through the family and now belong to James B. Ames of Cambridge, Massachusetts.

On the reverse of the framed pair appear two inscriptions in the hand of Charles Francis Adams 2d, grandson of the sitters, copied from older inscriptions written by Elizabeth Coombs Adams. On the reverse of J. Q. Adams is written: "Silhouettes cut in the President's House in 1828 by young Hubbard, cut with scissors. This of John Quincy Adams is very perfect as we all saw him in his study last year he was in the Presidents House.   ECA   Frame made by Mr. Arnold of Quincy with the acorn." On the reverse of Mrs. Adams: "Silhouette of Mrs. John Quincy Adams cut by Master Hubbard in the Presidents House, last year Mr. Adams was in the House 29. Cut with scissors, while looking at them and are very perfect—from E. C. Adams and I. Hull Adams to Mr. C. F. Adams, now Dec. 1891." In the margin appears the word "Quincy." Elizabeth Coombs Adams, daughter of John Quincy Adams' brother Thomas Boylston Adams, died in 1903 at the age of ninety-five. Isaac Hull Adams was her younger brother. Both were of an age to have known their uncle when he lived in the President's House.

The pair were reproduced, with Miss Elizabeth Ogden Adams' permission, in Bennett Champ Clark, *John Quincy Adams, Old Man Eloquent*, Boston, 1933, facing p. 254.

JARVIS F. HANKS (b. 1799)

Early in 1829, and but shortly after leaving the President's House to settle on Meridian Hill, Adams and his wife sat again for their shades. This event is recorded in his diary: "A Mr. Reynolds called to ask me to permit a boy, a Master Hankes to come and cut me out in paper which he said would not take him more than ten or fifteen minutes. I told him he might come tomorrow at twelve O'Clock." [1]

"Master Hankes," whose first name is spelled variously Jarvis or Jervis, was born in Pittsford, New York, in 1799, and is said to have served in the War of 1812. Subsequently he became a portrait painter, silhouettist, sign and ornamental painter, adopting the title "Master" about 1826. It is a little hard to see how Mr. Reynolds could have referred to him as a "boy," then upward of thirty years old (perhaps Adams misunderstood Reynolds' use of "Master" as meaning "boy"), but there is little doubt of the identity of the silhouettist.

[1] Entry of 24 March 1829.

146

67. THE ADAMS FAMILY. SILHOUETTES BY JARVIS F. HANKS, 1829

He came the next day as expected, and Adams wrote: "Mr. Persico came and took a sitting of two hours for my bust; and Mr. Reynolds came with master Hankes who cut me out and all the family in paper. I had my wife and myself; my son John, his wife and their baby, Mary Roberdeau and Abigail S. Adams, all cut out and pasted upon one Card." [2] The group is shown in Fig. 67; the writings is in Adams' hand. This group of shades now belongs to James B. Ames of Cambridge, Massachusetts. A duplicate of the silhouette of Adams, cut at the same time, belongs to Mrs. W. C. J. Doolittle of Barneveld, New York. It is framed with a lock of Adams' hair and bears an inscription in the hand of Mary Hellen Adams (Mrs. JA2) to the effect that it was cut on the day of Adams' inauguration, 4 March 1825—an obvious lapse of memory.

The striking similarity—almost identity—of the shades cut by Hubard and Hanks, and indeed of those cut by Williams twenty years before, attests their accuracy and assures us of good likenesses.

HORATIO GREENOUGH (1805–1852)

In 1818, young Greenough—only thirteen years old—made a chalk copy of J. B. Binon's great bust of John Adams then standing in Faneuil Hall.[1] Ten years later he made his now famous marble bust of John Quincy Adams. On 13 February 1828 Adams received a letter from his kinsman Josiah Quincy in Boston, endorsed "By favor of Mr. Horatio Greenough." Mayor Quincy wrote:

Permit me the liberty to introduce to your knowledge and notice Mr. Horatio Greenough of this city, a gentleman, distinguished for his early biass to the art of sculpture, and for the genius he has displayed in the exercise of it. . . .

He visits Washington partly from a strong desire to see that Capital previous to his departing again for Europe and partly for the purpose of obtaining a portrait bust of the President of the United States; for which object he has obtained a sufficient subscription here.

Permit me to hope that you will gratify your friends, and patronise him by granting his request; which I am assured you will do the more

[2] Entry of 25 March 1829. Mary Roberdeau, of Philadelphia, was a daughter of Isaac Roberdeau and a granddaughter of John Adams' Pennsylvania friend Daniel Roberdeau. JQA once wrote a poem to her reading in part: "Ages, since thy father's sire/And mine were faithful friends have fled. . . ./Thy father, too, at dawn of Youth,/My swelling bosom learnt to prize." Abigail Smith Adams (later Mrs. John Angier) was a daughter of JQA's brother TBA and elder sister of ECA.
[1] Oliver, *Portraits of JA and AA*, p. 179–185 (Fig. 91).

willingly as there is nothing *mechanical* in his mode of obtaining the likeness, and as it will require you to submit to no more inconvenience than is usual to the sitting for a common portrait.[2]

Adams was evidently taken by the young artist and agreed to sit to him in the "noble studio" which Greenough had engaged in the house of the portraitist Charles Bird King.[3] He noted the first occasion in his diary: "Returning from my morning walk round the Capitol Square, I stopped at Mr. C. B. King the Painter's, and sat about an hour to Mr. Greenough who began the taking of my Bust."[4] Greenough found much in this first meeting to record:

Mr. Adams gave me his first sitting yesterday morning. A President is a man, you know, and so I put him in. He is much fallen away in flesh since Cardelli modelled him, and the character of his head is improved by it. His brow is unique. He gave me this morning nearly two hours. I think I have a likeness of him.

Harding is here, and being desirous of studying upon an unfinished head, I offered to allow him to paint while I was modelling. Mr. Adams is very agreeable as a sitter; he talks all the while, has seen much of art and artists, and remembers everything. He told me the dates of Copley's life, and even corrected me with regard to Thorwaldsen. His enthusiasm (he was very eager this morning in describing the difference between Stuart and Gerard) is of the head. I shall not attempt (as Sully and others have done) to make him look cheerful. He does not and cannot. Gravity is natural to him, and a smile looks ill at home.[5]

By the completion of the fourth sitting, on 25 February, Adams gave tangible evidence that Greenough's skill had impressed him. Greenough proudly reported this sign of favor to his brother:

The President has given me a most gratifying proof of his respect for my talents,—an order for a marble bust of his father, to be placed on a monument in the granite church at Quincy and to be modelled after my own heart.[6]

Early in March, Adams, walking around Capitol Square as usual, met Greenough, who requested a last sitting. This final meeting,

[2] 27 Jan. 1828 (Adams Papers).
[3] Horatio Greenough to Henry Greenough, 21 Feb. 1828, *Letters of Horatio Greenough to His Brother, Henry Greenough*, ed. Frances Boott Greenough, Boston, 1887, p. 25.
[4] Entry of 20 Feb. 1828.
[5] To Henry Greenough, 21 Feb. 1828, *Letters*, p. 25–26.
[6] JQA, Diary, 21, 23, 25 Feb.; Horatio Greenough to Henry Greenough, 28 Feb. 1828, *Letters*, p. 31. Coincidentally, the fourth sitting occurred on the same day as the marriage of Adams' son John to Mary Catherine Hellen.

according to Greenough, brought a rare, unqualified approval from Adams:

I have finished the head of the President, and shall probably cast it on Monday. He thinks well of it, and says he should not wish the head other than it is. "It is a noble art," he said, as he stood before the work on the last day. He conversed in the most animated manner on architecture, and confirmed me in the opinion that the highest reasoning powers cannot pierce the circle of beauty, however usefully they may act for directors. The President has, as I have told you, given me an order for the bust of his father. I shall adopt the Hermes form and treat the hair *au naturel*.[7]

In May, Greenough left for Italy where the busts of the two Adamses and one of Mayor Quincy were to be cut in marble. These were finished and sent off to America early in 1829. At this time two busts of John Quincy Adams were made, one intended for Greenough's father and one which was subsequently acquired by the Boston Athenæum for $200. Adams was waiting in Quincy for the bust of his father which he intended to install in the Stone Temple. Early in July a bust was delivered to him from Greenough, "but it proved to be of me. I had not bespoken it, nor did I expect it." Next day, he wrote, "I spoke to Coll. Quincy of the Busts, and he said that the bust of myself had been sent to me by mistake, and belonged to Mr. Greenough's father, who had retained that of my father in its stead."[8] It was not until September that his own bust was returned: "After dinner a man named Rowe, came from the Athenaeum with an order for my Bust, done by Greenough which was delivered to him."[9] The Athenæum bust (Fig. 68) was paid for on 9 December 1829. The inscription, "ΓΡΗΝΩ/ΕΠ," is incised beneath Adams' left shoulder.[10]

A smaller version (probably Fig. 70) was among the pieces shown in an exhibition of sculpture by Greenough at 4 Summer Street, Boston, in 1831. Adams recorded his attendance: "Returning to Charles's house, I went with him and his wife, and I. H. Adams to the exhibition of Statuary by H. Greenough," which included "two small copies of his large busts of my father and of me."[11] Charles described Greenough's group of statuary as "very good."[12]

---

[7] To Henry Greenough, 8 March 1828, *Letters*, p. 31–32. See Oliver, *Portraits of JA and AA*, p. 231–232, 234; Cat. No. 215.

[8] JQA, Diary, 2, 3 July 1829.

[9] Same, 4 Sept. 1829.

[10] See Nathalia Wright, *Horatio Greenough, the First American Sculptor*, Phila., 1963, p. 59.

[11] JQA, Diary, 12 May 1831.

[12] *Diary*, 4:46 (12 May 1831).

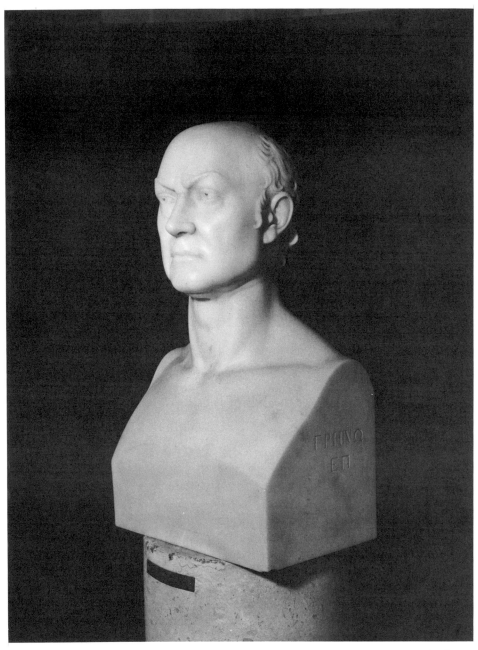

68. JOHN QUINCY ADAMS. MARBLE BUST BY HORATIO GREENOUGH, 1828

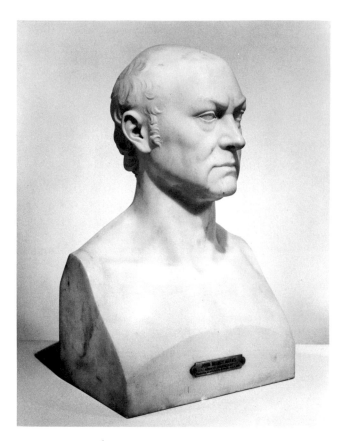

69. JOHN QUINCY ADAMS.
MARBLE BUST BY HORATIO GREENOUGH, 1828

A matching bust of Adams of the same size as the Athenæum bust (Fig. 69) was presented to The New-York Historical Society in 1858 by Augustus Howard. Nothing further is known of its origin. The third example (Fig. 70), one-half life size, was bequeathed to the Museum of Fine Arts by Greenough's widow in 1892. Whether it, or The New-York Historical Society's example came from Greenough's father does not appear. Greenough's career as a sculptor and examples of his work are well known, perhaps the most charming being the so-called "Forest Children" (Grace and Knyvet Winthrop Sears) now owned by the Massachusetts Historical Society.

One sour note sounds in the relations between the Adamses and Greenough. Unpleasantness seems to have arisen from the final accounting for the bust of John Adams, which had been commissioned in early 1828 and delivered to John Quincy Adams during the summer of 1829, prior to its installation in the Stone Temple in Quincy in

70. JOHN QUINCY ADAMS.
MARBLE BUST BY HORATIO GREENOUGH, 1831 OR BEFORE

October. Under date of 27 May 1830 Charles Francis Adams recorded: "Mr. Greenough called to be paid his demand for the expenses of the Bust, a stale thing for which he ought to have been ashamed." [13]

In 1850 Charles Francis Adams attended a gathering of his Harvard class, the class of 1825. He recorded in his diary that he did not think much of the class from the point of view of talent, but thought that the best known to the public was Greenough. Three years later, and after Greenough's death, a somewhat more mellow tone is evident in Adams' recollection of their association: "I had always been in pleasant relations [with him] ever since we were freshmen at Cambridge, and [his] loss I sincerely deplore." [14]

[13] Same, 3:246.
[14] Entry of 16 July 1850; CFA to Henry Greenough, 5 June 1853 (LbC, Adams Papers).

153

V

The Representative
1830–1848

"My countenance does injustice
in my old age to my heart."

CHRONOLOGY OF JOHN QUINCY ADAMS' LIFE, 1830–1848

1830

Completes notes on political parties in the United States which was to remain in manuscript until 1941. Is elected to the Board of Overseers of Harvard College, on which he served until his death.

Nov. 1: Elected to the 22d Congress as representative from the Plymouth district.

1831

Feb.–April: Composes *Dermot MacMorrogh, or The Conquest of Ireland,* in 4 cantos and 266 stanzas of *ottava rima.*

May: Becomes active in political Antimasonry.

July 4: In an oration delivered in Quincy, opposes the South Carolina doctrine of nullification as inimical to the Union and the Declaration of Independence.

Oct.–Dec.: Returns from Quincy to Washington and takes seat in Congress.

1832

Leads reform movement in Phi Beta Kappa Society to end secrecy. Serves as chairman of the House Committee on Manufactures which successfully frames a tariff of conciliation and compromise; continues as chairman of this committee until 1841.

March 13: Death of his brother TBA.

March 22–April 17: As a member of a special House committee, goes to Philadelphia to inquire into the affairs of the Bank of the United States, afterward submitting a minority report in which the Bank is cleared of all charges.

1833

March: Delivers with effect an extemporaneous speech in the House against

154

further tariff concessions to the South and against a policy of national protection of its special property interests.

Sept.: Birth of first grandson and namesake (JQA2), son of CFA and ABA.

1834

In the House defends the Bank of the United States and its president, Nicholas Biddle, and argues against the threatened withdrawal of public funds from it.

Oct. 23: Death of his son JA2 in Washington.

Dec.: Spokesman for the nation in memorial services for Lafayette.

1835

Supports President Jackson in House debate on crisis with France. Becomes chairman of a House special committee to administer the $500,000 bequest of James Smithson to the nation to establish an institution at Washington "for the increase and diffusion of knowledge among men"; begins efforts lasting many years to insure that Smithson's intention is carried out. Sits to Durand (Figs. 72–75).

1836

Plays an important role in the settlement of the Michigan-Ohio boundary dispute.

Jan.: In opposition to a speech in the Senate by Daniel Webster, again defends the President's policy in the crisis with France; begins to be referred to as "Old Man Eloquent" (see Milton's Sonnet to the Lady Margaret Ley).

May: Without JQA's being allowed to speak in opposition to it, a gag rule, by which all petitions relating to slavery are automatically tabled, is passed by the House; begins long and continuous struggle for repeal of the "gag" in its successive forms.

1837

Undertakes to present petitions to Congress from slaves themselves; wins a personal triumph but loses the issue. Enters ardently into the fight to prevent annexation of Texas, which has just established its independence from Mexico. Sits to Powers (Figs. 81–83), and to Clevenger (Fig. 85).

1838

June–July: Forces delay in the efforts to annex Texas. Publishes a report to his constituents in the form of a 131-page pamphlet: *Speech of*

John Quincy Adams, of Massachusetts, upon the Right of the People, Men and Women, to Petition; on the Freedom of Speech and of Debate in the House of Representatives . . . and the Petitions of More than One Hundred Thousand Petitioners, Relating to the Annexation of Texas to This Union.

Sept.: Sits to Page (Fig. 86).

1839

Proposes three constitutional amendments designed to end slavery in the United States, but the House refuses to receive the resolutions; loses favor with the abolitionists by publicizing his view that prohibition of slavery in the District of Columbia would require an amendment to the Constitution. At establishment of the Harvard Observatory, long advocated by him, becomes a benefactor and member of the committee charged with its oversight; reports a bill for an astronomical observatory as a suitable expression of Smithson's intent; delivers two lectures on the Smithson bequest at Quincy and Boston.

Sept.: Agrees to defend the freedom of Cinque and the other captive Africans who had seized the schooner *Amistad* off Cuba and brought it to Long Island.

Dec.: Saves the House from anarchy by assuming the Chair during a deadlock over its organization.

1841

Becomes Chairman of the House Committee on Foreign Affairs and serves until 1843. Sits to Lambdin (Fig. 94).

Feb. 24 and March 1: Successfully argues the case of the Africans of the *Amistad* before the United States Supreme Court, reasserting the basic right of *habeas corpus*.

1842

Jan. 25: In presenting to the House a petition from the citizens of Haverhill requesting the dissolution of the Union because of Southern slavery, incurs a resolution of censure.

Feb. 2: Begins to defend himself in the House against the charge of subornation of treason.

Feb. 7: Motion to censure is tabled.

Sept. 17: Receives public acclaim for his career in a ceremony at Braintree.

Sept. 27: Visits Plumbe's Daguerrean Gallery in Boston, there to be "taken" for the first of the many photographic likenesses that were to be made of him in his last years.

1843

July 6–Aug. 5: His vacation trip through New York State with ABA, JQA2, and Peter C. Brooks unexpectedly becomes a triumphal progress.

Sept. Painted by Marchant (Fig. 87).

Oct. 25–Nov. 23: At the cornerstone-laying ceremony of the Cincinnati Astronomical Observatory delivers a speech (published immediately) recounting the history of astronomy; is greeted with veneration and affection throughout Ohio as "Defender of the Rights of Man." Sketched by Mote (Figs. 96–97).

Dec.: Receives formal thanks from the government of Mexico for upholding in Congress "the cause of Mexico in the Texas Question, in respect to slavery, humanity, and the principles of justice."

1844

Painted by Bingham (Fig. 98), by Gibert (Fig. 102), and by Hudson (Fig. 104).

Dec. 3: After nearly nine years of unremitting effort, succeeds in having all gag rules withheld in the House, thus restoring the freedom of petition and debate in Congress.

1845

Feb.: His efforts to prevent annexation of Texas meet final defeat.

July–Sept.: Sits to J. C. King for his bust (Figs. 105–106), and to Healy (Fig. 108).

1846

The policies adhered to in his term as Secretary of State and President achieve fruition in the signing of the Oregon treaty with Great Britain, extending the northern boundary of the United States along the 49th parallel to the Pacific. The Smithsonian Institution is established as a learned organization. Sits to Billings (Fig. 120), and to Eastman Johnson (Fig. 121).

May: Together with thirteen other "Conscience Whigs," votes against declaration of war with Mexico.

Aug.: At Faneuil Hall in the last public meeting over which he presides, protests the return of a runaway slave to his master in New Orleans.

Nov. 20: Suffers a cerebral hemorrhage in Boston; recuperates at CFA's Boston home until early in February.

1847

Feb.: On return to the House of Representatives he is greeted by a standing tribute from all; is relieved of all committee work except that of the Committee on the Library of Congress, on which he has served since his first session; votes for peace resolution with Mexico; and speaks against indemnity for the owners of the *Amistad.*

March–June: Sits for his last portrait, to Powell (Fig. 122).

July: Celebrates his fiftieth wedding anniversary, at Quincy.

Dec.: Takes his seat in the House of Representatives as usual.

1848

Jan.: Continues to speak against President Polk's policy in the Mexican war. His last entry in his diary made on 4 January.

Feb. 21: Collapses in his seat during roll call on voting resolutions of thanks to American generals and troops in the Mexican War.

Feb. 23: Dies in the Speaker's Room at the Capitol.

Feb. 26–March 11: Funeral honors in Washington, Boston, and nationally; interment in Quincy.

1852

May 15: Death of LCA.

Dec. 16: Reinterment of JQA and LCA in the crypt of the Stone Temple in Quincy beside JA and AA.

JOHN WESLEY JARVIS (1780–1840)

Very little is known of the portrait of Adams (Fig. 71) said to have been painted by Jarvis. It could be said to bear a superficial resemblance to Adams, and the only information available is that it is thought to have been "probably painted, not from life, in New Orleans."[1] The same source gives the size of the picture as 30 by 25 inches and adds that it is said to have come "from the Adams family; Mrs. Hughes, Mobile, Alabama; Dr. Albert W. Sully, Philadelphia."

It was presumably painted before 1834, in which year Jarvis became paralyzed. No record of its painting or history, except as above, has so far come to light. It was reproduced in John and Alice Durant, *Pictorial History of American Presidents*, New York, 1955, p. 51,[2]

[1] W. R. Valentiner, *Catalogue of Paintings, Including Three Sets of Tapestries,* Raleigh: North Carolina Museum of Art, 1956, p. 42–43.

[2] The list of credits at p. 328 states that the portrait was then owned by Mrs. A. E. Rueff. The photograph was from the Frick Art Reference Library.

71. JOHN QUINCY ADAMS(?).
OIL ASCRIBED TO JOHN WESLEY JARVIS, BEFORE 1834

but is not listed in Harold E. Dickson, *John Wesley Jarvis, American Painter, 1780–1840*, New York, 1949.

Jarvis, who had been born in England, came to America and was apprenticed for a time to Edward Savage, the engraver. He painted a series of portraits of heroes of the War of 1812 for New York's City Hall and was considered one of the best portraitists of his day in New York. For a while, before his paralysis, he was associated with Henry Inman in New Orleans, where he painted during the winter months—hence the tradition that this portrait of Adams was painted there. We can only conjecture that if this painting be by Jarvis, and is indeed of J. Q. Adams, some other portrait or engraving of Adams, not now known to us, must have served as the artist's model.

159

LUIGI PERSICO (1791–1860)

"Mr. Persico came out this morning and took a profile likeness of my head in black crayons, as large as life, with the intention of moulding a bust from it." So Adams wrote in 1829, not long after he had stepped down from the Presidency.[1] The sculptor came again four days in a row, on the last occasion Adams noting: "Mr. Persico came and took a sitting of three hours; but during the greater part of which time I was reading the first Volume of Pelham, or the Adventures of a Gentleman. The most prolific School of Literature at present is Novel writing.... Before dinner I rode to the Capitol Hill, and at the House where Congress held their Sessions before they returned to the Capitol, I saw Persico's Busts of Thomas Low, and Charles F. Mercer, both finely executed, and excellent likenesses." Two more sittings on the next two days: "He touches and retouches with an anxiety of labour which belongs to the perfection of the Art. Never I believe was human scrutiny more closely applied to a face."[2]

The Adams family took great interest in this new likeness. Louisa wrote to her son Charles: "Your Father has been engaged sitting for a Bust to Mr. Perseco which bids fair to be a splendid thing—next to Stewarts Portrait the best thing that has ever been done and perhaps superior to that."[3] Adams himself wrote to Charles:

Persico of the Pediment is up Stairs moulding in clay a great man— *a beau ideal* which he is determined shall be a striking likeness of the last President of the United States. For the last ten days he has laid me under contributions of three Hours a day for sittings and looking grave. He forbids my smiling, because he says that is not *Presidential*, and that of course gives me an irresistible propensity to laugh. When that passes off, the dozing fit follows, and then comes the shocking incongruity of a *drowsy* President, which in Plaster of Paris will never do; however it may suit the Meridian of the half way house. And so to suit my Phidias I am compelled to "sit with sad civility"—not smiling, not dozing; but looking grave, and when he turns to work upon my ears or my whiskers, reading the Adventures of my Sybarite Spartan, otherwise called Henry Pelham the "Gentleman." ... Farewell, I must go and look grave for Phidias Persico.[4]

Adams wrote on the same subject that day in his diary, giving the background of his association with "Phidias Persico":

[1] Diary, 20 March 1829.
[2] Same, 26, 28 March 1829.
[3] 29 March 1829 (Adams Papers).
[4] 30 March 1829 (Adams Papers).

Persico came and finished the model in clay for my Bust. I gave him a sitting of about two hours. He has taken infinite pains to finish it, and has laboured upon it with the enthusiasm of an Italian Artist. He has also the feeling of gratitude for the aid and encouragement I gave him by employing him and furnishing him the design for the Pediment of the Capitol, which he has executed to universal Satisfaction, and for the subsequent contract which he has obtained for two Colossal Statues emblematical of Peace and War, which was authorized by an Act of Congress passed the last day of the late Session. The last official Act that I performed was the conclusion with him of that contract. I am gratified at having a Bust of myself made by him, because he is a very superior Artist, and because it will be the most perfect resemblance of me, which my Children will possess when I am gone.[5]

Luigi Persico, a Neapolitan, born in 1791, came to America in 1818 and lived successively in Lancaster, Harrisburg, and Philadelphia. During the Presidency of Adams he executed in sandstone, after a design suggested by Adams, a group of three allegorical figures portraying the "Genius of America" for the pediment over the Central Portico of the East Front of the Capitol. The sandstone figures are now in storage but were reproduced in 1959–1960 during the extension of the Capitol, carved in white marble by Bruno Mankowski. Similarly, the two colossal statues symbolizing Peace and War are in storage but have also been reproduced in marble and now stand in niches on each side of the East Central Portico. A third group Persico executed for the Capitol, the "Discovery Group," stood from 1844 to 1958 on the south cheek block on the East Front steps of the Central Portico, matched across the steps by Greenough's "Rescue Group"; both are today in storage. These commissions given to Persico, though aided by Adams' influence, evidence the high opinion held of his work.[6] The marbles of most of his various plaster models were apparently done in Italy, where he was in close contact (perhaps competition would be a better word) with Greenough. He died in Marseilles in 1860.

Two further sittings in April enabled the sculptor to complete the model for Adams' bust.[7] Not being content with the bust alone, Persico also took "a miniature portrait in crayons" of Adams, requiring four days work.[8] This miniature, entered in Adams' "Rubbish" list, has disappeared.

Early in May the artist called on Adams and took his leave. Then

[5] Entry of 30 March 1829.
[6] *Compilation of Works of Art and Other Objects in the United States Capitol,* prepared by the Architect of the Capitol, Washington, 1965, p. 365, 367, 378.
[7] JQA, Diary, 1, 6 April 1829.
[8] Same, 11, 15 April 1829.

he went to New York to embark for Liverpool, thence to Naples to undertake the two colossal statues for the Capitol; he took with him the model for his bust of Adams. In September he wrote his American patron from Naples: "From the place of my nativity, in the bosom of my family wherein I find myself happy, receive my thanks for all that you have done for me. To you I owe whatever I enjoy, distinction, honour, and occupation. May God bless you.... By my brother [Gennario] who will return to America next Summer, I shall send you the bust I had the honour to make of you." [9]

Time passed; the following year Luigi Persico wrote proposing to make a present to Adams of his bust in marble.[10] But artists, at least those with whom the Adamses came in contact, are known to be procrastinators. It was two more years before Adams received word from Gennario Persico that he had received from Luigi the bust and that he was to ship it to Charles Francis Adams at Boston. On receipt of this advice, Adams wrote to Charles: "I now enclose ... A Bill of Lading for a Box, Ship'd in the Brig Thorn Cleveland Master. Mr. Persico says it should be taken from the vessel and carried by hand and not by cart or waggon—it contains Mr. Persico's bust of me." [11] What had arrived was a plaster bust and hence brittle, but capable of being carried by hand.

Two and a half years more slip by, and the sculptor and his bust surface again in Adams' diary:

Persico invited me to go to his rooms on the Capitol Hill and see a collection of Pictures by some of the Masters of the Italian Schools which he brought with him from Italy upon Speculation, and wishes to sell, and a marble bust of the President, of which he proposes to make a present to him on the 8th of January next. Persico is desirous of further employment by Congress, and wishes to make friends. I advised him to visit Mr. Jarvis, Chairman of the Committee on the public buildings, and Mr. Polk, Chairman of the Committee of Ways and Means, and invite them to go and see his bust of the President, and to be careful not to omit making the present on the 8th of January. Just then a renewed fancy took Mr. Persico, to make a marble bust of me. He had entertained this fancy while I was President, and when his being employed by the public depended upon me. Before he went to Italy he had taken the mould of this bust in clay, and when he had been there about two years, he sent me a cast of it in Plaster of Paris; with some enquiry whether I should prefer to have it in marble. I was then not in public life, and alike indifferent [Oh, modest man!] to Busts whether in Marble or in Plaster.

[9] 24 Sept. 1829 (Adams Papers).
[10] JQA, Diary, 16 Sept. 1830.
[11] 9 April 1832 (Adams Papers).

I did not answer his Letter. He now begs me to give him one more sitting, that he may finish in higher perfection the model, and is fully determined to make the bust in marble and to send it to me. I desired him not to give himself that trouble but he insisted upon it; and I have no doubt will persist in his determination till he shall find it more convenient to desist from it and he knows that for me the intention is equivalent to the deed.[12]

And so the following month Adams sat again to the persistent sculptor, who "made some marks upon my Plaster bust."[13] From this entry we can conclude that the plaster of Paris bust that arrived in Boston on the brig *Thorn* in 1832 was in Adams' possession in January 1835 and was being used by Persico as the model for the proposed marble. From this time the plaster bust drops from sight, but not Persico. In May he wrote to Adams:

I have been in Raleigh N.Ca. with a view of restoring the mutilated Statue of Genl. Washington at that Capitol. I found it in such a state as to pronounce it irreparable. The Governor Mr. Swaine asked me an estimate for the execution of a new Statue, which I gave to him, and told me that he would try to raise the funds, in this month, by a subscription.

Should your Excellency write a letter either to the Governor, or to some leading Gentleman in that State, recommending me to their confidence, I might likely expect to return home from this country with a commission that would employ me at the arrival.

My reliance on your experienced goodness towards me, imboldens me to make the request.[14]

Such a request is eloquent testimony to Adams' "experienced goodness" to artists and sculptors with whom he came in contact.

Two more years passed before the marble bust was completed—whether in Italy or not is not clear. Persico offered it to Adams as a gift in 1837, as the following letter testifies: "I have selected this day to present you the bust I have executed, because it is a day you have rendered dear to my memory. The bust is now in the library of Congress, to your order. Accept my thanks for all you have done for me, and may God Bless you."[15]

The same day he wrote again: "Illustrious and benevolent man, accept in trust for posterity, your bust in marble, which I have executed with the view that when your useful career shall have closed, the features of the Patriot and Philandropist ever industrious for the good of his country, and of mankind, shall remain to be looked upon

[12] Entry of 26 Dec. 1834.
[13] Entries of 25, 27 Jan. 1835.
[14] 5 May 1835 (Adams Papers).
[15] 3 March 1837 (Adams Papers).

by succeeding generations, to incite them to a noble emulation of his virtues and his actions." [16]

At this stage of Adams' career the offer seems genuine and innocent enough, but he as always viewed the matter with the greatest discretion. He declined the offer, undoubtedly holding the marble bust to be of greater significance and value than the plaster one he had received five years earlier, and wrote his son: "Persico has finished my bust in marble, and it is the admiration as a work of art, and a likeness, of everyone who has seen it. He offered it to me as a present but I declined accepting it, as too valuable for me as a public man to receive as a gift. It is in the Library rooms of Congress and may perhaps remain there." [17] Adams accordingly wrote to Persico:

I have received with the deepest sensibility your Letter of yesterday rendered doubly precious to me, by your allusion to its date, and to associations in my own mind not less interesting to myself than to you.

The bust has been admired by many persons who have seen and mentioned it to me, as a likeness. No judge of Sculpture can behold it without admiring it as a work of art. It is too valuable for me to accept as a present. But let me suggest to you the idea of presenting it to the Library of Congress, where it now is, and where it may remain a monument of your unrivalled talent, of your grateful recollections, and of our disinterested friendship. There it will honour me by exhibiting to multitudes of after times the lineaments of my face, in the simplicity of nature, and the perfection of art. It will honour you as demonstration of the talent which it was my good fortune to recognise, to encourage and to patronize as far as was within my humble means. The artist and his friend and subject will go down together in that block of marble to the succeeding age and in that association my share of reward will be as precious in my estimation as yours of grateful generosity and of renown in the art of Praxitelas and of Michael Angelo. [18]

Though Adams saw no reason why Persico should not present to President Jackson his marble bust, his own relationship with Persico had been such that he leaned over backward lest any cloud be cast on it by the acceptance of his own bust in marble. Persico acceded to the suggestion and wrote to the Librarian:

On the third of March last, I requested you to keep the bust in marble I had placed in the Library of Congress, subject to the order of John Quincy Adams, as President of the United States. That bust I executed with the intention of presenting it to the original, as a testimonial of my gratitude

[16] Second letter of 3 March 1837 (Adams Papers).
[17] 23 March 1837 (Adams Papers).
[18] 4 March 1837 (LbC, Adams Papers).

for his kindness towards me: I did present it to him on the same day I made the aforesaid request; but he, in a very flattering note, declined the acceptance of it, and suggested to me, for my own advantage no doubt, the idea of presenting it to the Library of Congress.

In compliance with his suggestion, I beg the favor of your proposing it next session to the Senate, on my behalf, for their acceptance.[19]

Thus the record was kept straight, and Adams avoided any charges of having accepted gifts in return for official favors granted. But it was a fatal decision so far as the bust was concerned. For fourteen years it was preserved in the secure and safe confines of the Library of Congress in the Capitol, as were Stuart's portraits of the first three Presidents, painted in 1818–1820 for Doggett of Boston—safely kept, that is, until Christmas Eve 1851, when the Library was gutted by a disastrous fire which destroyed two-thirds of its contents. Persico's "perfect" bust of Adams, the likeness which had received high praise from the family as well as the public, was among the many treasures that did not survive.[20] To my knowledge it was never copied or reproduced in any medium and we can only imagine its perfection. To add to the misfortune, the plaster bust by Persico that had been in Adams' possession for several years is unaccountably lost.

JOHN GADSBY CHAPMAN (1808–1889)

Chapman was a young man when he painted Adams' portrait in 1832, but by then it was known that Adams was receptive to any artist. Chapman was born in Alexandria, Virginia, in 1808, and early received instruction from Charles Bird King, establishing himself as a professional artist in 1827. Not long afterward he went to Europe, traveling for a time with Samuel F. B. Morse and studying in Rome and Florence. His *Baptism of Pocahontas*, painted between 1837 and

[19] A copy of Persico's letter to John S. Meehan, dated 9 May 1837, is among the Adams Papers with a note from Persico transmitting it to Adams, addressed "To His Excellency John Quincy Adams ex President of the United States, at N. Biddle's Esqre." In the upper corner, written in Adams' hand, appears "Persico Luigi 12 May 1837 Phila.," and under that the words "Cash for his Voyage," bespeaking undoubtedly a combination of Persico's importunity and Adams' unfailing generosity.

[20] John S. Meehan, Librarian of Congress, reported to the Hon. James Alfred Pearce by letter, dated 7 Jan. 1852, describing in some detail the loss occasioned by the fire including "busts, in marble of Thomas Jefferson, J. Q. Adams [presumably that by Persico], and Gen. Lafayette, ... and portraits of Presidents Washington, Adams, and Jefferson, by Stuart; a portrait of President J. Q. Adams, by J. Cranch ..."; adding with respect to the latter portraits, "all belonging to private individuals, were in the Library at the time of the fire and were all destroyed" (DLC:Letterbook of the Librarian, 1849–1854, p. 214–216).

1840, one of the eight large historical paintings in the Rotunda of the Capitol, is perhaps his best-known work. For it he received $10,000; Trumbull had received $8,000 each for his four which were placed in the Rotunda in the late 1820's.

Early in February 1832, Adams began sitting to the young artist for a portrait commissioned by a Mr. Linton of New Orleans, a friend of the Senator from Louisiana, Josiah S. Johnston. Chapman at the time told Adams he wanted to do a painting of the removal of Washington's remains from Mount Vernon and thought it would be an excellent subject. Adams agreed, noting in his diary: "But his purpose will be disappointed."[1] He was right: Washington's dust has been allowed to rest undisturbed. A few more sittings took place in May, but by 12 May the young painter "was gone to Baltimore."[2] Adams dated this portrait in his "Rubbish" list as having been painted in 1833. Perhaps it was not finished until that year. No further mention of it has appeared and the portrait is one of the many so far lost.

Adams must have indicated that he was kindly disposed toward the young artist, for in 1847 Chapman wrote for help in connection with the niche in the Rotunda of the Capitol to which the *Baptism of Pocahontas* had been removed. When commissioned in 1837 to paint the picture, Chapman was the youngest of the artists selected. He claimed he had designed the picture expressly for the "nitch" designated by Colonel Preston—the actual decision having been left by Congress to the Vice-President and the Speaker of the House. This place was the space or "nitch" immediately to the left of the north door of the Rotunda, and there the picture hung for some six years until, as Chapman wrote Adams, it was "recently removed in order, as I have been informed, 'to give Weir's picture [*Embarkation of the Pilgrims*, completed in 1847] a better light.'" He was obviously hurt, for he continued:

The picture has its defects, of which no one can be more sensible than I am, and a charitable feeling towards what may be considered a first effort might have saved it from the degradation of its removal to give its place to another who possessed equal opportunity of suiting his picture to its intended light. . . . I confidently rely upon the justice of my position, and by no one I am sure, will I be more cheerfully sustained than by yourself, however indifferently I may be personally known to you."[3]

Adams' reply to Chapman has not been found. The painting was left where it was and was not restored to its original location.[4] But in

[1] Entries of 10, 14, 16 Feb. 1832.
[2] Entries of 1, 2, 12 May 1832.
[3] 8 Feb. 1847 (Adams Papers).
[4] J. George Stewart, Architect of the Capitol, to the Author, 23 May 1969.

1856 the old, low, wooden, copper-covered dome, with but a small opening at the top, was replaced by the present dome, with the result that the lighting on all the Rotunda paintings is substantially equal. Chapman's, which had in fact been removed to a worse light, no longer suffers "degradation" but shares the light with Weir's picture.

REMBRANDT PEALE (1778–1860)

It was in December 1833 that Rembrandt Peale, second son of Charles Willson Peale, visited Adams in Washington, telling him that there was an exhibition of his paintings in the city which he wanted him to see and asking him to sit to him for his own portrait. Adams promised to do both. A week later he described the paintings in the exhibition: "His Collection of Pictures of his own painting is pleasant. One of them a very good copy of Raphael's Madonna of the Chair; a Picture which I always delight to see—There were also several Portraits—one of Rammohun Roy the Hindu Christian recently deceased in England. Peale said he painted it but a few days before his Death. Also a Portrait of Mrs. Oliver, a fat Poetess." [1]

From that time until the end of March 1834 Adams sat to Peale a dozen or so times for one or two hours at a time. Of one occasion he recorded that Peale's painting "differs from that of any other Painter, who has tried his skill upon my face. He takes the likeness first in Crayons upon Paper, and copies from that in Oil upon the canvass. Mr. Peale's conversation is not so amusing as that of Stewart used to be; but his Portraits are among the best I have seen painted in this Country next to those of Stewart." [2] Early in January the following year Adams could report that Peale "had transferred a copy of the sketch he had taken with Crayons upon Paper to the Canvas—and now said he would take this sitting to paint the eyes." A sitting in early March was abridged by the entry of Mr. George Fay, the member of the House from Batavia, New York, with Mrs. Fay, "whose Portrait Mr. Peale is occupied in painting. I gave way of course." [3] A few more references in the diary for March and then silence, though Adams remained in Washington until late June.

In reminiscences published a few years before his death, Peale makes no mention of painting Adams' portrait but does refer to him in relating his own eye trouble: "Many persons are acquainted with the practice of John Quincy Adams, who is said to have renovated his eye-sight, by frequently pressing his eye-balls with his thumb and

[1] Diary, 6, 12 Dec. 1833.
[2] Same, 28 Dec. 1833.
[3] Same, 4 Jan., 8 March 1834.

167

finger, from the outer to the inner corner. I have tried it without advantage, and the occasional inconvenience of forcing some of the eye-lashes painfully inwards." [4]

The only further mention of Peale's portrait that has come to light is an entry in Adams' diary in 1841: "Mr. Isaac I. Smith ... came to request a lecture for the New York Lyceum. He said also that they proposed requesting me to sit for my portrait, but had not fixed upon the painter. They thought of Rembrandt Peale at Philadelphia. I said he had painted me once, and was not very successful in the likeness." [5]

Knowing that Adams' opinions of portraits of himself are suspect and remembering Peale's two extraordinary portraits of Jefferson, one must greatly regret that Peale's one likeness of Adams has dropped from sight. In his "Rubbish" list, Adams dated the painting in 1837, but it was at least well under way in 1834.

ASHER BROWN DURAND (1796–1886)

Two things happened in the early months of 1835, of disparate significance to be sure, yet each contributing its part to the honor and glory of this country. The preceding year France had dishonored her treaty with the United States by reneging on the first installment of her admitted debt for depredations on American shipping and property during the Napoleonic Wars. Jackson had taken a firm stand for enforcing payment in his State of the Union message; the possibility of war loomed; and the question was debated long and hard in Congress. Adams in the face of strong opposition proposed a resolution supporting Jackson's position. Heated debate ensued, modifications were agreed upon, and when the question was put, on 3 March 1835, the resolution carried unanimously. The country's honor was upheld. Adams wrote his son Charles that it was the greatest parliamentary victory of his career; and his son in later years was to refer to it as "the first of the great triumphs of Mr. Adams in the House." [1]

The other occurrence, in a quite different theater of interest, was the determination of the well-to-do New York merchant Luman Reed, fired by a sense of the greatness of his country's history, to gather together a collection, in duplicate, of portraits of the seven Presidents of the United States. Life portraits were to be taken of those still

[4] Rembrandt Peale, "Reminiscences," *The Crayon,* 3:164 (June 1856).
[5] Entry of 1 Oct. 1841.
[1] JQA, *Memoirs,* 9:212.

living, Adams and Jackson, and copies of the best available portraits (by Stuart of course) of those who had died.

For his artist Reed chose Asher B. Durand, by then a competent and skillful portraitist. At the age of twenty-four he had engraved Trumbull's masterpiece, *The Declaration of Independence*, and, later, Sully's full-length portrait of John Quincy Adams (Fig. 53). The former established his reputation as an engraver, the latter confirmed it. From engraving, Durand had turned successfully to portraiture; and in later life he was to make a new reputation as a painter of nature in the grand manner of the Hudson River School.

In engaging Durand to paint the series, Reed had written, "I intend to make presents of them to one of our public institutions of Science and Natural History. . . . It is not proper for me to mention the name of the institution until the presentation is made. . . . If possible, get that of the Hon. John Quincy Adams, also Jefferson, from an original by Stuart, and likewise Monroe. . . . I forgot the portrait of the genuine patriot John Adams, which I hope you will consent to copy for me, be it where it may . . . Washington and Madison you already have."[2] Durand was well known to Adams, who readily consented to sit again for his portrait. The great debate was over; the House had risen; Adams was flushed with victory and, for a moment, had time on his hands. Four portraits of him were painted by Durand, two originals and a replica of each; and there has always been confusion as to which is which.

Adams sat to Durand from 12 to 20 March, a total of some eleven hours, all instances recorded carefully in his diary, concluding: "I gave one more sitting of an hour this morning to Mr. Durand to finish my portrait; which is now perhaps the best likeness ever taken of me."[3] A few days later Adams received a letter from Charles Augustus Davis of New York:

I feel much obliged to you for acceding to the wishes of my friend Mr. Reed in permitting Mr. Durand the Artist to take your likeness.

I call'd to day with Mr. Reed to see the Work at Durands Rooms. And I can truly say I never saw so faithful a resemblance of life. The Whole *Character* of the face is there.[4]

Davis apparently was so impressed with Durand's portrait of Adams that during the next few weeks he had the artist paint a replica of

[2] To Durand, [June] 1835, John Durand, *Life and Times of Asher B. Durand,* N.Y., 1894, p. 109.
[3] Entry of 20 March 1835.
[4] 28 March 1835 (Adams Papers).

it, which he presented to Charles Francis Adams' wife, an incident recorded with pleasure in the young man's diary: "Found my wife looking at a Picture which Mr. C. Aug. Davis of New York has sent to her as a present. It is by Durand and of my father, a very good likeness. This is a compliment and of the highest kind." The following day he was still enthusiastic: "The more I look the better I like my father's picture, though it does not give his fire." A few days later he notes the unexplainable fact that Mr. Davis, who had given the portrait to Charles' wife Abigail, "came to inquire the name of the Artist who painted the picture of my father." Was this just a lapse of Davis' memory? The original portrait (Fig. 72) had been exhibited in New York at the National Academy of Design, and the replica (Fig. 73) was now to be on exhibition at the Boston Athenæum. "The [Athenæum] Gallery is tolerably good," Charles wrote, "with a sprinkling of fine names but not corresponding excellence. The picture of my father in its simplicity contrasts singularly with the pretention of the others." [5]

The simplicity and directness with which Durand chose to portray Adams, and which Adams' son recognized at once as a virtue in the likeness, were the characteristics of Adams' appearance at this time that came through to others when in his presence. Less than a year before Adams sat to Durand, a visitor to Quincy sent an impression of him for publication in *Niles' Weekly Register*:

The personal appearance of the ex-President himself corresponds with the simplicity of his furniture. He resembles rather a substantial, well-fed farmer, than one who has wielded the destinies of this mighty Confederation, and been bred in the ceremony and etiquette of an European Court. In fact, he appears to possess none of that sternness of character which you would suppose to belong to one a large part of whose life has been spent in political warfare, or, at any rate, amidst scenes requiring a vast deal of nerve and inflexibility. [6]

If there was yet no "sternness" in the countenance, Durand saw along with the simplicity a deep sobriety and control that were evident also to the young William H. Seward when he first visited the statesman at Quincy in 1831:

A short, rather corpulent man, of sixty and upward, came down the stairs and approached me. He was bald, his countenance was staid, sober, almost to gloom or sorrow, and hardly gave indication of his superiority over other men. His eyes were weak and inflamed. He was dressed in an

[5] CFA, Diary, 18, 19, 23 May, 4 June 1835.
[6] J. C. C[ourtney], "Mr. and Mrs. John Quincy Adams at Home," *Niles' Weekly Register*, 47:91 (11 Oct. 1834).

olive frock-coat, a cravat carelessly tied, and old-fashioned, light-colored vest and pantaloons. It was obvious that he was a student, just called from the labors of his closet. Without courtly air or attitude, he paused at the door of the parlor. I walked quite up to him, while he maintained his immovable attitude, and presented my letter of introduction. . . .

Our interview lasted three hours; he was all the time plain, honest, and free, in his discourse; but with hardly a ray of animation or feeling in the whole of it. In short, he was just exactly what I before supposed he was, a man to be respected for his talents, admired for his learning, honored for his integrity and simplicity, but hardly possessing traits of character to inspire a stranger with affection. Occasionally, indeed, he rose into a temporary earnestness; and then a flash of ingenuous ardor was seen, but it was transitory, and all was cool, regular, and deliberate. When I left him he thanked me for the call . . . and so we parted; and, as I left the house, I thought I could plainly answer how it happened that he, the best President since Washington, entered and left the office with so few devoted personal friends.[7]

That Durand and Adams achieved a ready respect each for the other is as clear from the course of events as it is from the several portraits. In June 1835 the second original was put in train and a careful note of the occasion made by Adams:

Mr. Durand with Mr. Luman Read were here after dinner. They came about the double collection of Portraits of the Presidents which Mr. Read has employed Durand to paint for him. One of which he intends to present to some public national institution, and the other he proposes to keep himself. I lent Mr. Durand the Portrait of my father, painted by Stuart in 1799, for him to copy,[8] and I promised to sit to him next Thursday morning for another portrait of me. That which he painted of me at Washington two months ago has been exhibited at New York, at the annual exhibition, and was thought an excellent likeness. Durand has painted a copy of it for Mr. Charles A. Davis, which he has presented to my son Charles's wife, and which is now at the Athenaeum exhibition in Boston. But instead of making another copy, Durand asked me to sit again, to which I assented.[9]

As Adams' diary entries reveal, sittings began soon afterward and continued a couple of weeks in Quincy and in Boston: "Mr. Durand

---

[7] F. W. Seward, *Seward*, 1:205–207. That Adams was capable at times of more animation, even joviality, than Seward saw or than Adams' portraits lead us to suppose is suggested by a newspaper correspondent at the Capitol just a few years earlier: "He wears the same old hat, with a band an inch and a quarter wide which he used to wear when Secretary of State; and now and then, he is observed to administer to some Kentucky member his old pump-handle shake of the hand!" *Boston Patriot*, 20 Dec. 1831, p. 2, col. 3. Also on this lighter side, see Philip Hone's description, below.

[8] See Oliver, *Portraits of JA and AA*, p. 136 (Fig. 64).

[9] Diary, 1 June 1835.

72. JOHN QUINCY ADAMS. OIL BY ASHER BROWN DURAND, MARCH 1835

73. JOHN QUINCY ADAMS.
OIL BY ASHER BROWN DURAND, BEFORE JUNE 1835

173

came about ten O'Clock, and I sat to him about two hours. He took also a sitting of my granddaughter Georgiana Frances, at the request of Mr. Read, who yesterday asked me to permit him to present the picture to me." A few days later: "I went to Boston, with Mrs. Adams, the child Fanny, and Mrs. Wilson. We stop'd at the Athenaeum, where Mr. Durand has a chamber in the upper story of the building. He took a sitting of the child till one O'Clock.... I returned at one to the Athenaeum, and sat to Mr. Durand till two.... Mr. Durand said he should want another sitting both of me and of the child, and promised to come to Quincy for that purpose, next Wednesday; and I engaged him to paint also a Portrait of my other Grand-child, Mary-Louisa, which I propose to give to her mother."[10]

Durand's work undoubtedly merited and clearly received full approval by all concerned. Adams wrote to him from Quincy in July:

I regret much that I had not the pleasure of seeing you once more, before your departure for New York to thank you for the excellent likenesses of my Grandchildren as well as myself which you have made permanent for the eyes of Posterity.

I accept with grateful sentiments to you the Portrait of my little Louisa, and pray you to offer to Mr. Read and to accept yourself those of my family with my own for that of her Sister Fanny.

Wishing you all the success in your new profession, which you can desire and which to judge from the specimens which you have left with us, and from those which you took with you, must certainly await you, I remain.[11]

The artist records his own progress and evidences his gratitude to his patron Reed in a letter written at this time:

I have been at work to some account since I wrote last, but, gadding about and looking at everything in and out of Boston most of the time, I have of course not made much progress, although I have four paintings begun; one of a beautiful little girl, the grand-daughter of Mr. Adams, which I paint at the request of Mr. Reed, to be presented to Mr. Adams; another, a portrait of the Hon. Edward Everett for Mr. Davis; ... a third, the head of President John Adams [after Stuart] which is almost done, as well as that of John Quincy Adams, an entirely new portrait from life, and much better than the one I did in Washington. I shall begin copies of Washington and his wife immediately. After Mr. Reed leaves me I shall have nothing to do but work and make the most of my time. I have dined once with Mr. Adams, and have promised to do so again tomorrow. His residence is eight miles from Boston, which renders it not

[10] Same, 9, 13 June 1835.
[11] 10 July 1835 (LbC, Adams Papers).

so convenient as I could wish for sittings in taking him and his grand-daughters' portraits. But as I have already said, no inconvenience shall interfere with my carrying out the wishes of Mr. Reed, who seems to think of nothing else while here but to promote my best interests.[12]

In due course Durand made a replica of the June portrait; no comment on the fact appears, but we know a double set was intended and two of the June version exist.

Both sets of portraits are undoubtedly good likenesses of Adams; Charles liked the first better every time he saw it, though Durand thought the second superior. The justifiable pride and satisfaction Adams must have felt at the time, after his parliamentary victory, is perhaps apparent though without a suggestion of smugness. Although the duplicate versions are similar—and often thought to be but one version in four copies—there are significant differences, but differences of a kind that might not be remembered or recognized if the two types were not seen together. In the first version, the March portrait (Fig. 72) and its replica (Fig. 73), Adams wears a maroon coat, with very little white showing below his stock, his eyes looking away from the observer. In the June pair (Figs. 74 and 75) the coat is navy blue, a considerable portion of shirt appears below the stock, and he looks the observer squarely in the eye.

With Adams' diary and other pertinent records now available for the first time, the provenance of the four paintings can readily be reconstructed. The first to be disposed of was the replica (Fig. 73) of the March portrait, and it was given by Mr. Davis to Charles' wife. The last member of the family to own it was Arthur Adams, a grandson of Charles, by whom it was presented to Harvard. It now hangs in the John Quincy Adams Dining Room of Adams House in Cambridge. In the course of time it came to be thought that this portrait was a copy after Durand by William Page and that it was painted about 1840. Page did paint a portrait of Adams (Fig. 86) in 1838, but the only similarity is in the pose.

The March 1835 original portrait (Fig. 72) and a companion portrait of Madison by the same artist were purchased for $300 from the artist in 1870 by The Century Association in New York, in whose dining room both have hung ever since.

The June pair (Figs. 74 and 75) were of course delivered to Mr. Reed. One of them—perhaps it can be presumed to have been the original—he kept in his own collection; the other, together with Durand's

<hr>

[12] Durand, *Life of Asher B. Durand*, p. 109.

74. JOHN QUINCY ADAMS. OIL BY ASHER BROWN DURAND, JUNE 1835

75. JOHN QUINCY ADAMS. OIL BY ASHER BROWN DURAND, JUNE 1835

77. JOHN QUINCY ADAMS.
ENGRAVING BY JOHN WESLEY PARADISE, CA. 1834

76. JOHN QUINCY ADAMS. OIL BY AN UNKNOWN ARTIST

paintings of the other six Presidents, Reed presented on 14 December 1835 to the Brooklyn Naval Lyceum. On the disestablishment of the Lyceum in 1892 they were transferred to the United States Naval Academy Museum at Annapolis, Maryland, where they now hang. Fig. 75 shows the portrait, now at Annapolis, which I guess to be the June replica.

The portrait Mr. Reed kept for his own gallery (Fig. 74), also accompanied by likenesses of the other Presidents, he was not long to enjoy. He died in June 1836, to the understandable distress of Durand. "The fatal hour has come," Durand wrote. "Our dear friend is dead. The funeral will take place on Thursday afternoon. Come and look for the last time on the man whose equal we never shall see again. I can say no more." [13]

For some years Reed's collection of paintings was retained by his family. Adams saw them in 1840: "I went with Mrs. De Windt and Mr. and Mrs. Downing to the house of the late Mr. Luman Reed whose collection of pictures is still kept by his widow and family. ... The pictures are chiefly by Cole and Durand who is now in Europe. ... The first seven presidents of the United States are ranged in their order, myself and Jackson painted by Durand; and the rest good copies by him from Stuart." [14] Ultimately, Reed's heirs were obliged to dispose of the collection. A private subscription was raised to purchase the collection and to found with it the New York Gallery of Fine Arts. Two years later, in 1858, the new gallery's collection was in turn transferred to The New-York Historical Society, where it formed a valuable and significant nucleus of a great collection of paintings.

The Durand likeness of Adams has long been a popular one and has been reproduced in engravings and otherwise more than any other. So far as we have been able to discover, all of the engravings are of the March version, which is not surprising because Durand kept that original in his own possession for thirty-five years, very likely for the very purpose of having it engraved.

The only painted copy of Durand's likeness of Adams that has come to light is that owned by the Chicago Historical Society (Fig. 76). Nothing is known of its provenance or by whom or when it was painted, and it could well have been taken from an engraving. The earliest known engraving of Fig. 72 is that done by J. W. Paradise (1809–1862) for Longacre and Herring's *National Portrait Gallery of Distinguished Americans* (Fig. 77). It is a line engraving of vigor

[13] Same, p. 124.
[14] Diary, 20 Nov. 1840.

No. 17. JOHN QUINCY ADAMS.

79. JOHN QUINCY ADAMS.
WOOD ENGRAVING BY HOWLAND BROTHERS, CA. 1850

JOHN QUINCY ADAMS.
Sixth President of the United States.

78. JOHN QUINCY ADAMS.
LITHOGRAPH BY NATHANIEL CURRIER

80. JOHN QUINCY ADAMS. BRONZE BUST BY EDMOND T. QUINN, 1930

and faithfulness and in an area of but a few square inches well repro-
duces Durand's likeness. Nathaniel Currier, at a later date not yet
ascertained, adapted his earlier lithograph of Adams after Stuart (Fig.
32) by doing little more than changing the facial likeness from
Stuart's to Durand's (Fig. 78). It is not convincing, but recognizable.
An eccentric variation is that by Howland Brothers (Fig. 79), done as
a wood engraving in 1850 for the *American Phrenological Journal and
Miscellany*; it is one of those familiar reversals overlooking the fact
that the coat buttons on the wrong side. A more recent derivation from
Durand's Adams, or perhaps from Paradise's engraving (Figure 77),
and less satisfactory, though prominent, is the bronze bust in The Hall
of Fame for Great Americans, at New York University (Fig. 80),
done by the sculptor Edmond T. Quinn, and unveiled on 8 May 1930.

HIRAM POWERS (1805–1873)

Only a few days after the inauguration of Martin Van Buren as 8th President of the United States in 1837, and at a critical point in Adams' crusade for the defense of the right of petition guaranteed by the Constitution, we find Adams again sitting for his portrait, this time to be in marble. "Hiram Powers," he wrote, "a native Artist born in Vermont, is taking a mould of me in clay for Casts, and proposes taking it with him to Italy. He is self-formed and promises to rival Greenough. He is engaged to make a marble Statue of Mr. Calhoun for the South Carolina Nullifiers."[1]

Adams spent two or three hours a day for the next week sitting to Powers, but saw only the molded clay. The final sitting prompted him to note in his diary: "This is probably the last time that a counterfeit presentment of me will be made in this world; and likenesses enough of my face and person will be left to survive me. My likeness has been taken in the course of my life by sixteen Painters, five Sculptors, and one medalist. Stewart, King, Harding and Durand have painted me twice. My face has been copied in my sixteenth and my seventieth year. They show what I am, and what I was."[2] Yet the sight in Washington of Powers' clay inspired him to compose a sonnet:

To Hiram Powers

Sculptor! Thy hand has moulded into form
The haggard features of a toil worn face:
And whosoever views thy work shall trace
An age of sorrow, and a life of Storm.
And canst thou mould the *Heart?* for *that*—is warm;
Glowing with tenderness for all our race:
Instinct with all the sympathies that grace
The pure and artless bosom where they swarm.
Artist! may Fortune smile upon thy hand;
Go forth! and rival Greece's art sublime:
Return; and bid the Statesmen of thy Land
Live in thy marble through all after time.
Oh! snatch the fire from Heaven, Prometheus stole,
And give the breathless block, a breathing soul.[3]

[1] To CFA, 23 March 1837 (Adams Papers).

[2] Entry of 1 April 1837. Emerson, writing at the same time, saw what he was: "If he see John Quincy Adams, then he learns that a man may have extreme irritability of face, voice and bearing, and yet, underneath, so puissant a will as to lose no advantage thereby. A steady mind, a believing mind wins the world" (*Journals of Ralph Waldo Emerson*, ed. Edward Waldo Emerson and Waldo Emerson Forbes, Boston, 1909–1914, 4:233–234).

[3] 25 March 1837 (LbC, Adams Papers).

The plaster model apparently was finished in March, and the sculptor sailed for Italy from New York in the fall, after extracting from Adams the promise of a letter of introduction to Richard H. Wilde, the poet and ex-Congressman who had gone abroad to live in Florence.

Powers, born near Woodstock, Vermont, had early moved to Ohio. Here as a youth he worked for a time in a clock and organ factory and later in the mechanical department of Dorfeuille's Western Museum in Cincinnati. Having had some success in modeling wax figures for a representation of Dante's *Inferno*, he moved to Washington in 1834 and pursued the art of sculpture seriously and successfully. In 1837 he went abroad and spent the remainder of his life in Florence, where he died in 1873. It was in the early 1840's that he completed his *Eve* and *Greek Slave* which firmly established his reputation as the foremost American sculptor of the day.

In Florence, Powers soon became a close friend of his fellow countryman, the sculptor Horatio Greenough, who aided him not only by admiring his work but by lending him workmen and marble and introducing him to those who could be helpful. Many of Powers' busts and statues of prominent Americans, completed in Italy, are extant, that of Greenough in the Museum of Fine Arts in Boston being a good example of his talent. Greenough himself particularly admired Powers' busts of Webster and John Quincy Adams (Fig. 81), purchasing the latter for $1,000.[4]

It is difficult to tell exactly when the marble of Adams was completed. Writing to Charles Francis Adams many years later, Powers said, "I was a long time about it."[5] That it was in Greenough's possession by 1841 is apparent from Richard H. Wilde's glowing account of it to Adams: "His bust of yourself is one of the most perfect things of the kind I ever saw both as it regards likeness, expression and beauty of execution. Mr. Greenough has acquired it and estimates it as a master piece."[6] Edward Everett mentions it twice in such a way as to suggest it was not completed until late in 1840. Everett wrote on 8 November, "I called on Mrs. Greenough.... I found the Greenoughs charmingly situated amidst pictures of the Ancient Masters, books, and music. A bust of President Adams by Powers was pronounced by Greenough the finest bust, Ancient or Modern which he has ever seen."[7] In his "American Sculptors in Italy," written during

---

[4] Nathalia Wright, *Horatio Greenough, the First American Sculptor*, Phila., 1963, p. 210.

[5] 22 April 1873 (Adams Papers).

[6] 23 Jan. 1841 (Adams Papers).

[7] Edward Everett, Diary, 8 Nov. 1840 (MHi).

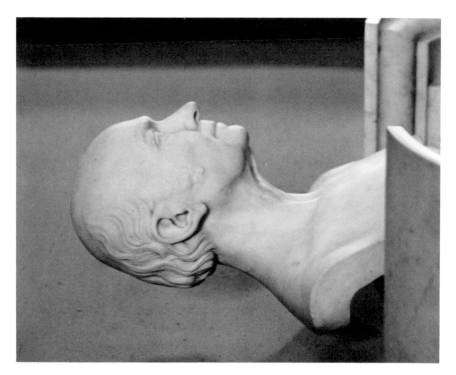

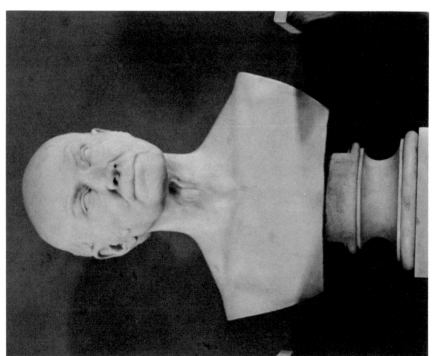

81. JOHN QUINCY ADAMS. MARBLE BUST BY HIRAM POWERS, 1840

his 1840–1841 residence in Florence, Everett wrote: "[Powers] has now on hand very perfect models of the busts of Presidents John Quincy Adams and Van Buren, and an admirable bust of General Jackson in marble, of heroic size."[8] Though not conclusive, these remarks suggest that in November 1840 Greenough possessed the marble and that, on visiting Powers, Everett had seen only the plaster. Perhaps a fair guess might be that the marble was completed toward the end of 1840.

Though Powers' works were applauded by all who saw them, he suffered, like many another artist, from lack of commissions and often found it difficult to support his family. Wilde tried to help him, and wrote on several occasions to Adams to enlist his aid, proposing that the Government commission an equestrian statue by Powers: "Let the rider be an *Indian* ... add a *Buffalo*, in the act of being struck or standing at bay, and you have a most animated groupe. Place it in the centre of the Capitol Square, and it tells you what the country once was. What it now *is* is told by the edifices round it."[9] Wilde wrote again in 1844, and in 1846, when a project giving Powers a commission for an equestrian statue of Washington was before the Senate, in each instance enclosing long extracts from letters from the sculptor telling of his difficulties and of works he had under way.[10] Some years later, in 1859, Powers' marble statues of Franklin and Jefferson were purchased for the Capitol, and now stand in the Senate and House wing respectively.[11]

Not long after Adams' death, an article appeared in the *Quincy Patriot*, entitled "The Tomb of John Q. Adams," signed by Grace Greenwood. A description of the "purely republican," unostentatious tomb, "a plain granite structure with no monument," was followed by a eulogy on the life and character of the great patriot whose dust lay beneath. Mention was made of the tablets commemorating John and Abigail Adams in the Stone Temple and the fact that there was a bust of John Adams (made by Greenough),[12] but of John Quincy Adams there was none, though in the author's opinion there should be. "There is a place for it," she wrote, "on the left of the pulpit. I was told that there was a noble one by Power[s], owned by a gentleman in Boston. Here there is a fine opportunity for the owner to win the admiration of the public, and the gratitude of 'pilgrim strangers,' by

[8] *Boston Miscellany*, 1:54 (Feb. 1842).
[9] To JQA, 23 Jan. 1841 (Adams Papers).
[10] 25 Feb. 1844; 8 March 1846 (Adams Papers).
[11] *Compilation of Works of Art and Other Objects in the United States Capitol*, Washington, 1965, p. 270–271, 274.
[12] See Oliver, *Portraits of JA and AA*, p. 231.

presenting this bust to the Quincy church." The author added, "A friend in company, the gifted artist M. R. Kellogg, late of Florence, took an admirable sketch of the tomb for me. I prize it above everything." [13] The artist was undoubtedly the portraitist Miner K. Kellogg, well known to Powers and Greenough in Florence, and presumably the one who had told Miss Greenwood of the bust in Boston.

By 1841 Greenough had bought Powers' bust of Adams. Whether he brought it with him when he returned to the United States in 1842 for a short period is not known, but it must have been in Boston and domiciled in his house or in that of a member of his family by 1848 (Greenough and his brother Henry were in Florence that year) when Grace Greenwood learned that the "noble" bust was owned by a "gentleman in Boston." In 1853 Charles Francis Adams, perhaps recalling the article in the *Patriot*, wrote from Quincy to Henry Greenough, after Horatio's death:

A few weeks before the decease of your brother Horatio . . . I had a conversation with him respecting the bust of my father by Powers, which belonged to him. It grew out of my asking him if he could furnish me a mate to that he had made of my grandfather, for the inside of the church at Quincy. While he declined doing this from himself, he was kind enough to say that he would let me have that by Mr. Powers, as he had always kept it with the idea that it might be required for some public use. I proposed to see him again upon the subject to consult more fully than we could do at that moment, being in the street, to which he assented. Not long afterwards I went to Washington, and I never saw him afterwards.

May I now enquire of you how this matter stands. Can I hope to obtain this bust still, or shall I be obliged to turn in some other direction, perhaps to Mr. Powers himself? I understand that you are the person to whom I must apply for information. If mistaken in this, I pray you to pardon this intrusion, and to let me know the proper course to take.[14]

At the same time Charles noted in his diary "This has been delayed perhaps too long, but I have had so many things on my mind that I have scarcely known which to take first." [15]

Not unpredictably the matter dragged on. It was almost a year before Charles received a reply to his request: "I have consulted Mrs. Horatio Greenough in relation to the price of Powers bust of your late father and she is ready to part with it for $500. This amount is less by $100 than the price my brother received for his last bust and is *only one half* of that charged by Powers for all busts of late years." [16]

[13] *Quincy Patriot*, 19 Aug. 1848, p. 1, col. 5.
[14] 5 June 1853 (LbC, Adams Papers).
[15] Entry of 7 June 1853.
[16] Greenough to CFA, 8 May 1854 (Adams Papers).

There must have been other discussions, for in the following month Charles accepted the offer:

After a careful re-examination of the bust of my father in its present position, the difficulty does not strike me as so great as I thought it at first. . . . I presume that the bust is now under some engagement at the exhibition, and I am not yet prepared with the place upon which it is permanently to rest. Yet whenever a period may be agreed upon for its ultimate transfer, I shall be pleased to close the transaction, and with it, I hope, one of the things which have cost me no small anxiety for some years.[17]

Greenough replied that the "bust will be at your disposal at the closing of the Athenaeum Exhibition," or earlier if he should request it.[18]

A delay was incurred while a base was made for the bust, Adams writing to Greenough early in November: "I am informed that this week the work may be done which is to make the base of the bust Mrs. Greenough was kind enough to promise me. Will you be kind enough to send me an order for it upon the Trustees of the Athenaeum?" Greenough answered that he had "just seen Mr. E. A. Crowninshield who tells me that you can have the bust at any time." A little later Adams wrote: "I inclose my check on the Merchants Bank for $500 payable to your order. Will you be kind enough to transmit in return the necessary evidence that will show my right to the bust?" A final letter from Greenough, written from the Somerset Club, closed the matter: "I duly received your favor of 18th enclosing check for $500. I presume you received my order for the bust, and enclose a bill of the same, receipted by my brothers Ad[ministrato]r which I suppose is the only form of giving you a title to it."[19] So it was that the bust was finally acquired.

The bust was installed over the tablet in the Stone Temple in time for the morning service on 19 November 1854, and on that day Charles Francis Adams recorded in his diary his sensations: "Upon opening the door I had the great satisfaction to perceive that it was all complete. The effect was very good, though in some particulars I saw where it might have been improved. The bust appeared another thing, and entirely satisfied me.... I was glad I had come to witness the completion of a filial duty which I have lived to execute.... I have waited the opportunity to obtain this bust, which has happened very favorably and now my responsibility ceases."

[17] To Greenough, 13 June 1854 (LbC, Adams Papers).
[18] 15 June 1854 (Adams Papers).
[19] CFA to Henry Greenough, 5, 18 Nov. (LbCs); Greenough to CFA, 9, 20 Nov. 1854 (all in Adams Papers).

Powers' likeness of John Quincy Adams continued to be held in high esteem by Adams' son. Twenty years after the purchase from Mrs. Greenough, Charles obtained from Powers himself, a replica of it. "The bust has arrived safe in the house of my son," he wrote Powers, "who is delighted to have an opportunity of placing it in his new house.[20] As I have decided to make him a present of it, I remit herewith a draft on Messrs. Baring Brothers & Co. of London at ten days sight for the sum of £122, payable to your order, conformably to your memorandum sent to him."[21] To this Powers replied from Florence:

Your letter with bill on ————— for £122.0, duly reached me. But not being negotiable here, I inclosed it to Messrs. Baring Brothers & Co. and said, that if necessary, I begged that they would forward it to you for correction. Otherwise, that they would place the amount to my credit. They have replied today, that they have credited my account with the above sum, having had notice from you in regard to the matter.

I hope that the bust will be put in a good light. The marble is of a harder and more translucent quality than the first one and requires a stronger light to bring out the details. The first one was executed in marble with my own hands *entirely*. For when it was done, I had no workman capable of it. I was a long time about it and before it was finished I began to despair of ever making my living by the *"sculpturizing* business." My friend Greenough paid me $300 Dollars (Tuscan) for it.

I hope that your son J. Q. Adams Esq. is satisfied with my work, but I have not heard from him.[22]

This replica (Fig. 82), in marble, 23⅝ inches in height, bears the inscription "H. Powers Sculp." It now stands in the Stone Library, adjoining the Old House, opposite Cardelli's marble bust of Adams (Fig. 27).

In 1865 the *Historical Magazine* reported the sale at auction on 18 October of the "House and Furniture of the Late Edward Everett," President of Harvard College and brother-in-law of Charles Francis Adams' wife. The details of the objects and prices they brought are as heart-rending as always in such circumstances; for example: "The bookcases were still surmounted with the busts which ornamented them in Mr. Everett's life.... The busts included those of Webster, Clay, Marshall, Franklin, Joseph Warren, J. Q. Adams, W. H. Prescott, Walter Scott, some of the Roman Emperors, and some female

[20] JQA2 had recently completed a new house, which he called Merrymount, on the Adams property at Mount Wollaston on Quincy Bay.
[21] 28 March 1873 (LbC, Adams Papers).
[22] 22 April 1873 (Adams Papers).

82. JOHN QUINCY ADAMS.
MARBLE BUST BY HIRAM POWERS, 1873

heads. The first choice was sold for $9.50; subsequent ones at differ-
ent prices ranging from $1 to $5." [23] As noted before, Everett had
been a friend and admirer of both Powers and Greenough in Florence
in the 1840's. It is not unlikely that some of the busts sold at the
1865 auction were by Greenough or Powers. There stands in the long
hall at the Old House, just behind the front door, a plaster bust of
John Quincy Adams by Powers (Fig. 83). Perhaps it is the original
plaster made in 1837 or a reproduction—even that disposed of at
Everett's sale.

[23] *Historical Magazine*, 9 (1865):367, quoting the *Boston Advertiser*, 19 Oct.
1865.

189

83. JOHN QUINCY ADAMS.
PLASTER BUST BY HIRAM POWERS

Comparison of Powers' busts of Adams with other contemporary likenesses bears out the accepted opinion that Powers' were excellent likenesses. They justify the family's efforts to obtain them for public and private display. An engraving by Forbes & Co. (Fig. 84), 4 inches high, of one of Powers' busts served as the frontispiece to the eighth volume of the *Memoirs of John Quincy Adams*, published in 1876.

EUNICE MAKEPEACE TOWLE

Coming down the steps of the Capitol late in September 1837, Adams was accosted by "a man by the name of Towle" with the request that he sit for his portrait to be painted by Mrs. Towle. True

190

84. JOHN QUINCY ADAMS. ENGRAVING BY FORBES & CO., 1876

to his custom, Adams accompanied Towle to his house, where Hiram Powers also had his studio. There he met Mrs. Towle and saw her collection of portraits of President Van Buren (a patient of Mrs. Towle's husband), R. M. Johnson, Polk (then Speaker of the House), Thomas Hart Benton, Amos Kendall, and Henry A. Wise, the latter "unfinished." "I was not overambitious to appear in such company, meme en peinture, as old Count Löwenhielm said he would not like to reside at Delft. Nor was I charmed with the execution of Mrs. Towle's Portraits."[1] But with his usual courtesy he promised to sit during the winter session of Congress if he had time.

He was as good as his word, and his diary entries over the next few years evidence what a chore obliging an artist sometimes could be. "I sat about an hour to Mrs. Towle," he wrote, "for my portrait and she requested a second sitting for this day week. She says she was a pupil of Harding's but she is of a lower order of skill as an artist. Her like-

[1] JQA, Diary, 30 Sept. 1837.

191

nesses are strong, but they have the sign post hardness of outline." "I was detained till Noon before I could go, for a second sitting to Mrs. Towle, who will make a hideous object of me." Two weeks later he "gave her a short, cold and rather drowsy sitting." On a later occasion he sat in the presence of Mr. Towle, who talked politics; "however I preferred to divert the conversation." Before she finished what Adams termed a "strong but not a pleasing likeness," [2] the artist was taken sick and no further mention of the subject appears for three years when, at the renewed request of "Dr. Towle," Adams recommenced sitting. "I walked to the capitol hill and gave a sitting of nearly an hour to Mrs. Towle. Her portrait of me painted in October 1837 is hideous. She says she was taken ill at that time, was unable to finish my portrait or any other, and has scarcely painted half a dozen since. It were well if she knew that the word applicable to all her works is not paint, but daub. The poor woman said she had met with domestic affliction since my former sittings by losing a little boy her Son; a calamity in which I deeply sympathized with her." And later: "After the adjournment of the house, I walked over and gave a sitting of two hours to Mrs. Towle, during which once or twice I fell asleep. This infirmity of old age frequently happens to me, to mortify my pride; and to remind me how near I am to the caducity of the last Scene of all." At his last sitting Adams "told her my objection to it was that it was too much like the original." [3] A few months later Dr. Towle told Adams his wife wanted to paint "the President" (presumably John Tyler), and asked for a letter of introduction. Adams wrote, "This I declined upon my general rule, which he did not take amiss. He asked to borrow Stewart's last Portrait of my father, to which I consented." [4]

The portrait of Adams has not come to light, which is perhaps just as well, though we might be curious to see one more example of what to Adams was both "hideous" and a "strong likeness." Mrs. Towle's portrait of Van Buren now belongs to Columbia University, but little more about the artist or her gallery of portraits has been discovered.

SHOBAL VAIL CLEVENGER (1812–1843)

Scarcely a month after Adams had taken many hours out of his busy life to sit to Mrs. Towle, we find him similarly engaged with the sculptor Clevenger. This man had been born in Ohio and had learned

[2] Same, 25 Oct., 1, 15, 22, 29 Nov. 1837.
[3] Same, 3, 8, 14 Dec. 1840.
[4] Same, 19 April 1841.

the rudiments of stonecutting from David Guion of Cincinnati when only twenty years old. His efforts met with success, and from about 1836 to 1840 he modeled busts of many of the distinguished men of the day in Philadelphia, Washington, Boston, and New York. The New-York Historical Society has seven examples of his work, all in plaster. In 1840 he went to Italy and joined the company of American sculptors there, becoming an intimate friend of Greenough and Powers. What promised to be a distinguished career was, however, cut short by consumption, and he died in Florence in 1843.

Like many another artist who passed through Washington during the early part of the 19th century, Clevenger was able to take a likeness of Adams. The first record we find of their meeting was in 1837: "I called this morning at the rooms of Mr. Clevenger at the Capitol Hill, above the Bridge, and sat to him for a plaster bust about a Quarter of an hour." Ten days later: "I gave a sitting of an hour to the young Sculptor Clevenger who is taking my bust, but from having risen so early, was slumbering almost all the time he was at work."[1] Although modeling a sleeping sitter may have had its drawbacks, Adams' wife thought Clevenger had done well. She wrote to her son: "Your Father has been sitting for another Bust by a Native Artist from Ohio a very young Man Mr. Clevenger. When I saw it, it was an admirable likeness; but that was at the second sitting. The poor fellow seems to expect to make a large Sum of money out of it; as he is very poor, and evidently has genius, I wish he may succeed—Your Father says it is horridly like—He never looked handsomer or better than he does now."[2] Louisa was always an admirer of her husband's appearance; she had made the same remark more than twenty years before when they were both sitting to Leslie.

Whether the young artist made a large sum of money out of Adams' bust is not known, but he obtained many commissions at the time. In November, Adams found him at the Boston Athenæum finishing a bust of Mrs. Webster, who had given him nine sittings, and also saw "good busts" of Judge John Davis and Isaac P. Davis as well as an unfinished one of Daniel Webster.[3]

The Providence (Rhode Island) Public Library possesses a small marble bust (Fig. 85) which I believe to be that done by Clevenger. No records have been found of the provenance of the bust except that it was presented to the Library in the latter part of the 19th century

[1] JQA, Diary, 27 Dec. 1837; 6 Jan. 1838.
[2] To CFA, 26–28 Jan. 1838 (Adams Papers).
[3] JQA, Diary, 22 Nov. 1838.

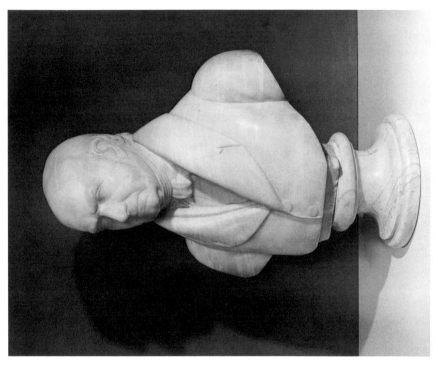

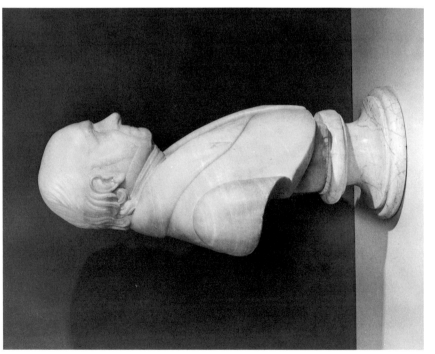

85. JOHN QUINCY ADAMS. MARBLE BUST BY SHOBAL VAIL CLEVENGER, 1837

by George F. Leete, who was a Trustee of the Library from 1875 to 1884. The marble lacks any inscription, but the likeness is unmistakable and resembles closely Durand's portraits of 1835 (Figs. 72–75). The only other busts done in the 1830's are those by Powers (Figs. 81–83) and the "perfect" likeness by Persico which was destroyed in the burning of the Library of Congress. It seems safe to conclude therefore that Fig. 85 is the "admirable likeness" by Clevenger.

GEORGE FREEMAN (1789–1868)

Only a year before Adams compiled the "Rubbish" list, he sat on several occasions in Washington to George Freeman, a miniaturist. Perhaps the reason he failed to list Freeman's likeness was that he never saw it finished.

A record of these sittings appears in three diary entries: "Mr. G. Freeman, a Miniature Portrait Painter ... wishes to take my picture and I engaged to call upon him at his lodgings to-morrow." A few days later: "Sat for my miniature to Mr. Freeman, lodging at Mr. M'Leod's." Lastly he recorded calling on Mr. Freeman, who had packed his trunks to go to Baltimore and Philadelphia, but unpacked and took a three-hour sitting, "which entirely exhausted my patience."[1]

Mrs. Adams reported these sittings to her son Charles, mentioning that Mr. Freeman wished to have the likeness to take to England to be engraved. He had also brought with him a portrait of Van Buren as a specimen of his work which, she said, "is a remarkably fine likeness greatly embellished and beautified and yields a *handsome* proof of the Painters skill." She added: "He has taken Mrs. Madison but I believe it is not completed yet." A week later the portrait won her approval as "a beautiful likeness of Mrs. Madison with which your Father is quite enchanted."[2]

Freeman, who was born in Spring Hill, Connecticut, went to England about 1813 for twenty-four years and is said to have painted Queen Victoria and Prince Albert. Apparently his best-known work is the miniature painted in Philadelphia of Mrs. Edward Biddle. H. B. Wehle said of him: "But for the miniature Freeman painted of this lovely lady he would probably be almost forgotten today."[3]

With comments such as the foregoing in mind, we must again regret that still another likeness of Adams is lost.

[1] Entries of 8, 12, 16 March 1838.
[2] To CFA, 8–14, 18–21 March 1838 (Adams Papers).
[3] Harry B. Wehle, *American Miniatures, 1730–1850 ... and a Biographical Dictionary of the Artists* by Theodore Bolton, N.Y., 1927, p. 49, 86–87.

FREDERICK BASHAM

Near the end of the "Rubbish" list, Adams included a "mask" done in 1839 at Washington by an "Englishman." The tricks memory plays are odd. The "Rubbish" list was compiled in April 1839. Two diary entries in 1838 give clues to the "Englishman."

"Mr. Fowler had called at the House yesterday," Adams noted, "and requested me to come this morning and have my eyes opened; that is, the eyes of my bust. I went accordingly, and an Englishman named Basham, opened one of the eyes, requesting me to call again to-morrow morning to open the other." The next day, "I called this morning at Mr. Fowler's; but Mr. Basham had opened the second eye of my mask; and released me from farther attendance." [1] Nothing further is known of the mask, and it has not been found.

Basham is described in Groce and Wallace's *Dictionary* as "Modeller, plaster worker, architect, draftsman." He was in New York from 1837 to 1852, and exhibited some sort of drawing at the National Academy in 1842. The Mr. Fowler mentioned might have been Trevor Thomas Fowler, the portrait and genre painter who did portraits of Harrison and Clay in 1840, or perhaps Orson Squire Fowler, the phrenologist.

WILLIAM PAGE (1811–1885)

The time is mid-September 1838; Adams, seventy-one years old, has passed a troubled, sleepless night at his home in Quincy. His diary reveals how it was spent:

The weight of years presses me down with constantly growing aggravation, and trifling causes of excitement multiply upon me, which in the prime of life I should not even have felt. Worn out with fatigue by two successive almost sleepless nights, I took to my bed last Evening before the stroke of the Curfew bell. There was then a feeble radiation of Northern light. About midnight I awoke and looking out at the Eastern window in front of my bed saw a light surpassing that of a full moon, and which I took first for the morning dawn within a quarter of an hour of the Sun's rising. But I slept again till a quarter past three, when Sirius was half an hour risen. I brought out Bode's Uranographia from my closet, laid him on my bed and found the position of Procyon which I had forgotten. Renewed also my acqaintance with Betelgeuse, Bellatrix, and Rigel the three brightest stars of Orion. Then dressed, visited my plantations; finished my Letter to William Ladd, and made up some documents for the Post Office.

[1] Entries of 29, 30 May 1838.

In this pessimistic frame of mind, but optimistic course of action, he recorded further events of the same day. "Soon after dinner I had visits from Mr. Francis Jackson and Mr. Ellis Gray Loring, whose special object was to have a Portrait of me taken, for a company of Gentlemen in Boston, and they requested me to sit for that purpose, to a young promising Portrait Painter from New-York named Page; to which I consented. Mr. Loring is to give me notice of the time and place, which is proposed to be next week at some house in Boston."[1]

Page was of course the young artist William Page who became one of the early important American art theorists. He moved to Italy to live, divorced his first wife, and married the sister of Henry Stevens, a prosperous bookseller of London, who advanced large sums to aid his brother-in-law, who was constantly in financial distress. Page's best-known paintings are his self-portrait and and the portrait of his second wife, both painted in 1860–1861, and now belonging to the Detroit Institute of Arts. Henry James characterized him as "That strange dim shade of William Page, painter of portraits, who peeps unseizably, almost tormentingly, out of other letters ... who offers the rare case of an artist of real distinction, an earnest producer, almost untraceable less than half a century after his death." But, after still another half-century, he was called "the American Titian."[2]

The first sitting was arranged by letter from Loring to Adams: "Mr. William Page, the Painter, is now in Boston, and would like, if convenient to you, to have you sit to him, Thursday morning, 20th. inst. at 10 o'clk. His room is at No. 22 School Street, 3d Story. If inconvenient to you to attend on that day, will you please let me know, by mail, the time that would better accomodate you."[3] Eight sittings by Adams are recorded. The first at 22 School Street; "Mr. Ellis Gray Loring was there nearly all the time." The following week Adams "gave a sitting of 3 hours to Mr. Page, whose manner of painting is different from that of any other painter who has taken my Portrait. The first sitting, he took the outlines of the face in Charcoal; and this day he filled up the space between the lines with a thick daubing of oil colours. It has no pleasant aspect, but his finished Portraits of Harding the Painter, of Mrs. Ellis G. Loring and two other Ladies which he has at his room, give proof of no ordinary talents." At a later sitting early in October Adams' son Charles came in "but did

[1] Entry of 14 Sept. 1838.
[2] Henry James, *William Wetmore Story and His Friends*, Boston, 1904, 1:47; Joshua C. Taylor, *William Page, the American Titian*, Chicago, 1957.
[3] 18 Sept. 1838 (Adams Papers).

not like it. He thinks it fails not in the likeness of the features, but in the expression. Dr. Parkman was also there and thought well of it." [4] A few days later the portrait was seen by Edmund Quincy (son of Josiah Quincy, one of the "company of Gentlemen in Boston" who had commissioned the portrait), who characterized it as "an admirable one I should think." [5] Further sittings took place on 3 and 9 October. Then Page went to Quincy to dine with Adams, who took him to the Stone Temple in Quincy. "I shewed him the tablet surmounted by the Bust of my father executed by Greenough, and the Epitaph of my father and mother written by me. We returned to dine. . . . Mr. Page took with him the engraved print of the stone temple which I keep suspended in my Library. He wishes to paint in the back-ground of my Portrait a distant view of the Stone Temple." [6] Two days later he gave the "Eighth and probably last sitting to Mr. Page, although the Portrait is yet far from being finished. He was unwell and worked with flagging Spirits." [7] But a month later he sat again, promising even one more sitting.

What in fact turned out to be the last sitting took place under circumstances very pleasing to Adams, which he noted in his diary:

I went to Mr. Page's painting room and sat about half an hour; at 11. O'Clock there came in quick succession about 20 gentlemen, the subscribers for whom this portrait had been painted—among whom were Richard Fletcher, Abbott Lawrence, Josiah Quincy jr., Jonathan Phillips, Isaac P. Davis, Joseph T. Buckingham, George Parkman, Ellis Gray Loring, Francis Jackson, [Henry G.] Chapman, [Francis G.] Shaw, a son of Robert G. Shaw, and some others, with whom I was not personally acquainted. After viewing the Portrait, Mr. Loring addressed them, and said that it would now be necessary to determine what disposal to make of it. Mr. Phillips was then chosen Chairman of the Meeting, and with five others was appointed a Committee to withdraw and report Resolution to the Meeting for adoption. The[y] went accordingly and soon returned with a Resolution that the Portrait should be presented to the City of Boston, to be suspended in Faneuil Hall. This Resolution was unanimously adopted, and the same Committee were charged with the Office of presenting the picture to the City authorities. They then passed a vote of thanks to Mr. Page, for the handsome execution of the work; and a motion was made for a vote of thanks to me, for the favour of sitting to the Painter, upon which I interposed, and said that I felt this would be an inversion of the part suitable to be performed between them and me.

[4] JQA, Diary, 20, 25 Sept., 2 Oct. 1838.
[5] Edmund Quincy, Journal (MHi:Quincy Papers).
[6] JQA, Diary, 11 Oct. 1838. Confirmed by CFA in his diary for the same date: "Dined at the Mansion, Mr. Page, the artist who is taking my father, being there."
[7] JQA, Diary, 13 Oct. 1838.

That the thanks were due from me to them, and that I offered them with the deepest sensibility to their kindness. That when requested by two of them to sit to the Artist, I had cheerfully complied without knowing or enquiring what was the purpose of the proposal, nor had a conjecture entered my mind upon this subject till I was now made acquainted with it. That I intreated them to believe that I felt it as an honour doubly precious, in the act itself, and in the delicacy of the manner in which it had been performed, and if the return of my thanks to them was not expressed in elegance of language suitable to the occasion, I hoped they would attribute the deficiency of words to the pressure of an overburdened heart. Mr. Phillips, the Chairman, made a brief complimentary reply, and the meeting dispersed.[8]

Adams reported the compliments to his son, who recorded of his father that "The feeling in the City is much more favorable to him than it has been for many years."[9]

The *Quincy Patriot* shortly afterward confirmed what Adams had reported, and listed as subscribers, in addition to those he had named, Daniel P. Parker, Nathan Appleton, Thomas L. Winthrop, Lucius M. Sargent, Samuel Appleton, William Sturgis, Francis C. Gray, Nathaniel I. Bowditch, Edward Tuckerman, Timothy Gilbert, J. V. Himes, H. C. Fifield of Weymouth, Samuel Philbrick of Brookline, and William Jackson of Newton.

The portrait (Fig. 86) is a fine painting, but, though it is an unquestionable likeness, I incline to Charles' reaction to it in not liking Adams' expression. He looks like a man, as Emerson said of him a few years later, "who cannot live on slops, but must have sulphuric acid in his tea."[10] Adams' left hand rests on a sheet of paper, perhaps intended to represent a congressional bill, though more likely introduced as an artist's trick to enable him to include his own signature unobtrusively. (The first three letters of Page's name are legible.) In the distance, behind the high-backed chair in which Adams sits, the Stone Temple can be seen. After the painting was completed, Adams called on Page to get back the engraving of the Stone Temple, but was told that it had been taken by Dr. George Parkman for him. A year later he went with Dr. Parkman to Faneuil Hall to see the portrait, "which is placed in the centre of the East end of the Hall, immediately under the Bust of my father."[11]

And there the portrait stayed until 1876, when it was deposited by the City of Boston in the Museum of Fine Arts. At that time a copy

[8] Same, 16 Nov. 1838.
[9] CFA, Diary, 16 Nov. 1838.
[10] *Journals of Ralph Waldo Emerson*, ed. Emerson and Forbes, 6:350.
[11] JQA, Diary, 30 May 1839.

86. JOHN QUINCY ADAMS. OIL BY WILLIAM PAGE, 1838

was made of it by Horace Robbins Burdick which now hangs in Faneuil Hall on the balcony wall to the left of the platform.

Like many another artist to whom Adams sat, Page sought his help to further his own professional advancement. In March 1839 Adams wrote to Page enclosing, "in cheerful compliance with your request," a recommendation addressed to William L. Marcy: "Mr. William Page supposing the testimonial of my estimate of his merits as a Portrait Painter may be of service to him, has requested a line from me expressing my opinion in that respect. I take pleasure in complying with that request; and in saying that from his success in painting portraits of several persons of my acquaintance which I have seen, as well as of my own, I consider him as an Artist of Talent unsurpassed in this Country."[12] Seven years later, when many an artist was trying by all means within his power to obtain the commission to fill the niche in the Rotunda that had been given to Inman, Page wrote for assistance to Adams:

As I understand that something is about doing in reference to that picture for the "Rotunda" at Washington, which was once given to be painted to Mr. Henry Inman of N. York, since deceased, And as I well *know* that he had never even made a commencement of the same, I take the liberty to ask you to interfere in my behalf, that the commission may be given to me.

Some eight years since, when I had the honor of painting a portrait of you, now [in] Faneuil Hall in this city you were pleased to express such a favorable opinion of me and my endeavours, that I am now the more bold to ask this of you, as the intervening time I can well assure you has not been without its struggles on my part to increase my ability for such a work and I am now bold to say that my present skill and knowledge of Art are at the least equal to that of any other Painter this country can now claim. And if the votes could be obtained from all the Artists of the country for that man who would be likely to paint the best picture, next to himself, I have great confidence I should obtain their sanction to do it.

I hope that you will excuse this speaking of self, when I say that it is only on my competency to the task that I would found any claim.

With the greatest respect for your honor and worth as well as gratitude for the kindness which you showed me through the occasion abovementioned as well as since when you were pleased to write to Hon. Wm. L. Marcy on my behalf I remain your since humble friend.[13]

Page's self-professed humility may be open to question; Healy and Powell also sought Adams' support in the competition for the Rotunda niche. Powell's *Baptism of Pocahontas* was chosen to complete the series.

[12] 1 March 1839 (LbC, Adams Papers).
[13] 16 Feb. 1846 (Adams Papers).

S. M. CHARLES

The portrait of Adams done by the young artist Charles in 1839 is lost; but its painting provided the stimulus for Adams to compile the so-called "Rubbish" list of all likenesses of himself, done to that date, which is described and reproduced in the Introduction and which forms the starting point of the study of Adams' iconography. As little is known of Charles as of his portrait of Adams. Charles Henry Hart, the art historian, refers to a miniature of Andrew Jackson said to have been inscribed "S. M. Charles, 1836," and in 1931 Frederic F. Sherman mentions a self-portrait inscribed "Painted by S. M. Charles at Washington 1840." Groce and Wallace in their *Dictionary* could find no substantiation of either portrait.

The young artist approached Adams in Washington with a letter of recommendation from Joseph Gales, who with William W. Seaton was editor of the *National Intelligencer*, and asked him to sit for him, which of course Adams consented to do.[1] Seven sittings, in all, were given between 1 April and 20 April, and Adams' diary comments on the several occasions provide some picture of Charles and his ability which lessens our disappointment at not being able to locate the picture itself.

"I was occupied this day," Adams wrote, "till past one, with my task [preparing his memorial address to be delivered at The New-York Historical Society on the occasion of the fiftieth anniversary of the inauguration of Washington], and then went and gave a sitting to Mr. Charles for my Portrait. The tension of mind all the morning was so great that when the pressure was taken off, an exposition of sleep came over me, and I was dozing all the time of the sitting to Mr. Charles. He told me that he had heard Stuart once painted such a sitter—asleep." After a third sitting Adams wrote: "A poor job. His colours are vermilion, Chremnitz, a mixture of white lead and silver, Yellow Ochre, Black ivory, ultramarine blue, made of lapis lazuli and madder lake. These are all mixed up with Oil. Mr. Charles is ambitious to do well, but as yet hardly reaches mediocrity." By the time of the fifth sitting Adams could only declare that Charles was "making a portrait of me different from any other and so like that it looks like a Caricature." On that occasion the artist showed Adams his three-volume set of the copperplate engravings of Sir Joshua Reynolds, for which he paid $200, though to Adams they appeared "very indifferently executed." Finally, on 20 April, the task was completed: "I gave

[1] JQA, Diary, 30 March 1839.

202

my seventh and last sitting for my Portrait to Mr. Charles, who told me that he was forming his style upon the model of Sir Joshua Reynolds; but that he was a young man. This is the thirty-fifth time that my likeness has been taken by Artists for Portrait, miniature, bust or medal, and of the whole number Parker's miniature [Fig. 6], Copley's portrait in 1796 [Fig. 11] and Stewart's head in 1825 [Fig. 57], with Persico's bust now in the library room of Congress are the only representations of my face, satisfactory to myself."[2]

These sittings to Charles are but further evidence, if any be needed, of Adams' complete willingness to sit for his portrait to whoever might apply, apparently regardless of his qualifications. Though there are many lost portraits, it is this constant responsiveness on Adams' part that accounts for the extraordinary legacy of likenesses that has been left.

EDWARD DALTON MARCHANT (1806–1887)

On 16 November 1840 Adams left Quincy for Washington to attend once more the opening session of the House of Representatives. He traveled by way of Hartford, New Haven, and New York, where he stayed from the 18th to the 21st. Apparently he got in touch with the artist Edward D. Marchant shortly after his arrival in New York, though what prompted the meeting is obscure. "I had parted yesterday from Mr. Marchant," Adams wrote, "with the understanding that as I was to be here only this day, and could give him only one sitting he had given up the purpose of painting my portrait. After concluding to stay till Saturday, I went to Mr. Marchant's and told him I could sit this day and to-morrow if it should suit him, and accordingly I sat nearly two hours before, and one after dinner."[1] It would almost seem that Adams could not resist the opportunity to sit for his portrait, or else considered it an obligation he owed to artists in general. The next day was largely devoted to portraiture. "After breakfast sat 2 hours to Mr. Marchant, who has taken a good likeness though the portrait is unfinished. He requested of me a line of recommendation to Mr. Gallatin whose portrait he is very desirous of taking. He has those of General Jackson, General Harrison, Henry Clay, Mr. Ewing of Ohio, Chancellor James Kent and some others. Mrs. Marchant and her sister, both comely women, came in and joined in conversation

---

[2] Same, 1, 3, 6, 13, 20 April 1839.
[1] Diary, 19 Nov. 1840.

while he was at work." [2] The same entry disclosed Adams' discussion with Mrs. de Windt about her disappointment with Pelton's engraving of Blyth's pastel of Abigail Adams for the edition of her *Letters* which had just appeared; and his visit at the home of the late Luman Reed, whose collection of pictures by Cole and Durand was still kept by his widow and family.

No further reference to Marchant appears in Adams' diary or correspondence for three years. Then Adams received a letter from the officers of The New-York Historical Society asking him to sit for his portrait: "The New York Historical Society, being desirous to preserve in its Archives the portraits of distinguished individuals, especially such as have aided to enrich the history of our country, the Executive Committee respectfully request that you will sit for your portrait, to Mr. Marchant of this city. Should you consent to thus gratify the Society, we, as well as Mr. Marchant, will feel obliged if you will appoint a time when you can conveniently see him for that purpose and he will call on you." [3]

Late in August, Marchant called on Adams in Quincy to inquire if he had heard from the Society:

I said I had; but that having been immediately afterwards absent from home a month, and under some uncertainty whether it was the wish of the Committee that Mr. Marchant should come here to paint the portrait, or wait till my passage through New-York, I had hitherto delayed answering their Letter. He said he had now come to take the time that might suit my convenience for the work. Mr. Marchant had already painted my portrait in November 1840 at New York. But as I could then give him only three sittings in two days, he was not satisfied with his own work, and wishes to do it over again. He had now with him a miniature copied from his former picture, but our Ladies thought it bore no resemblance to me. Mr. Marchant is at present engaged in painting certain portraits at Providence, and will come the week after next to take mine. [4]

Adams sat from the 13th to the 16th of September. "Mr. Marchant ... was employed the whole day and evening upon my portrait: painting from the life in two long sittings before and after dinner, and the remainder of the day copying from the portrait which he painted of me at New-York in 1840. He was suffering all day with a severe headache." [5]

On 16 September, Adams noted that after a whole day's activity, and half a dozen sittings from breakfast "till evening twilight," Mar-

[2] Same, 20 Nov. 1840.
[3] 26 June 1843 (Adams Papers).
[4] JQA, Diary, 25 Aug. 1843.
[5] Same, 14 Sept. 1843.

87. JOHN QUINCY ADAMS. OIL BY EDWARD DALTON MARCHANT, 1843

88. JOHN QUINCY ADAMS.
ENGRAVING BY GEORGE PARKER, 1845

chant finally "finished." The family thought it a better likeness than
the 1840 portrait. Adams saw it as "more laboured and finished; but
the likeness is not so strong." [6] Even his son Charles was involved:
"My time was somewhat wasted in waiting for Mr. Marchand a painter
who has been taking a likeness of my father and who wishes to see
the pictures of him by Copley and of my grandfather by Stuart which
are at my house." [7]

From all of these entries it is clear that by the end of September
1843 there were in existence at least three portraits of Adams by
Marchant: the 1840 likeness; the miniature taken from the 1840
likeness which the Adams ladies thought "bore no resemblance" to
Adams; the new 1843 likeness for The New-York Historical Society,
at least partly taken from the 1840 portrait. As will be seen later,
there was still another 1843 likeness with notable differences from
the others.

The Historical Society's portrait (Fig. 87) was given to the Society
by the artist in 1844. Shortly afterward it was engraved (Fig. 88) by

[6] Same, 16 Sept. 1843.
[7] CFA, Diary, 19 Sept. 1843.

206

the English engraver George Parker, then working in Boston, for *The American Review*, in which it appeared in May 1845.[8] Parker's engraving was also reproduced, among other places, in Hurd's *History of Norfolk County*,[9] where it was noticed by the younger Charles Francis Adams.

The miniature (Fig. 89) whose resemblance to Adams the ladies disparaged, only 5 by 4¼ inches in size, was purchased by Charles Francis Adams Jr. from the artist in 1885 or 1886 and is now owned by Mrs. Thomas Nelson Perkins Jr. of Westwood, Massachusetts. Said to have been taken from the 1840 original, it shows the sitter's bow tie with the ends tied out sideways rather than hanging down. The present ownership and provenance of the 1840 original is unknown, unless it be one of those mentioned below.

In 1886, only a year before Marchant died, Charles Francis Adams Jr. ordered a replica to be made by Marchant from The New-York Historical Society's 1843 portrait, as the following letter from Adams to the Trustees of the Thomas Crane Public Library in Quincy reveals:

While the Crane Memorial Hall was in process of construction, Mrs. Crane intimated to me that it would be very gratifying to herself and family if I would place in it a portrait of my grandfather, John Quincy Adams, for whom Mr. Crane during his life entertained great regard. . . . I was not at the time acquainted with any portrait of J. Q. Adams which to me was satisfactory. There was none which I cared to have copied. Some two years afterwards, the history of Norfolk County appeared, and in that volume I found among the illustrations a steel engraving of a portrait of President Adams, with which I was not familiar. I had never heard that such a portrait existed. It was painted apparently about the year 1843, by E. D. Marchant.

As a result of considerable enquiry on my part, I learned that the portrait in question was the property of the New York Historical Society. Going to the rooms of the Historical Society, I there found it, and on examination concluded that it was to me a more agreeable portrait of my grandfather than any with which I was acquainted, although many had been painted of him. Upon further enquiry I was gratified to find out that Mr. Marchant, the artist, was still engaged in painting and I requested him to make a replica of the original, painted now more than forty-three years ago. This he did most successfully, and it affords me the utmost gratification to now present it, in accordance with Mrs. Crane's request, to the Crane Memorial Hall.[10]

[8] *The American Review: A Whig Journal of Politics, Literature, Art and Science*, vol. 1, no. 5, frontis. (May 1845).
[9] D. Hamilton Hurd, *History of Norfolk County, Mass.*, Phila., 1884, p. 354.
[10] *Quincy Patriot*, 7 Aug. 1886.

89. JOHN QUINCY ADAMS. OIL ON IVORY
BY EDWARD DALTON MARCHANT, 1840–1843

The Quincy Public Library, which now embraces the Crane Memorial, still owns the Marchant 1886 replica (Fig. 90), but lacking the space to hang it, has long kept it in storage. It is signed by the artist in red at the lower left but the date is illegible. This portrait lacks the clarity of outline found in Marchant's other Adamses, a defect which may be blamed either on the age of the artist at the time it was painted or on a deterioration of the portrait itself. There is in the Stone Library, adjoining the Old House in Quincy, another handsome Marchant likeness of Adams (Fig. 91), also signed, in red, "E. D. Marchant." This may be either a replica Charles Francis Adams had made for himself in 1886, or possibly the original 1840 version which

91. JOHN QUINCY ADAMS.
OIL BY EDWARD DALTON MARCHANT

he might have purchased from Marchant at the time he acquired the miniature (Fig. 89) or while negotiating the painting of the replica for the Thomas Crane Public Library (Fig. 90).

Yet the tale does not end there. Still another similar likeness of Adams (Fig. 92) hangs in the American Embassy, Grosvenor Square, London. The Embassy staff says the painting is "without benefit of complete documentation," but describes it as "Size of Canvas 29½ by 24½ inches, Painted by E. D. Marchant, 1843; No other information." Unlike the other three known examples, which closely resemble each other, the Embassy portrait discloses notable differences,

92. JOHN QUINCY ADAMS.
OIL BY EDWARD DALTON MARCHANT, 1843

both in facial expression and in the treatment of the sitter's collar
and bow tie. The pose and general appearance, however, are so similar to Marchant's other portraits of Adams that it is unlikely this is
an original; it is probably only a modified replica. No satisfactory
evidence has come to light to indicate its origin or exact date of painting, but there is no reason to doubt that it was painted by Marchant.
A faint lead to its early history appears in *Current Opinion*, 76:171
(February 1924), where it is stated that this portrait, or one looking
like it, "accompanied Col. Harvey on his return to private Life." This
reference is presumably to Colonel George Harvey, Ambassador to
the Court of St. James's from 1921 to 1923.

A comparison of the Marchant likeness in almost any of its versions
with other contemporary portraits of Adams makes it readily understandable why his grandson found it "a more agreeable" likeness than
any others with which he was acquainted.

AUGUSTE EDOUART (1789–1861)

"Mr. Edouart is a Frenchman," Adams wrote at Washington in March 1841, "who cuts out profiles in miniature on paper, and came and took mine. He says he has a collection of them 85000 in number. He took one also of my father from a shade taken in 1809, which with those of my mother, my wife, myself, and our sons George [and John] then boys 8 and 6 years of age, we have under glass in one frame. He gave me a full length profile of President Harrison, in the attitude of delivering his inaugural address."[1] Not long afterward he was back again: "In the Evening Mr. Edouart the man of shades, came and left with me full length profiles of my father, President Tyler, and myself."[2] The likeness of Adams (Fig. 93a) is one of the few whole-length likenesses of him that were taken. His face in profile is familiar, the long pointed nose readily recognizable, but his dress suggests a heavier man than would be expected from the profile of his face alone.

Adams later stopped at Edouart's house and saw his collection: "He has a curious collection of the figures of many distinguished men of this country assembled together and standing in one hall in relative positions to each other, forming a very pleasant tableau and many of them striking likenesses."[3]

Most striking and characteristic in Edouart's work are his choice of pose and the elegance of his groupings or tableaux. A minor but distinguishing feature, a "snipped out white collar on the men,"[4] is evident in his silhouette of Adams. By folding the paper and cutting the "shade" in duplicate, Edouart was able to produce counterparts for himself and the sitter. Adams makes no mention of having received a counterpart, and no example has come down in the family. The two versions of Adams' "shade" which we have are owed to Edouart's practice of retaining one of the counterparts for his own scrapbook where it was available for further replication. Even so, as we shall see, these examples barely survived the vicissitudes of time.

Edouart's career as a silhouettist began in 1825; in 1839 he came to the United States. After an extraordinarily active practice of his art for ten years, during which he cut many thousands of silhouettes of distinguished Americans, he set sail for France on the *Oneida* in 1849. A storm wrecked the vessel in Vazon Bay, off the coast of

[1] Diary, 11 March 1841.
[2] Same, 11 June 1841.
[3] Same, 15 June 1841.
[4] Helen K. Greenaway, "Notes on Profile Cutting in America," *Auction*, 2:15 (March 1969).

Guernsey. Although there was no loss of life, much of the cargo disappeared. According to one account most of Edouart's 50,000 duplicate silhouettes were lost, but in fact fourteen folio volumes, containing the principal portion of the American collection, were saved. These volumes, or scrapbooks, the shipwrecked silhouettist presented to Frederica Lukis (or Lukens), the daughter of the family which befriended him.[5]

For many years the collection dropped from sight until early in the 20th century when Mrs. F. Nevill Jackson, of London, through a response to her advertisement inserted in *The Connoisseur* in 1911, discovered and procured all or most of the long-lost volumes, although at this distance it is difficult to be certain of what was in fact recovered. In 1913 a large part of her collection of originals was exhibited at the gallery of Arthur S. Vernay, an antique dealer of New York, who published a catalogue of it.[6] The New-York Historical Society's copy of Vernay's catalogue contains two bits of revealing marginalia. On page 114, otherwise blank, there is written in ink:

When Mrs. F. Nevill Jackson purchased the original Edouart silhouettes in or about 1911 she had each page of the original albums photographed on 5 x 7" glass negatives and then sold most of the originals. She issued a catalogue of the photographs of the American silhouettes [after 1921],[7] and sold a few prints from her negatives, the originals of which had been scattered (the Metropolitan Museum of Art has 2330 of them in four of the original albums, the bequest of Rev. Glen Tilley Morse who bought the unsold remainder of the originals offered in this catalogue by Vernay).

The negatives were brought to this country by Mrs. Jackson's son and heir, Mr. Bernard H. Jackson, who sold them to The New-York Historical Society in 1952. A few were broken but most of them are intact and from them prints of nearly the entire collection are available.

Also written in ink in the margin of page 17 and keyed to the listing of the silhouette of John Quincy Adams is the note: "Bought from

[5] Ethel Stanwood Bolton, *Wax Portraits and Silhouettes*, Boston, 1914, p. 61.

[6] *American Silhouettes by August Edouart. A Notable Collection of Portraits Taken between 1839–1849*, New York [1913].

[7] *Catalogue of 3,800 Named and Dated American Silhouette Portraits by August Edouart, 1789–1861.... Discovered by Mrs. F. Nevill Jackson ...* [London, n.d.]. On the cover appears a silhouette likeness of President Tyler with a legend to the effect that it "now hangs" at the White House, having been "presented to the American Nation by Mrs. F. Nevill Jackson shortly after its discovery in England in 1911." The text (at p. 2) announces that "Photo facsimiles can be obtained, price £1 10s each, from Mrs. Nevill Jackson, taken from the original cuttings once in her possession, now no longer available.... There should be in every Museum and Reference Library in America, this complete pictorial record as shown in these lists ... in its entirety, price £800 in facsimile size, 7½ inches each figure; or £500 4½ inches each figure." The catalogue is arranged alphabetically by subject; the nineteenth entry is "Adams, John Quincey, ex-Pres. (Washington, March 10, 1841)."

93a. JOHN QUINCY ADAMS.
SILHOUETTE BY AUGUSTE EDOUART, 1841

Vernay by Mrs. Frank B. Powell of N.Y.C. (a descendant of J.Q.A., who still has it in 1956)." What must be this silhouette is reproduced as Fig. 93a from The New-York Historical Society's negative. The present whereabouts of the original is not known. At the foot of the figure is the inscription, "John Quincy Adams Ex Prest. / Washington 10th March 1841." This silhouette, like the others of which the Historical Society has negatives, is the bare shade only, without embellishment.

John Quincy Adams
11. March 1841.

John Quincy Adams Ex President
Washington 11 March 184

93b. JOHN QUINCY ADAMS.
SILHOUETTE BY AUGUSTE EDOUART, 1841

But the harvest is even richer. On 15 October 1955, at the Norvin H. Green sale at Parke-Bernet Galleries, there was acquired by John D. Schapiro of Baltimore a volume, bound in what appears from a photograph to be old (1849?) leather, of several hundreds of Edouart's silhouettes. During Mr. Schapiro's ownership the pages of this volume were photographed and the photographs bound together, with a typewritten index. This volume of photographs is now owned by The New-York Historical Society. Inside the cover is a notation that the cover of the original volume was 9¾ by 11½ inches in size, and the pages 8 by 11. Following the index, the first photographic page exhibits a bill, dated "Feby 3, 1923," recording the sale by E. F. Bonaventure Inc. of 536 Madison Avenue, New York, to Miss Sarah C. Hewitt of "1 Vol. Silhouettes of eminent [then the figure 343 interlined] Americans by Edouart—net $1200." [8] The volume is a scrapbook of silhouettes, arranged on the pages singly, in pairs, or in groups, each superimposed upon a page providing as a background an attractively embellished library, drawing room or outdoor scene, tastefully sketched in ink (comparable to the lithographed backgrounds of William H. Brown's silhouettes). Almost without exception each of the figures is accompanied, above, below, or to the side by the autograph of the subject.

The original volume was disposed of by Mr. Schapiro a few years ago, and the present owner, who wishes to remain anonymous, kindly gave me a photograph of the page showing John Quincy Adams, reproduced here as Fig. 93b. Adams appears almost identical to his shadow in Fig. 93a, standing at a window, facing a table and book-strewn floor (a familiar Adams prop). Beneath him is inscribed, "John Quincy Adams Ex President / Washington 11th March 1841." On the curtain which covers the bookcase opposite Adams is written in his hand as a sort of guarantee of genuineness, "John Quincy Adams / 11 March 1841." Several explanations can be offered for the difference in the dates given in the inscriptions on Fig. 93a (10 March) and Fig. 93b. The 11th of March is the date on which Adams inscribed his signature on the silhouette, and Edouart appears on Adams' list of visitors and in the diary only on that date. However, it seems quite possible that Edouart actually cut the shades on 10 March, as is claimed in the inscription on Fig. 93a; that he returned on the next day, by which time he had superimposed the shade upon its background, finally offering it to Adams for his signature.

[8] It appears that Bonaventure had acquired the volume in Paris (Hannah R. London, *Shades of My Forefathers*, Springfield, Mass., 1941, p. 68).

Auguste Edouart; James R. Lambdin

The preceding page contains three newspaper clippings (undated except for an ink notation, "April 1842"). One of these commences "From Washington (Correspondence of the Herald) Congressional Sketches," and another, "A correspondent of the New York American" —both containing laudatory biographical sketches of Adams. In the first, the description of Adams' appearance complements nicely the image cut by Edouart: "Mr. Adams is now seventy years of age, and begins to show the marks of time. His figure is of the medium height, and he seems to have become much broader of late; his head is nearly bald with silver sprinkled locks."

There is no doubt that Edouart and William Henry Brown were the foremost "shade men" of their day. Edouart took his art seriously and published in 1835, shortly before coming to America, *A Treatise on Silhouette Likenesses* in which he described himself as "Silhouettist to the French Royal Family, and patronized by His Royal Highness, the late Duke of Gloucester and the principal nobility of England, Scotland and Ireland."[9] Glances at the collections of Edouart's silhouettes at the Metropolitan Museum of Art, the negatives owned by The New-York Historical Society, and the reproductions of the volume once owned by Mr. Schapiro all lend credence to this boast.

JAMES REID LAMBDIN (1807–1889)

On 20 February 1841, before the United States Supreme Court, Justice Taney presiding, Adams commenced his great argument in the *Amistad* case. At issue was the status of a cargo of Africans who had been illicitly sold into slavery in Havana, had subsequently killed the crew of the schooner *Amistad* in which they were imprisoned, and had taken charge of the vessel until intercepted by the United States coastal survey brig *Washington* off New London. Public interest in the case ran high; the issue was one of great moment to slaveholders; and Adams found himself, as usual, lined up against many of his old political enemies, Southern plantation owners and "Northern men of Southern principles." After months of diligent, dogged hard work, he made a brilliant argument before the Court over a period of several days, and a decision was rendered in favor of his clients. The Africans were ruled to be free. It was Adams' greatest court victory.

[9] Bolton, *Wax Portraits*, p. 56–57.

At the age of seventy-four he had resisted the appeal to take the case on the grounds that he was too old and by the passage of time had become too inexperienced, but he was persuaded by the argument that it was a matter of life and death for the unfortunate Africans.[1] How extraordinary on any count, and how fortunate it is for us, that, with a matter of such moment at hand, Adams could find time for portraiture! Only a week before the argument he managed to sit for his portrait on four occasions to the painter James Reid Lambdin in Washington. Thus there has been preserved for posterity a likeness of the aging advocate almost at the very moment of his victory in the cause of freedom.

Lambdin was a well-known Philadelphia portrait painter, an officer of the Pennsylvania Academy and an Honorary Member of the National Academy. He had been born in Pittsburgh and had early studied under Sully. How his meeting with Adams was arranged we do not know, but Adams' diary records the occasions on which he sat. "Mr. Lambdin called at 9 O'Clock this morning, and borrowed my father's last Portrait by Stewart, to take a copy of it. He rode with me to the Capitol, and took it with him. I sat to him nearly an hour in the room of the Committee of Post-Offices and Post-roads, until the meeting of the Committee when we were obliged to retire." He sat again in the same room on 13 and 15 February and for the last time on the 16th: "Gave a final sitting of half an hour to Mr. Lambdin.... He returns to Philadelphia to-morrow. [James I.] McKay who was there said the Portrait was an excellent likeness."[2]

After Lambdin's departure nothing was heard of the portrait for three years. In April 1844 the matter appears again in the diary:

Mr. Lambdin is a painter usually residing at Philadelphia, who two or three years ago painted a portrait of me and from whom I have not since heard till this morning, when he called on me, and requested me to sit for him again. He has the portrait still, and says it has been much approved as a likeness, by all persons acquainted with me who have seen it. He

[1] Old in years he was, but not in spirit. Philip Hone describes him at a dinner party in New York only a few days before the argument: "I dined with Mr. Barnard; a small and very pleasant party and an excellent dinner of French cookery and good wine. The party consisted of Mr. John Quincy Adams, Richard Bayard, Gouverneur Wilkins, Abbot Lawrence, Mr. Jackson of Philadelphia, and myself. Mr. Adams was, as usual, the fiddle of the party. He talked a great deal; was gay, witty, instructive, and entertaining. It is a privilege and an era in one's life to see him as he was on this occasion. A man must be stupid indeed who can listen to this wonderful man for three or four hours, as I have done to-day, without being edified and delighted" (*The Diary of Philip Hone, 1828–1851*, ed. Allan Nevins, N.Y., 1927, 2:526 [26 Feb. 1841]).
[2] Entries of 11, 16 Feb. 1841.

218

has made a copy of it, which he intends to present to the Astronomical Society of Cincinnati and wishes me to give him one or two sittings for finishing touches to the present time. I agreed to meet him to-morrow morning at 10 O'Clock.[3]

Only a short time before this, in November 1843, Adams had addressed the Astronomical Society on the occasion of the laying of the cornerstone of its observatory. His address had been well received, and forthwith the eminence on which the observatory stood had been named "Mount Adams."[4] At the Capitol, Adams sat once more to Lambdin: "His former portrait was there and is one of the strongest likenesses that has ever been taken of me. He has also likenesses of President Tyler, W. Wilkins and the Senators Mangum of North Carolina, and Morehead of Kentucky." After a sitting two days later Adams noted that Lambdin had "finished the copy of his former portrait of me, and is now finishing a smaller copy, from which he proposes to hav[e] an engraving made." The task was finished the following day. "I gave the last sitting of a full hour this morning to Mr. Lambdin, who finished his third and last portrait of me. He asked me also to stop on Monday morning at Haas's Daguerreotype shop, and having a likeness of me taken there for him to which I agreed."[5] He did agree but apparently put off the task. Lambdin wrote from Philadelphia to renew the request:

You were kind enough to offer, whilst sitting for your portrait, to give Mr. Haas a sitting for a full length miniature Daguerreotype for my benefit. Being obliged to leave for home rather suddenly I was unable to call and arrange with you for the sitting. If Mr. Haas has not seen you on the subject, will you do me the favour, if consistent with your engagements, to give him an opportunity to take the picture. It will greatly facilitate the completion of my picture, which is now likely to swell out to a full length Portrait. Mr. H. informed me that he could take it in a few minutes any morning at 10 o'clock.[6]

Adams called on Haas promptly, but the daguerreotypist was not ready for him, and the next day was "dark and beclouded." The third day Haas "took three more Daguerreotype likenesses of me, one of which is for Mr. Lambdin at Philadelphia."[7]

Adams has nothing further to say of the portraits and only two of

[3] Entry of 9 April 1844.
[4] For a fuller account of the occasion and its significance, see the section on Marcus Mote, below.
[5] Diary, 10, 12, 13 April 1844.
[6] To JQA, 29 April 1844 (Adams Papers).
[7] Diary, 3 May 1844.

95. JOHN QUINCY ADAMS.
OIL BY JAMES REID LAMBDIN, 1844

94. JOHN QUINCY ADAMS. OIL BY JAMES REID LAMBDIN, 1841

them have come to light: Fig. 94 is now owned by The Pennsylvania Academy of the Fine Arts, having been acquired in 1933 from the John Frederick Lewis Memorial Collection, without any indication of how or where Mr. Lewis had obtained it. It is deposited on indefinite loan to the University of Pennsylvania. Fig. 95 is owned by The Union League of Philadelphia, whose records are silent as to its source. The two are near enough alike for one to be a copy of the other, and we may conclude that the artist did not carry out his intention to give the copy to the Cincinnati Astronomical Society.[8] The third portrait, perhaps swelled out to life size, has not been discovered.

Lambdin's likenesses of Adams were approved by those who saw them. From this distance and in comparison with other contemporary portraits and Haas' daguerreotype (Fig. 127), Adams' expression appears gentle, almost humorous, rather than stern and severe as he often found it to be. It is perhaps for this reason we find no disparaging remarks of his about this likeness.

WILLIAM HENDRIK FRANQUINET (1785–1854)

Only a month or so after sitting to Lambdin, and the day after receiving his silhouette by Edouart, Adams received a visit from the Belgian painter Franquinet. "Mr. Franquinet is a portrait painter in crayons," Adams wrote, "who came with a recommendatory letter from judge Cranch, and a request that I would sit to him for a drawing of my bust for the judge, which I consented to do at 7. next Monday morning. Mr. Franquinet had with him a Portrait of judge Cranch and one of a young Lady in New-York to show as samples of his art, very good."[1]

Franquinet was born in the Netherlands on Christmas Day 1785 and spent his early days in Europe. He was in London in the 1830's exhibiting in a number of galleries and then came to America. He worked in Washington and New York and died in New York in 1854. Examples of his work were at various times exhibited at the Boston Athenæum, the National Academy, and the Pennsylvania Academy.

[8] The Astronomical Society does not own such a portrait nor is there a reference to a portrait by Lambdin in its records, now held by the Cincinnati Historical Society (Mrs. Lee Jordan, Librarian of the Historical Society, to the Author, 11 Nov. 1968). It is possible that with the failure to secure from Lambdin the likeness of Adams desired for the Observatory, a decision was reached in 1847 to turn to William Henry Powell; see below, p. 274.

[1] Diary, 12 June 1841.

Adams was as good as his word and received the artist the following Monday at 7: "Mr. Franquinet came and began his portrait of me in crayons. He breakfasted with us and asked me for another sitting tomorrow morning to which I consented. He is a native Belgian, an experienced Connoisseur in the art of painting, and greatly admires the last portrait by Stewart of my father in his 90th year. But his likeness of me is already a failure, and will in no respect equal that which he has taken of judge Cranch." A second sitting was given the next day, "but his work as a likeness is a total failure. He breakfasted with us. He is a native of Maestricht, and saturated with the love of painting from his childhood." Adams enjoyed the company of artists and conversed freely with them, but when it came to likenesses of himself he was myopic. At a final sitting the next day the artist claimed that all who saw the portrait thought it "an admirable likeness." But in the sitter's view, "the harshness of the features is softened almost into smooth insignificance and the character of my countenance is lost." [2] And so, unfortunately, is the portrait.

The artist appears for the last time a year later. "Mr. Franquinet a painter from French Flanders, recommended to me heretofore by judge Cranch came this morning and invited me to his chamber at Brown's hotel, to look at a portrait of Henry Clay, which he has just finished. I did not at first recollect Mr. Franquinet, who told me that his permanent residence now is at No. 12 Park Place, New York." [3]

No further mention of the artist or the portrait of Adams has been found among the family papers. The portrait was presumably given to Adams' cousin Judge William Cranch, Chief Justice of the Circuit Court of the District of Columbia, but it is now unlocated.

JAMES H. BEARD (1812–1893)

"Mr. Beard," Adams wrote in his diary in 1842, "is a painter by profession and brought me a letter from John Cranch of Cincinnati. Mr. Beard wished to paint my portrait, and I promised to sit tomorrow morning, from 9 to 10 O'Clock at a small building at the head of the Pennsylvania avenue recently built as a painting studio." [1] The pattern for the rest of the month was a familiar one.

Beard, who was born in Buffalo, became an itinerant painter at

[2] Same, 14, 15, 16 June 1841.
[3] Same, 23 April 1842.
[1] Entry of 3 Aug. 1842.

the age of seventeen and worked in Pittsburgh, Cincinnati, New Orleans, and other Southern cities. Most successful as a painter of children, he was also an animal and genre painter. One of his sons, Daniel Carter Beard, became the well-known Boy Scout leader. It was while living in Cincinnati that Beard had become acquainted with Cranch and thus was able to obtain an introduction to Adams.

Adams kept his engagement and sat to Beard the day after their meeting, reporting that "he had with him a portrait of President Harrison, painted by himself of barely tolerable execution. But he appears to have a theoretical knowledge of the principles of his art." We know what to expect a few days later: "Gave a sitting from 9 to 10 to Mr. Beard. His progress is not encouraging. It is the most hideous caricature that I have ever beheld." Once again he called on the artist and found his door locked; a few days later he had no leisure for sitting; later still he found Beard "quite unwell and unable to work."[2] At another time he found with Beard a son of William Brent at work with his palette. Two final entries describe the unhappy result, for which we are, of course, prepared. "I gave a sitting of an hour to Mr. Beard, who asked for one more, which I promised. It is a sad exhibition of caducity. Young Brent was there; and read to me a very flattering and ambitious character of me in an early number of the Democratic review."[3]

Brent was probably reading "Glances at Congress, By a Reporter" in the issue for October 1837. How Adams must have enjoyed the account:

Who that has seen him sitting beneath the cupola of the hall, with the rays of light gathering and glancing about his singularly polished head, but has likened him to one of the luminaries of the age shining and glittering in the political firmament of the Union. . . . Never absent from his seat, never voting for an adjournment, vigilant as the most jealous member of the House. . . . We look upon a more than king, who has filled every department of honor in his native land, still at his post; he who was the President of millions, now the representative of forty odd thousand, quarrelling about trifles or advocating high principles. . . . He appears passive, but woe to the unfortunate member that hazards an arrow at him; the eagle is not swifter in his flight than Mr. Adams. . . . Nothing daunts him—the House may ring with the cries of order—order!—unmoved —contemptuous—he stands amid the tempest, and, like an oak that knows its gnarled and knotted strength, stretches his arm forth and defies the blast.[4]

[2] Entries of 4, 6, 8, 10, 13 Aug. 1842.
[3] Entry of 22 Aug. 1842.
[4] *The United States Magazine and Democratic Review*, 1:78–79.

Brent must have been a welcome antidote to Beard's efforts.

Lastly, "I gave this morning the last sitting to Mr. Beard for my portrait, and he finished it. A living ruin. He has also painted my cousin, Judge William Cranch, within one year of my own age." [5]

The record of the "living ruin" has disappeared.

UNKNOWN "COLORED MAN"

In July 1843, Peter Chardon Brooks, informed that their family physician prescribed a change of air for his daughter, Mrs. Charles Francis Adams, organized a trip to Niagara Falls and invited John Quincy Adams to accompany them. Adams gladly assented. Their route led them through Springfield, Pittsfield, and Lebanon, to Saratoga Springs, Champlain, Quebec, Montreal, Ogdensburg, and Niagara Falls; returning by way of Buffalo, Rochester, Auburn, Utica, Albany, and Springfield.

At Utica the Adamses stayed with a family connection, Alexander Bryan Johnson, a banker and publicist, who had married John Quincy Adams' niece Abigail Louisa Smith Adams, daughter of his brother Charles. There exists in several versions a manuscript autobiography of A. B. Johnson, who, proud of his ties with two Presidents of the United States, described at length the visit to Utica, in the last days of July and the first days of August, of his uncle-by-marriage. In detailing the numerous visitors to the ex-President, Johnson recorded that:

Among them was a poor sickly colored man who frequently wrote poetry. . . . But he was also, a painter, and expressed a desire to take a portrait in oil colours of Mr. Adams and the president kindly consented. It was to be forwarded to Quincy when completed. The poor man faithfully performed his promise and in due time, delivered to me a portrait which I forwarded to Quincy. It was not a bad painting nor a bad likeness, considering who was the artist.[1]

The identity of the artist and the whereabouts of the painting are unknown, but the account is a touching recognition of the part Adams was playing in maintaining the right of petition in relation to the slavery issue. This trip west and another that grew out of it, described

[5] Entry of 25 Aug. 1842.
[1] From a typescript in the possession (1965) of a descendant, Alexander Bryan Johnson of Darien, Connecticut. For an account of the Adams-Brooks party's tour of New York State and the relations of the first A. B. Johnson and the Adamses, see L. H. Butterfield, "Alexander Bryan Johnson and the Adams Family," in Charles L. Todd and Russell T. Blackwood, eds., *Language and Value*, N.Y., 1969, p. 183–206.

224

later,[2] convinced Adams, to his surprise, of his great popularity as a defender of liberty and the constitutional right of petition. We are not without likenesess of Adams at this period of his life, but it would have been of interest to have preserved one by a member of that race for whom he had done and was still doing so much.

FRANKLIN WHITE

Whether in Washington or traveling or at home in Quincy, it was always the same: at all times of the year artists sought out Adams to take his portrait, and he always consented to sit. He recognized his position as a public figure, and it had to be duty and not vanity that prompted him to be so acquiescent in what was a time-consuming chore, with the result, as he often termed it, "hideous!"

August 1843 provides a typical example, all we know being what Adams, at home again in Quincy, confided to his diary: "Franklin White, a painter of portraits by trade, had called on me, before I went upon my late journey, and requested me to sit to him for my portrait, which I promised to do, after my return. He came this morning and claimed the performance of my promise. And this afternoon he came again and took a sitting of one hour." A second sitting followed inevitably: "It must be extremely difficult for any painter to take a favourable likeness of me now, for I cannot sit five minutes or three or even one, without falling into a doze.... This irresistible spell has made it impossible to take a good daguerreotype likeness of me, and it baffles though not in equal degree the skill of the portrait painter, who cannot give life or animation to a countenance all the muscles of which are all the time lapsing into slumber." A third sitting was also "somnolent." A few days later, he recorded: "Mr. Franklin White had been here on Saturday but found himself so unwell that he could not take a sitting at that time, but agreed to come again this day. He came accordingly, took a fourth sitting of an hour, and finished the portrait. He is a timid, unobtrusive man, who in the performance of menial services for Harding, himself a third rate portrait painter, acquired the talent of taking likenesses in Oil colours, but he can scarcely claim to be called an artist."[1] This entry was followed by the statement, quoted in the Introduction, that this was about the forty-fifth time Adams had sat for his portrait.

[2] See below, p. 227, 229–230.
[1] Entries of 7, 9, 15 Aug. 1843.

Like many others, White's portrait has dropped from view. No clue to it or to the artist's history has been uncovered.

MARCUS MOTE (1817–1898)

While at Buffalo in the summer of 1843, on the trip taken for the health of his son Charles' wife, Adams was approached by Professor Ormsby MacKnight Mitchel, a well-known Cincinnati scientist, who brought a pressing invitation to him to deliver the principal address on the occasion of the laying of the cornerstone of the Cincinnati Astronomical Observatory.[1]

Despite his advanced age and the chilling prospect of another long and arduous trip, the proposal was a tempting one and offered Adams an opportunity to express himself publicly on the subject of astronomy, which had long been a primary intellectual concern and to the advancement of which he had contributed in many ways.

His interest in Harvard College's efforts to build what would have been the first astronomical observatory in the country had been manifest at least as early as 1815. In 1816 he had given to Harvard for the use of the observatory a copy of Johann Elert Bode's *Uranographia,* "the best and latest Collection of Celestial Charts that has been published"; and in 1823, in an effort to bring the observatory into being, had subscribed a thousand dollars for the projected building. But, that effort coming to nothing (until 1839), Adams in 1825, at the outset of his Presidential term, turned his thought to the creation of a national observatory and urged it upon a Congress that then and afterward was disposed to grant no funds for astronomy. Notification to the Congress by the President in 1835 of a generous legacy in excess of half a million dollars to the United States by the Englishman James Smithson for the creation of an "establishment for the increase and diffusion of knowledge among men" seemed to Adams to provide a heaven-sent opportunity to bring an observatory to realization. But conflict persisted in the Congress about how the fund should be administered and to what purposes it should be put. The matter of a national observatory was still undecided in 1843, when Cincinnati was making ready its observatory. Only after that milestone, and the establishment of the Naval Observatory in 1846, did Adams shift the direction of his thinking about Smithson's bequest, and, still seeking

[1] The observatory, long since demolished and superseded, is a dominant feature of a panoramic view of the city in an 1848 daguerreotype reproduced in Oliver Jensen and others, *An American Album,* N.Y., 1968, p. 46–47.

to adhere to the intent of the donor, concur in the decisions that led to the founding of the Smithsonian Institution. But his commitment to the advancement of astronomy never ended.[2]

Needless to say, Adams accepted Professor Mitchel's invitation and on his return to Quincy commenced preparing his oration, a major intellectual effort in which he was to attempt no less than the whole history of astronomy.[3] On 25 October he set out on the trip west, by way of Albany, Buffalo, Erie, Cleveland, Columbus, and on to Lebanon on 7 November, twenty-two miles from Cincinnati. He traveled by train, steamboat, and canal boat, always on display to crowds; the trip became a trial of physical endurance. At Lebanon he stopped at the Golden Lamb Hotel, then temporarily known as the Williamson Hotel. The town's citizens turned out in force to greet the great statesman, the welcoming committee including two former Governors of the state, aged Jeremiah Morrow and Thomas Corwin. By an odd chance there had been a circus in Lebanon the day before, the Great Philadelphia Zoological Garden combined with the New York Institute, which featured in its parade two prodigious elephants harnessed to a car in which rode a band, also a lion drawing an Ancient Triumphal Car. The city was therefore in a gala mood, and people from all over the county were on hand to see, hear, and shake hands with Old Man Eloquent. During the evening Adams was sketched by a young artist named Marcus Mote.

Mote had been born in Ohio in 1817; he was a self-taught artist and a Quaker, exercising his profession under the disapproval of his Quaker Meeting, yet persevering gently though firmly until he had established a reputation. He painted many portraits of Lebanon residents, but his best-known painting is the large canvas *Indiana Yearly Meeting of Friends, 1844*, showing in a charming, if stiff, style a village square thronged with carriages and wagons and people gathered for the meeting. His old notebook reveals that he received 75¢ to $1.00 for his portrait sketches. In 1850 he formed the Daguerrean Gallery, and in 1864 moved to Richmond, Indiana, where he became recognized as one of the best artists of the Middle West outside of the

---

[2] JQA to John Thornton Kirkland, President of Harvard, 30 Nov. 1815, 19 May 1816; to Judge John Davis, 15 Sept., 4 Oct. 1823, 16 Oct. 1825 (LbCs, Adams Papers); JQA, First Annual Message to Congress, 6 Dec. 1825, Richardson, ed., *Messages and Papers*, 2:313–314; Bessie Zaban Jones, *Lighthouse of the Skies*, Washington, 1965, p. 8–31, 308–309; same, "Diary of the Two Bonds, 1846–1849," *Harvard Library Bulletin*, 15:369 (Oct. 1967); JQA, *The Great Design, Two Lectures on the Smithson Bequest*, ed. Wilcomb E. Washburn, Washington, 1965.

[3] Printed and published in 72 pages, Cincinnati, 1843.

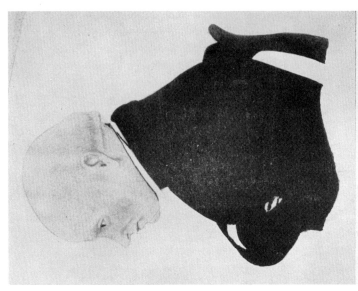

3. *John Quincy Adams, November 7, 1843*

From a drawing from life at the Williamson Hotel, Lebanon, Ohio, by Marcus Mote, a Quaker artist. Now in the Golden Lamb Hotel, Lebanon, Ohio.

97. JOHN QUINCY ADAMS.
DRAWING BY MARCUS MOTE, 1843

JOHN QUINCY ADAMS

Caricature Drawing Made by Marcus Mote With Lead Pencil in November, 1843, as Mr. Adams was being Entertained at Dinner in Lebanon, Ohio. He was on his way to Cincinnati to Dedicate the New Observatory on Mt. Adams

96. JOHN QUINCY ADAMS.
DRAWING BY MARCUS MOTE, 1843

metropolitan centers. He was also one of those rare men who cannot grow a beard.

It was during the evening, or at the large dinner party held in Adams' honor at the hotel, that Mote made his sketches, Adams noting the event in his diary:

A young Quaker limner of 19 or 20, took an egregious caricature likeness of me in pencil and told me that he took it for the bold and intrepid manner in which I had defended and sustained the right of petition; for which I thanked him. Afterwards he said another idea had occurred to him which was, that if I would adhere with patience and perseverance to the principles that I have asserted and maintained, all would ultimately be well. I told him I thanked him for his advice and hoped to profit by it. This dialogue was exceedingly diverting to Mr. Green who was present.[4]

The two sketches, Figs. 96 and 97, though "egregious caricatures," are yet readily recognizable and show ability and some humor. Some years ago they were "borrowed" from the proprietor of the Golden Lamb Hotel (Robert Jones, a cousin of the artist), and have never been returned. The reproductions here are taken from photographs of the sketches made many years ago. We are told that each bears Adams' autograph. On the full face, Fig. 96, written in Mote's hand, perhaps long after the sketch was made, appears: "From Life, John Quincy Adams, Eleventh Mo. 1843, His own autograph, while speaking in Old Baptist Church. Drawn at Lebanon, O. His visit to Cinti. to lay cornerstone for Mt. Adams Observatory." On the profile, Fig. 97, Mote wrote: "From life at the Williamson Hotel, Lebanon, O. 11 Mo. 1843. Present were Tom Corwin, Judge Burnet of Cinti. O., and Hon. Jos. H. Grinnell of Bedford, Mass."[5]

If a look of fatigue can be detected on Adams' face in these sketches, an explanation can readily be found in the physical tribulations of his journey and from his own description of the welcoming ceremonies:

At 11 o'clock we left Dayton and rode 22 miles to Lebanon; before reaching which we were met by a large deputation from the Astronomical Society of Cincinnati consisting of Judge Burnet, Mr. John C. Wright and others. Also by a carriage and escort with which we entered Lebanon in procession, where Mr. Thomas Corwin, heretofore a distinguished member of the house of Representatives of the United States, and late Governor of the State of Ohio welcomed me, at the Presbyterian Church [Mote called it Baptist], by an address of splendid eloquence. These premeditated

---

[4] Entry of 7 Nov. 1843.

[5] MS biography of Marcus Mote, written by Opal Thornburg, Archivist and Historian Emeritus of Earlham College, Richmond, Indiana, portions of which were very kindly lent to the Author.

addresses by men of the most consummate ability, and which I am required to answer off hand without an instant for reflection, are distressing
beyond measure, and humiliating to agony. After these ceremonies, we
walked in procession to the hotel, where crowds met and followed us. Mr.
Bellamy Storer came in from Cincinnati and sundry others. Through the
whole evening there came a succession of visitors, among whom many
Ladies. Supper, from which I retired early nearly worn out with fatigue.[6]

It was not until the day following Adams' address at the laying
of the cornerstone that the site of the Observatory was, by acclamation,
named Mount Adams.

This trip, and its prelude in the one earlier in the year, disclosed to
Adams what he had not truly realized—his enormous popularity, not
only because he was one of the last survivors of those who had played
an important part in the infant years of the Republic, but because of
his unending efforts to maintain "the rights of the people," including
women and slaves, to petition for redress of grievances, as guaranteed
by the Constitution but lately suppressed by the "slavocrats" and their
Northern allies in Congress. Everywhere he went in the old Northwest
and Middle West, which he had never visited before, Adams found
to his astonishment and secret delight that the mass of the people
wished to pay tribute to his principles and his courage in defending
them.

In May 1836 the House of Representatives had passed, over Adams'
strenuous objections, the first of its gag rules tabling all petitions that
touched on the subject of slavery. In each new session thereafter the
"gag" was renewed in the same or variant forms until 1840, when it
was made a standing rule. Yet the irrepressible Adams persisted, presenting thousands of petitions, signed by hundreds of thousands of
Americans, calling for the abolition of slavery and the slave trade and
for the restoration of the right of petition. None was received by the
House. The cause seemed hopeless. So it was that night in Lebanon in
November 1843 that Adams took such pleasure in the young artist
Mote's "idea" that if he "would adhere with patience and perseverance
to the principles" he had asserted, "all would ultimately be well." He
did persevere, and when, at the opening of the second session of the
Twenty-Eighth Congress in December 1844, Adams moved that the
25th Standing (or "gag") Rule be rescinded, the House supported

[6] JQA, Diary, 7 Nov. 1843. On the effort to commemorate the occasion by
commissioning a portrait of JQA to hang in the Observatory, see above, p. 219, and
below, p. 274.

him by a vote of 105 to 80. The right of petition even relating to slavery was established. "Blessed, ever blessed be the name of God!" Adams allowed himself to exclaim in his diary.[7]

GEORGE CALEB BINGHAM (1811–1879)

In 1967 E. Maurice Bloch's *George Caleb Bingham: The Evolution of an Artist* (Berkeley and Los Angeles), was published with its companion volume, *George Caleb Bingham: A Catalogue Raisonné*. Bingham's life and the wide extent of his work are now accessible to all. Most of his life was spent in Missouri, though he studied at the Pennsylvania Academy in 1837, lived in Washington, and studied abroad in Germany on two brief occasions. His genre paintings, such as those of boating on the Mississippi River, are probably his best-known works, though he painted many portraits. There can be no doubt that his sojourn in Washington, with the opportunity to paint such distinguished public figures as John Quincy Adams and Daniel Webster, must have enhanced his reputation at home.

Three portraits of Adams are attributed by Bloch to Bingham—one original and two modified replicas. For external evidence we have Adams' diary entries of May 1844 which mention his sitting to both Bingham and Cranch, Adams' cousin, at the same time: "I sat to Mr. John Cranch and Mr. Bingham who occupy jointly the painting room for my portrait." A week later he sat again, commenting: "I gave a sitting of an hour this morning to Mr. John Cranch and Mr. Bingham: neither of whom is likely to make out either a strong likeness or a fine picture." Further sittings took place on the 23d, 24th, and 27th; on the 28th Bingham finished his portrait.[1]

C. B. Rollins, in "Letters of George Caleb Bingham to James S. Rollins," states that Bingham painted a portrait of Adams in 1840, "a small copy of which, painted on a walnut board, Bingham presented to my father in 1840 and it is still in the family." The tale he tells of how the portrait came to be painted is probably apocryphal but not impossible. Bingham had a studio in Washington, and one day

a gentleman whom he did not know, dropped into his studio, and after some casual conversation their talk drifted into a discussion of the Bible.

[7] Entry of 3 Dec. 1844. See Bemis, *JQA*, 2:447. By far the best account of the long struggle over the right of petition and the various gag rules is in Bemis, chs. 17, 18, 20.
[1] Entries of 14, 21, 29 May 1844.

98. JOHN QUINCY ADAMS.
OIL ON PANEL BY GEORGE CALEB BINGHAM, 1844

Bingham had studied the Bible years before in New Franklin under the Rev. Justinian Williams, the minister cabinet-maker to whom as a boy he had been apprenticed. . . . Bingham said he soon discovered he knew much more about the Bible than his caller, and worsted him on every issue raised. The man was so impressed with Bingham's theological knowledge that he said: "Young man, if you know as much about painting portraits as you do about the Bible, you are an artist and I'll give you a sitting." In this way, he came to paint the portrait of Adams.[2]

The tale continues that Adams was so pleased that he tendered more than the price agreed upon and that Bingham declined it. Adams himself never received the portrait or either of its replicas and it is hard to see why he should have agreed to pay anything. Much more likely he simply acceded to the request of his young cousin Cranch's associate to sit to him.

It is clear from Adams' diary that the original portrait was painted in 1844, not 1840. It is reproduced in Bloch's *Evolution of an Artist* as No. 34. The painting is in oil on a small panel, 10 by 7¾ inches. Bloch believes that the picture was undoubtedly acquired by Major James S. Rollins from Bingham himself, then inherited by his son George Bingham Rollins, passing on his death to his daughter, Mrs. John D. (Margaret Rollins) Von Holtzendorff. From her it went to the present owner, James Sidney Rollins II, of Columbia, Missouri. The likeness (Fig. 98) is unmistakable.

A second example (Fig. 99), also painted in oil, and on a panel 10 by 7⅞ inches, is now owned by The Detroit Institute of Arts, the gift of Mrs. Walter O. Briggs. Written on the back of the painting are two old inscriptions. One in ink reads: "Born 1767 / [J]ohn [Quincy] Adams / Painted in his 81st year [. . .] (aetat 8[ ]) / Taken by Bingham of Washington / and presented to Rev. Jeremiah Twitchell of / New Orleans / La." The other inscription, in pencil, reads: "Portrait of J. Q. Adams / Aug 4 1850 / and presented to Rev. Jer[emiah] Tw[it]chell / of N[ew] O[rleans]." These inscriptions are ambiguous at best and err in at least one respect. In 1844, when we know Adams sat to Bingham, he was seventy-six years of age, and he died in 1848. This portrait is undoubtedly a replica by Bingham or a copy by another hand of the 1844 painting mentioned above. It was very likely made in 1850, which explains the date 4 August 1850. In later years the picture was acquired by Oliver R. Barrett and then by his son Roger W. Barrett of Chicago; it was sold at auction at Parke-Bernet Galleries in 1953. Despite minor differences between

---

[2] *Missouri Historical Review*, 32:9 (Oct. 1937).

100. JOHN QUINCY ADAMS.
OIL BY GEORGE CALEB BINGHAM, CA. 1850

99. JOHN QUINCY ADAMS.
OIL ON PANEL BY GEORGE CALEB BINGHAM, 1850

the two likenesses, in each Adams is painted full-faced, looking at the viewer. Fig. 99 is illustrated in *Evolution of an Artist* as No. 35.

The third example catalogued by Bloch (Fig. 100) is considerably different from the other two but undoubtedly derived from one of them. Adams is shown, turned slightly to his right and looking to the viewer's left. The bald dome of his head is somewhat elongated and there is a certain lack of expression. There are also differences in the treatment of his cravat and the visible part of his shirt front. It appears in *Evolution of an Artist* as No. 36, and is described as being in oil on canvas, 29¼ by 24½ inches, painted, in Bloch's opinion, about 1850. It was presumably acquired from the artist by James S. Rollins, and inherited by his son Curtis Burnham Rollins, passing on his death to his daughter, Mrs. W. D. A. Westfall, of Columbia, Missouri, by whom it was sold in 1969 to its present owner, the National Portrait Gallery.

WILLIAM HENRY BROWN (1808–1883)

Second only to Edouart as a silhouettist was William Henry Brown, originally from Charleston, South Carolina. Brown was not quite so prolific or elegant an artist, perhaps, yet his shades are true to life and his subjects people of the first importance. His early career was as an engineer, but from the early 1830's until 1859 he cut silhouettes, up and down the Eastern seaboard. Finally the popularity of the camera cast its shadow in turn on Brown's art and he became known as the "Last of the Silhouettists." He cut shades of many prominent Americans, sometimes of most elaborate composition. His first cutting of importance was said to have been of Lafayette, and his most pretentious, that of a volunteer fire company in St. Louis, Missouri, 25 feet long, containing a likeness of every member of the company.[1]

In 1845 Brown's best-known work, *Portrait Gallery of Distinguished American Citizens with Biographical Sketches*, was published in Hartford by the lithographers E. B. and E. C. Kellogg. It contained many full-length silhouettes with stylized background and accompanying biographical sketches. Most of the first edition of this work was destroyed by fire, but the book was reissued in 1925 and again in 1931. Among others included are shades of John Quincy Adams, described as "From life by Wm. H. Brown. Lith of E. B. & E. C. Kellogg," and of Marshall, Jackson, Harrison, Calhoun, and Clinton.

[1] Bolton, *Wax Portraits*, p. 62–65.

101. JOHN QUINCY ADAMS. LITHOGRAPH OF SILHOUETTE
BY WILLIAM HENRY BROWN, CA. 1844

That of Adams (Fig. 101), said to have been cut in 1844, is a strong likeness. No record of when or where it was cut or where the original silhouette is, has so far turned up among the Adams Papers or elsewhere.

JEAN BAPTISTE ADOLPHE GIBERT (1803–1889)

In the late 19th century there hung (and had hung for many years) in the offices of the State Department of the United States a splendid portrait of John Quincy Adams. Then it disappeared, without explanation. The gap was filled in 1891 by the purchase on 24 January by the State Department from Seaton Munroe, for the sum of $600, of a portrait of Adams, painted, according to the records of the Department, "from life," by Jean Baptiste Adolphe Gibert. Munroe had received the painting from his mother, Mrs. Columbus Munroe, daughter of William Winston Seaton, editor of the Washington *National Intelligencer* and a long-time friend of Adams. The portrait now hangs in the inner corridor of the Secretary of State's suite.

It was later discovered that the first portrait, which had mysteriously disappeared, was hanging in the American Embassy in London —and there it hangs today—a fine likeness of Adams painted by Edward Dalton Marchant and described above (Fig. 92).

The origin of Gibert's painting is not clear. Adams' diary records four or five sittings to the artist during the latter part of April and in May 1844: three sittings in April, and one in May described as "the last sitting."[1] Then a final entry records a half-hour's sitting to retouch the portrait, and adds that Gibert had also painted another portrait from the daguerreotype likeness taken by Anthony and Edwards—"a hideous likeness."[2] Since the portrait turned up in the hands of Seaton's daughter, we can perhaps assume that it was Seaton who commissioned it.

Whatever we may think of the portrait (Fig. 102)—and it seems neither a pleasing nor a good likeness—Adams' wife apparently approved of it, as attested by her letter recommendatory to Charles Bird King a year later:

A long and friendly acquaintance must authorize the privilege which I take of recommending Mr. Antoine Gibert an eminent Artist to your kind patronage and attention.

[1] Entries of 24–26, 29 April, 1 May 1844.
[2] Entry of 22 May 1844.

102. JOHN QUINCY ADAMS.
OIL BY JEAN BAPTISTE ADOLPHE GIBERT, 1844

238

This Gentleman is desirous of pursuing his profession in the City of New York, and the fine Portraits which he has painted of some of our most distinguished men attest his talent, and the success of his likenesses.

Should it be in your power to promote his views in his Art, I shall be sustained in my conviction of his stile by the Royal Academy of Paris; and shall feel personally grateful for the encouragement of this Gentleman, to whom, myself and family feel very friendly as well for his own merits, as for old acquaintance sake; the recollection of which times past, have always been so pleasurable to Your friend,

L C A [3]

Little is known of Gibert, who was born in Pointe-à-Pitre, Guadeloupe, 24 January 1803, and who lived for several years in Washington, dying, it is believed, in Rome in 1889.

The portrait, signed "A. Gibert 1844," was reproduced in *Scribner's Magazine* for November 1906,[4] and in Richard S. Patterson, *The Secretaries of State: Portraits and Biographical Sketches*, Washington, 1956. There is no ready explanation of the confusion with respect to Gibert's first names. Adams' wife referred to an Antoine Gibert, of whom she spoke feelingly as if he were an old friend—and her letter was written only a few months after the painting of the Gibert portrait. The Department of State records describe the painter as Jean Baptiste Adolphe Gibert. We can only conclude that they are one and the same person and that the family, or at least Louisa Catherine Adams, favored the likeness and the artist.

JOHN CRANCH (1807–1891)

It was during one of the lulls in the normal routine of being painted, after retiring from the Presidency, that Adams consented to have his portrait taken by John Cranch, a son of his first cousin Judge William Cranch, and well known to the family. Only a few years before, in 1826, Adams had attended a commencement at Columbian College (now George Washington University), from which young Cranch was graduating, and had heard him deliver a poem on painting, "for which," Adams observed, "he has a strong natural propensity." [1]

Nevertheless, in 1830 Cranch was a relative beginner in the art of portraiture, and we could wish to see his likeness of Adams. Two sittings in April were recorded in the diary, but no comment was

[3] 29 March 1845 (Adams Papers).
[4] Vol. 40:615.
[1] Diary, 20 Dec. 1826.

made by the sitter on the success of the portrait.[2] It is entered in the "Rubbish" list under 1834, but no diary notes other than the two mentioned have been found. After painting Adams, Cranch spent four years in Italy studying his profession, and then returned to paint portraits for some years in New York, Cincinnati, and Washington. Before his departure for Italy, Adams gave him a letter of introduction to Charles R. Leslie, who had painted Adams in 1816 (Fig. 22):

The bearer of this letter Mr. John Cranch is a young friend and relative of mine, who is entering upon the career in which you are so far advanced, and proceeds to Europe for improvement in the profession. As he proposes going to Italy before going to England, some months, perhaps years may elapse before he will deliver this; but at whatever time it may be I shall take as kindness to myself any attention for which he may be indebted to you: and am well assured that any service which you can render him in promoting the object of his pursuit will be equally well bestowed and gratefully received.[3]

In what may have been a letter of transmittal of the above letter, Adams wrote Cranch: "I hope and trust you will succeed in the object of your voyage of which there is little doubt if you take care to keep always the control of yourself."[4]

Where Adams' portrait went on completion is not known, but it found its way into the safekeeping of the Library of Congress and was destroyed in the fire which swept the Library on Christmas Eve 1851.[5]

There is preserved a photograph of a later portrait of Adams by Cranch (Fig. 103), painted pursuant to the following request, in which, curiously enough, Cranch makes no reference to the 1830 portrait:

May I ask you to do me the kindness to sit to me for your portrait. It would be a great gratification to my Father and all our family to have your portrait painted by myself, and I feel sure I shall be able to make one that will be satisfactory.

I know that you have had sufficient experience of the various operations of painting, sculpture and Daguerreotype, to be quite tired of them. Still I hope you can spare a little time for one more portrait, which I promise you shall be painted with all reasonable expedition.

I have no studio of my own to paint in at present. I paint sometimes at Mr. Bingham's room—at the foot of the hill, near the Capitol grounds. If

[2] Same, 14, 16 April 1830.
[3] 25 May 1830 (LbC, Adams Papers).
[4] 4 July 1830 (LbC, Adams Papers).
[5] *Compilation of Works of Art and Other Objects in the United States Capitol,* Washington, 1965, p. 396. See also above, p. 165n.

103. JOHN QUINCY ADAMS.
OIL BY JOHN CRANCH, 1845

you could find time to call there, at 9 or 10 oclk in the morning you will find me ready with my palette and pencils.

I should like very much to make a beginning *tomorrow* morning if it should be perfectly convenient to you,—if not tomorrow, any other morning at the same hour you should mention. I am afraid I am troubling you, but my earnest desire to paint your portrait is my only excuse. Will you be so kind as to give me an answer by Mr. Brooks—and let me know whether it would be perfectly convenient to you to sit to me four or five times, an hour at a time—beginning tomorrow morning or any other day you may fix upon.[6]

From mid-May until June that year Adams, in Washington, was sitting on several occasions to both Cranch and Bingham. Cranch had requested the sitting for the portrait, Adams wrote, "for his father, judge William Cranch, my cousin. At 9 this morning I sat to him in

[6] 18 April 1844 (Adams Papers).

241

a small hut or shanty at the foot of the capitol hill and northern corner of the Pennsylvania avenue. An hour and a half exhausted his patience and mine, and I promised him another sitting tomorrow morning." He sat again the next day to both.

A week later we hear gloomy forebodings: "I gave a sitting of an hour this morning to Mr. John Cranch and Mr. Bingham, neither of whom is likely to make out either a strong likeness or a fine picture." He sat again on 28 May, but they requested one more sitting. He gave another hour to Cranch the next day, an hour a week later "to retouch his portrait of me and yet he did not finish"; and "Another last sitting" on June 7.[7]

As Adams himself might have said, the portrait is not a pleasant one but is probably a good likeness and compares favorably with daguerreotypes and with paintings and engravings taken from daguerreotypes of the same period. The portrait was last known to belong to the Reverend Christopher R. Eliot of Cambridge, Massachusetts, and during his ownership in 1935 was photographed. Its present whereabouts is unknown, although a dealer has reported orally to me that he has seen a portrait answering the description of that by Cranch in Ossining, New York—but in whose possession he characteristically declined to disclose.

Two other likenesses of Adams by Cranch, taken from a daguerreotype, will be discussed later.[8]

JOHN W. MASON

Adams spent every summer in the Old House in Quincy, but never in idleness. An 1844 diary entry exhibits a not untypical midsummer-morning's activity at age seventy-seven:

I went to Boston this morning with Mrs. Charles Adams, Alexander S. Johnson and my grand-daughter Mary Louisa. . . . I went first to the Emancipator and Morning Chronicle Office where I found the Revd. Joshua Leavitt. I delivered to him the manuscript copies of the proceedings in the District and Circuit Courts of the United States in Georgia upon the case of the Antelope. I had received a Letter from Mr. Charles T. Torrey in jail at Baltimore, requesting the loan of these papers for the use of his counsel. Mr. Leavitt promised to have them forwarded.

After doing his duty he was free to look after his own interests. The entry continues:

[7] JQA, Diary, 13, 14, 21, 28, 29 May, 5, 7 June 1844.
[8] See below, p. 298–299.

I then went to Charles's Office and thence to the bottom of commercial wharf on board of the new ship John Quincy Adams, just built for Mr. Daniel P. Parker who has given to it this name. Built at Medford of 650 tons burden already nearly laden with a cargo of cotton fabrics and bound to Canton in China. She has a sculptured figure head likeness of me, larger than life of about 8 feet in stature, and considered as a strong resemblance, with the name and the family arms carved upon the stern. Mr. Parker had assembled a few of his friends and mine to meet me there; and after taking me all over the ship and introducing to me the master workmen, ship carpenters, block-makers, riggers and caulkers, and especially the carver of the head and stern, Mr. Mason, had a temperance collation of cakes, grapes, apricots and limonade served up in the cabin where Coll. Josiah Quincy [1802–1882] introduced by a short sentiment complimentary a toast so flattering that I could not fix it in my memory. I was so overwhelmed with humiliation that I had not the power of articulation left and only muttered a few incoherent words and hid my head for shame. Coll. Quincy relieved the dulness of the scene by his usual smartness of wit, and he called on the Sailor's preacher the Revd. Mr. Taylor, who made a short and amusing Speech. Mr. Abbott Lawrence and Mr. Gould joined in the conversation, and a number of Ladies cheered the company with their smiles. About half past 12. I took my leave and the company dispersed. I gave a parting blessing of silent prayer for the destiny of the ship and returned through Faneuil Hall Market to Charles's Office.[1]

His young cousin Alexander Smith Johnson confirmed part of the day's events to his father, Alexander Bryan Johnson of Utica, in a letter dated 9 August: "On Saturday, I went to Boston with Mr. Adams to visit the new ship J. Q. Adams, a fine vessel of 650 tons, for the China trade. Her figure head is a full length statue of Mr. Adams, excellently done; and on her stern are his arms and motto—Libertatem, Amicitiam, Fidem. He was addressed and replied very fittingly."[2]

The figurehead, not surprisingly, has disappeared, and no paintings of the ship have been found. Mr. Mason the carver was John W. Mason, who had served his apprenticeship under Laban Beecher of Boston, who carved for the *Constitution* the figurehead likeness of Andrew Jackson. Mason was active in Boston from 1836 to the 1850's and did figurehead and other carving on clipper ships.

From Marion V. Brewington, the Director of the Kendall Whaling Museum at Sharon, Massachusetts, we learn that the *John Quincy*

[1] Entry of 3 Aug. 1844.
[2] Quoted in Alexander Bryan Johnson, MS Autobiography (draft in possession of Leonard J. Wyeth Jr. of Dayton, Ohio [1963]; photoduplicate of Alexander Smith Johnson's letter in Adams Papers Editorial Files).

Adams was built by Paul Curtis, who later distinguished himself by building some of the fastest of the clippers, and was launched at Medford on 27 July 1844. She was apparently 661 tons, and her dimensions 144.4 by 31.8 by 21.3 feet; a full model with a deck cabin, two decks, three masts, square stern, and no galleries. During her career she made voyages almost as fast as the true clippers.

We can only speculate whether Mason's 8-foot Adams was an 1844 likeness or possibly harked back to his Presidential days.

WILLIAM HUDSON JR. (b. 1787)

A year after his trip west to dedicate the Observatory of the Cincinnati Astronomical Society, Adams was residing, as was usual, in Quincy before the opening of Congress. In September he was visited by Thomas Loring, who had been a member of the Massachusetts House of Representatives a few years before, and who now desired to obtain a portrait of Adams. He brought with him William Hudson Jr., a portrait painter of Hingham, and Adams obligingly consented to sit to him, though he could scarcely keep his eyes open half the time. Loring and Hudson stayed for dinner.[1]

After a few more sittings Adams complained: "It is so irksome and so time consuming that he has agreed to reduce the sittings to one hour a day, and I have agreed to give him as many sittings as he shall desire. He improved the likeness very much this day." The next day he noted that Hudson "inclines to take the hands and we had a long consultation how to dispose of them." The problem of the right hand was disposed of by simply omitting it! The last recorded sitting was two days later when Hudson "took another sitting for my portrait, which he has so much improved, that the family are all pleased with the likeness. The spy glass in the hand will distinguish it from all other portraits of me."[2] The spy glass also "disposed" of the problem of Adams' left hand, and was probably prompted by Adams' recent connection with the Cincinnati Observatory as well as his long-time interest in astronomy.

Hudson was active as an artist in Virginia in 1818, and from 1829 to 1856 lived in or near Boston, later moving to Brooklyn, New York. Like so many of his contemporaries, he exhibited his works at the Boston Athenæum and the National Academy. His portrait of Adams (Fig. 104), though stiff and formal, is not an unpleasing likeness, and

[1] JQA, Diary, 17 Sept. 1844.
[2] Same, 24, 25, 27 Sept. 1844.

104. JOHN QUINCY ADAMS. OIL BY WILLIAM HUDSON JR., 1844

the family approved of it. The records of the Hingham Historical Society, which now owns the painting, are sparse as they relate to it, but it appears that the Society received the painting about 1914 from Thomas L. Sprague, descendant of a business partner of Thomas Loring.[3]

JOHN CROOKSHANKS KING (1806–1882)

Scottish-born, King came to America in 1829 and worked for some years as a machinist. Hiram Powers, whom he met by chance, encouraged him to take up sculpture. He devoted the rest of his life to it, principally carving marble busts and cameos. He met Adams through a letter of introduction from Allen C. Spooner, a lawyer who shared offices with Adams' son.

At home in Quincy, Adams tells of his first meeting with King in July 1845:

Mr. King wishes to take my head. He gave me his Address in Boston, and I am to call on him from time to time as I may find it convenient for the work. He dined with us, waiting for Gillet's 3 O'Clock Stage in which he returned to Boston. He is a Scot by birth, but has resided as an artist several years at Cincinnati, at New Orleans, and 4 years at Boston. He showed me a head of Audubon, the Louisiana naturalist, on a cameo breast pin—the head carved upon a conk shell from the West Indies. He was struck with the Portrait of Edward Boylston in our middle parlour, and enquired who was the painter of it. There could be no stronger proof of his exquisite eye as an artist than this discovery at the first glance of the merit of that picture.[1]

So Adams sat, willingly, to King, time and again, an hour or two at a spell, a dozen times in all but continually noting his usual discouragement with the result. "He labours his work very much, but I fear he is not likely to obtain a likeness." Mr. King's "progress in taking my bust is inconceivably slow and ... to my judgment has not yet reached one feature of likeness to my face." Finally, at the last sitting, King was pleased with the result, and numerous visitors thought it a good likeness. "I am not myself deeply impressed with the resem-

[3] Information received from Mrs. Frederick C. Cheney of the Hingham Historical Society.

[1] JQA, Diary, 12 July 1845. The Boylston portrait so admired by JQA was painted ca. 1723 in Barbados by an artist whose identity is not known and was presented to JA by Ward Nicholas Boylston. It displayed "a gentleman in the fashionable dress and wig of the time of George the first and holding in his hand a Letter addressed to the Revd. Edward Wigglesworth" (JQA to Rev. John Andrews, 16 Oct. 1839, LbC, Adams Papers).

blance; but he has done me no injustice, having rather softened than otherwise the harshness of my features."[2] This was strong praise from Adams.

A month later Adams stopped at Amory Hall to see King and the bust. King mentioned his intention to make a cameo for himself and that he had received four orders for copies of the bust. Every person who has seen it, he stated, thought it an "excellent likeness."[3] The bust is exactly contemporaneous with Healy's portrait of Adams (Fig. 108), both having been sat for at the same time, and together they give a lifelike representation of the old gentleman at the time, though his expression was severe, and neither to his satisfaction revealed the true sentiments of his heart.

Charles Francis Adams was not so well pleased with the bust. He reported: "At this I looked with every disposition to be pleased. It is a likeness, certainly, but not an agreeable one. The artist proceeding on a false idea of representing him in action has given to his face and particularly his lip an exaggeration, which approaches to deformity. I said what I could but I am no flatterer, and yet feel too well disposed to a poor artist to run down his work."[4] Thus spoke the third-generation art critic.

The bust was exhibited at the National Academy of Design in 1848 as Item 119, stated to be owned by King.[5]

Which of the two known examples is the original is not clear. One (Fig. 105) is in the United States Capitol, acquired in 1849, presumably from King although the records are incomplete. It is in the room in which Adams died, then the Speaker's room, on the second floor of the House wing, a room now required to be euphemistically designated as the "Congressional Ladies Retiring Room, H–235." There it stands high on a pedestal, inscribed under it the words: "John Quincy Adams who, after fifty years of public service, the last sixteen in yonder Hall, was summoned thence to die in this room, 23 February 1848." The other bust (Fig. 106) stands fittingly on the platform of Faneuil Hall in Boston, opposite Binon's great bust of John Adams,[6] together flanking a marble of Daniel Webster.

The following letter from King to Adams, written in Boston in 1847, gives a clue as to how many copies there may have been and how sculptors suffered from plagiarism:

[2] Entries of 22, 24, 31 July, 21, 26 Aug., 3, 9, 10, 13, 16, 18, 20 Sept. 1845.
[3] Entry of 21 Oct. 1845.
[4] Diary, 28 March 1846.
[5] *National Academy of Design Exhibition Record, 1826–1860* (NYHS, *Colls.*, 74 [1941]), p. 278.
[6] Oliver, *Portraits of JA and AA*, p. 184 (Fig. 91).

JOHN QUINCY ADAMS
who,
after fifty years
of public service,
the last sixteen
in yonder Hall,
was summoned thence
to die in this room,
23 February 1848.

105. JOHN QUINCY ADAMS.
MARBLE BUST BY JOHN CROOKSHANKS KING, 1845 OR AFTER

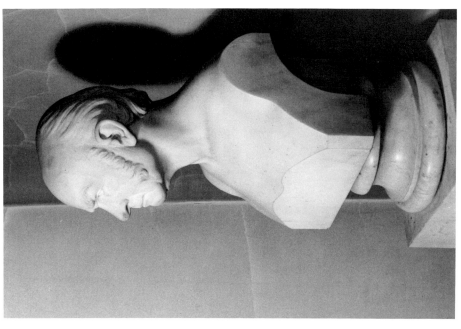

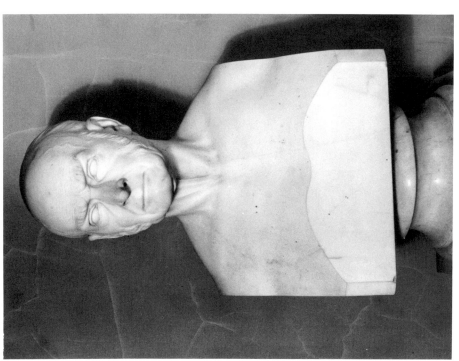

106. JOHN QUINCY ADAMS. MARBLE BUST BY JOHN CROOKSHANKS KING, 1845 OR AFTER

107. JOHN QUINCY ADAMS.
ENGRAVING BY
CHARLES KENNEDY BURT, CA. 1870

You will confer a great favour by writing to me your opinion of the bust that I modelled of you. I regret to state that a cast of it has, by some unfair means, been put in the hands of an Italian pedlar, who can sell casts for less than half of what I can afford them.

I had only eight subscribers, and can conceive of no other way in which the Italian could obtain a cast, but from one of them.

I would respectfully suggest that the protection granted to Authors should be extended to sculptors. As it is, we have to go through the tedious and expensive operation of *patenting* our works, as if they were spinning Jennies, or other mechanical inventions. But for the expense and delay I should have secured my bust of you against all pedlars.

Trusting that you will pardon the liberty I have taken with you.[7]

It was from a photograph of King's bust of Adams in the Capitol that Charles Kennedy Burt made the engraving ultimately utilized in the six-cent United States Ordinary Stamp, series 1938 (Fig. 107). Born in Edinburgh in 1823, Burt became a portrait, historical, and landscape engraver; by 1850 he was working in New York. His obituary in the *Boston Evening Transcript*, 28 March 1892, states that "a head of Queen Victoria, executed by Mr. Burt for the Canadian government for a postage stamp, was on its issue rated by philatelists as 'the queen of stamps.'"

GEORGE PETER ALEXANDER HEALY (1813–1894)

Much of our knowledge of Healy's life comes from his own *Reminiscences* and his daughter's *Life*, but the definitive work on this prolific and popular 19th-century artist remains to be written.[1] His career,

[7] 28 Sept. 1847 (Adams Papers).
[1] George P. A. Healy, *Reminiscences of a Portrait Painter*, Chicago, 1894; Mary Bigot [Madame Charles Bigot], *Life of George P. A. Healy ... Followed by a Selection of His Letters* [Chicago, 1913?].

however, is generally familiar to all, and his works are now eagerly sought after by collectors.

Without a background of formal training, Healy set up a studio in Boston, his birthplace, at the age of eighteen. There his early portrait of the socially prominent and attractive Mrs. Harrison Gray Otis opened the city's doors to the able young portraitist. It was not long before his commissions earned him enough to follow the established practice of the day of going abroad to study, to Paris in his case, which he did in 1834. Following the accepted routine of copying Old Masters in the Louvre, he quickly attracted attention, and his reputation kept him constantly supplied with willing sitters.

The commission he received which is most significant to this book was the request of Louis Philippe, King of France, to paint for him a series of portraits of American Presidents. To do this Healy returned to the United States in 1844. Years later, after an active and successful career in the East, he moved to Chicago, where, except for a brief return to Europe following the Civil War, he spent the remainder of his life. His paintings, both portrait and historical, can be found in many museums and private collections. His familiar portrait of Lincoln hangs in the White House State Dining Room; another is in the Corcoran Gallery of Art.

Adams' first record of meeting Healy was in Washington, in 1842, when he made a short return trip to America from France: "In the Evening we had as visitors Captain Talcott with Richard Cutts junr., and Charles A. [*i.e.* B.] King the painter, with Mr. Healy also a painter, an American recently from Paris, where he painted a full length portrait of the king Louis Philippe and also one of his finance Minister Guizot, ship'd as presents by the Americans at Paris to Congress, or to the President's house, but they have not yet arrived." [2] Three years later they met again in Quincy:

Mr. Healy the Painter was also here. He came from Paris commissioned by King Louis-Philippe to paint for him the portraits of the late General Andrew Jackson, Henry Clay and me. He came just in time to paint Jackson before he died. He has since painted Mr. Clay, and now comes for me. He returned immediately to Boston, being engaged to be there at two o'clock. I agreed to sit for him two hours next Wednesday, from [12?] or half past 12 o'clock at Mr. Charles Hubbard's room in Tremont row, No. 11. He said that the king had charged him to say that he would have sent a formal request to the persons whose portraits he desired, but that might have made it necessary to enlarge the number, which a necessity for some limitation had restricted him to 3 living characters. Healy says Mr. Clay

[2] Diary, 18 May 1842.

asked him why his Majesty had not thought of our present President [Polk] as one of the Americans whose portraits he thought it worth his while to possess.[3]

Healy's reply to Clay was not preserved.

True to his promise Adams stopped at Hubbard's painting rooms but was told that Healy was at Harding's painting rooms, where Page had painted him before. He went there, meeting President Quincy of Harvard at the door, and sat to Healy for about an hour. He did the same on 10 September, recording, with some humor, "1845—in the 15th year of the reign of Louis Philippe of Orleans King of the French, by whom Mr. Healy comes commissioned to take my portrait for his gallery of pictures." They talked that day about the France of 1778 and of 1815: "I had much to remember," Adams wrote. They also spoke of post-1815 France.[4] It was of one of these sittings that Healy wrote to his daughter:

After I had made a sketch, I asked permission to measure the head with my compass. He said: "Do you know, Mr. Healy, that of all the artists I have sat to, only you and Copley used the compass? I saw Copley paint my father's whole-length portrait and then he measured every part of the face with care, and also the length and thickness of the arms and legs and the body generally. . . . You are sure to like the portrait Copley painted of me. He took great pains with it and sent it as a present to my mother in acknowledgment of some service I had been able to render him. Stuart, when he, in his turn, painted my portrait, said that Copley's head was still very like me." I told Mr. Adams that one of my first studies was a copy of that head.[5]

Healy in his *Reminiscences* remembered Adams' conversation as "most varied and interesting; so much so that at the time I took a few notes after each sitting, and these, by some chance escaped destruction, whereas most of my papers were burned in the Chicago Fire or have been lost in my frequent travels. . . . John Quincy Adams was a most courteous gentleman."[6] In his letter to his daughter, Healy continued his account of the first sitting: "I asked him whether it had not been a little hard on him to sit to so many artists, and whether he was like Webster, who looked upon us as so many horseflies; brush them off on one side and they return on the other. 'No, sir; whether it be the result of a patient nature or for a more flattering reason, I

[3] Same, 30 Aug. 1845.
[4] Same, 3, 10 Sept. 1845.
[5] Bigot, *Life of Healy*, p. 52–53.
[6] Healy, *Reminiscences*, p. 153, 156, 157.

must say that some of my pleasantest hours have been spent in sitting to artists. There are of course some dull men in your profession, but among my most agreeable acquaintances I count several painters.' " [7]

Adams continued to sit during September, sometimes to Healy alone, at other times to S. E. Dubourjal as well. On one occasion he noted that

Healy has now received the two Portraits of Andrew Jackson and of Henry Clay which he has painted for Louis Philippe King of the French. There is a mystery in the art of Portrait painting. I have seen perhaps 20 portraits of Henry Clay and as many of Andrew Jackson—generally good likenesses, besides caricatures. These are different from them all. There is a delusion in them. They are true as a mirror—Tableaux parlans. When you look at them you feel as if they were speaking to you. My own will be fearfully like—for my countenance does injustice in my old age to my heart. It was not so when Parker painted me in 1795, and Copley in 1796. It was not so when Van Huffel painted me at Ghent in January 1815, or Leslie at London in September 1816. My sufferings since that time from the injustice of some of my cotemporaries, from declining health and from the destroyer Time have furrowed my brow, and distorted my face till my naturally tender heart has almost become a petrifaction.[8]

During the sittings Adams and Healy continued their reminiscences on art and on Adams' life abroad, which were recorded both in Adams' diary and in Healy's letter to his daughter. On one occasion, seeing busts of Voltaire and Franklin, Adams commented that the two men were representative of their respective countries, Voltaire "keen, satirical and energetic and devilishly intellectual," beside whom Franklin's head appeared "a good, strong English head," with a "countenance that is very fine, great and good, especially when you contrast it with that cruel mocker beside him." [9] In conversing on painters, Adams spoke at some length of his admiration of Rubens. Healy replied that he considered Rubens "one of the greatest geniuses that ever lived, in spite of a certain coarseness which sometimes marred his pictures." To this judgment, Adams responded: "Yes, that is quite true, but how one forgets it as one studies the *Descent from the Cross*. . . . The other day, as I looked at your portraits of Jackson and of Clay, I said that it seemed more like seeing the real men than their counterfeit . . . and that is eminently the case with Rubens." [10]

Although at early sittings Adams had worn a black silk stock, Healy

[7] Bigot, *Life of Healy*, p. 53.
[8] Diary, 20 Sept. 1845.
[9] Bigot, *Life of Healy*, p. 54.
[10] Same, p. 58.

later asked him to wear a cravat, and it was with the latter he was painted.[11] Writing to his daughter, Healy reported that when, at the end of the sitting, on 23 September, "I placed the portrait in its frame for Mr. Adams to see, I told him that I trusted he might not see in it ... a tiger. According to Mr. Frothingham, I had made of Jackson an old lion, of Clay a fox, and of himself a tiger! He looked at the portrait with evident satisfaction. I congratulated him that this was his last sitting. He most courteously assured me that it was no subject for congratulation, as he had greatly enjoyed his intercourse with me."[12] But it was not the last sitting.

Adams noted a few days later: "Healy's is such a picture of naked nature that I cannot look at it without shame. Conscious of its extreme likeness to my features at the present time, it brings me to that test which the ploughman poet Burns seems to think impossible of seeing myself as others see me. Mr. Healy wished that the Ladies of my family should some day next week visit the rooms and if on seeing my portrait they should think some further touches of the brush would improve it he would then ask for another sitting."[13] Another sitting *was* had, the result (Fig. 108) bringing from Adams an accolade: "Mr. Healy's picture is the strongest likeness of me that ever was painted, and I told him that I hoped it was the last portrait that ever would be painted of me.... Mr. Healy requested that any of my friends who wished to see my portrait should come on Saturday morning. His portraits of General Andrew Jackson and Mr. Clay painted for Louis Phillippe, King of the French, and that of Colonel Richard M. Johnson are all there and all incomparable likenesses."[14]

Charles Francis Adams met his mother at Healy's rooms to see his father's picture a few days later and found it "very good." Mrs. Adams agreed that it was the "strongest likeness" ever done of her husband. The portraits of Jackson, Clay, and Johnson she considered were all admirable, but they had "perhaps never been so elaborately finished" as Adams'. Healy was asked if he would have any objection to having a copper engraving made of the portrait before it went to France; he replied that it was his intention to obtain permission of the King to have engravings made of the three portraits ordered by him.[15] A few months later Adams' diary reveals, "About two or three months since he [Healy] sent mine to Boston to be engraved.... [H]e has made also for the King of France copies of several other portraits of

[11] JQA, Diary, 25 Sept. 1845.
[12] Bigot, *Life of Healy*, p. 58–59.
[13] Diary, 27 Sept. 1845.
[14] Same, 23 Oct. 1845.
[15] Same, 30 Oct. 1845; CFA, Diary, same date.

108. JOHN QUINCY ADAMS.
OIL BY GEORGE PETER ALEXANDER HEALY, 1845

persons distinguished in our Revolutionary History, and among them, of Gilbert Stuart's portrait of my father, painted *while* he was President of the United States, which is at Quincy with the portrait of my mother by the same Artist. That of my Father, was borrowed of me by Mr. Healy and kept by him several weeks." [16]

In February 1846 Healy pursued Adams in the hope of obtaining the commission for the last great painting for the Capitol Rotunda; Inman, who had started it, had died before its completion, and it was generally agreed an entirely new work would be required. They discussed together a possible subject for the picture, and Adams took some part in discussions with the Congressional committee charged with the project. But Adams, a friend to all artists, seems to have lent his help to other competitors as well. Adams' interest in Healy was shared by others of the family, his wife not long after noticing that "Mr. Healey left the City yesterday on his way to Boston to embark for France; from whence he is to return to paint the great Daniel, and the equally great John C. Calhoun." [17]

Healy was obviously fascinated by Adams. Not only did he make several replicas of his original portrait of him (Fig. 108), but he also included his likeness in his greatest historical painting, the gigantic canvas hanging in Faneuil Hall depicting *Webster's Reply to Hayne,* during which Webster made his celebrated plea for "Liberty and Union, now and forever, one and inseparable." On that canvas Healy has recorded the debate in the Senate on Foote's resolution (26 January 1830). Among some hundred and fifty persons, Webster stands, the principal figure, warming to his oratorical task.

It was to memorialize that event and those words of Webster's that have become so much a part of the national store that Healy undertook his ambitious painting; and with his admiration for Adams he wanted him to be recorded as part of it. Edward Everett, in describing the "grand historical picture of this debate," noted: "The passages and galleries of the Senate-Chamber are filled with attentive listeners of both sexes. Above a hundred accurate studies from life give authenticity to a work in which posterity will find the sensible presentment of this great intellectual effort." [18]

One of those "studies from life" is of Adams, seated in the picture (Fig. 109) in the front row of the gallery immediately to the left of

[16] Entry of 24 May 1846; see Oliver, *Portraits of JA and AA*, p. 171 (Fig. 85).
[17] To ABA, 24 July 1846 (Adams Papers).
[18] "Biographical Memoir," *The Works of Daniel Webster*, Boston, 1851, 1:c. The Massachusetts Historical Society owns what seems to be a preliminary gouache sketch by Healy for the large canvas. In the sketch, likenesses have not been attempted except for the principal figures.

109. WEBSTER'S REPLY TO HAYNE. OIL BY GEORGE PETER ALEXANDER HEALY, 1846

an oval portrait of Washington. He is readily recognizable, as he appeared at the age of seventy-nine in 1846, portrayed as a spectator at the great debate sixteen years before. Adams' likeness was introduced into the picture without his consent, probably taken from a daguerreotype. His diary explains the situation:

> I met at the Capitol Mr. Healy, the Painter, and went with him to Plumbe's Gallery where they took two Daguerreotype full-length likenesses of me. Both very indifferent. Mr. Healy wanted to introduce me as a spectator into the Historical Picture of Daniel Webster answering Robert Y. Hayne in the United States Senate on Foote's Resolution in 1831. Which picture he is to paint for certain Whigs of Boston to be suspended in Faneuil Hall. I told Mr. Healy that I must decline being introduced into that picture, not having been at that time in the Senate, nor in public life at all, nor present in the Senate chamber at the scene. I was residing in this City in Private life. . . . Healy told me that . . . the picture [along with a companion one of John C. Calhoun to be hung in Charleston, South Carolina] would be henceforth, a great labour of his life.[19]

Whether Adams ever saw the picture when finished is doubtful.

Partly because of the numerous replicas which Healy painted of his portrait of Adams, an interesting question is posed as to which is the original portrait, the painting of which is described by Adams and Healy, and which the first replica. In 1954 Healy's granddaughter, Marie de Mare, published an account of her grandfather in which, referring to the portrait of Adams, she states:

> Adams's family agreed so heartily with his praise that they ordered a portrait for themselves, and as he had done for Jackson, Healy let them have this first work, assured of new sittings from Mr. Adams for the Versailles painting. Thus it was that another portrait of John Quincy Adams, dated Washington, December 10, 1845, was presented the following year to His Majesty. It hung at Versailles through the Revolution of 1848, the Second French Republic, the Second Empire and the Third Republic. It weathered many storms.[20]

There is no doubt that the portrait of Adams delivered to the French King (Fig. 108), 28¾ by 22 inches in size, is in fact signed and dated over the sitter's left shoulder "Geo. P. A. Healy Pin[xt] / Dec 10th / 1845," and that it hung for a time in the Historical Gallery at Versailles, later at the Musée Imperial, Versailles, and is now in the Musée de la Coopération Franco-Américaine, in the Château de Blérancourt, Aisne, France, with the other portraits of prominent

[19] Entry of 20 July 1846. JQA, otherwise accurate in his recollection, was in error as to the year in which the debate took place.
[20] *G. P. A. Healy, American Artist*, p. 152.

I I O. JOHN QUINCY ADAMS.
OIL BY GEORGE PETER ALEXANDER HEALY, CA. 1845

American figures collected by the French King. It is also true that
there has for a long time been in the possession of the Adams family
a comparable portrait (Fig. 110), somewhat larger, 32 by 26 inches,
now belonging to Charles Francis Adams of Dover, Massachusetts.
But except for Marie de Mare's statement there is no evidence that
Fig. 110 is the original and Fig. 108 the replica. The date of 10 December is scarcely two months after the recorded sittings, and as late
as 30 October Adams noted in his diary the request to have an engraving made of the portrait before it went to France, a request quite
inconsistent with a gift of the original and the promise of further
sittings for another. The complete absence of mention by Adams of

III. JOHN QUINCY ADAMS.
OIL BY GEORGE PETER ALEXANDER HEALY, 1858

any further sittings is significant in the light of his custom of recording such events. An examination of the two portraits from an artistic
point of view corroborates the conclusion that Fig. 108 is the original.
It is a far more delicate, detailed, and sensitive rendering of the likeness; Fig. 110 (and all its derivatives, for it is the one that remained
in this country, probably for some time in Healy's possession) is bland
by comparison.

Another replica (Fig. 111) was painted in 1858 at the request of
the collector Thomas B. Bryan and was one of a group of seventeen
Presidential portraits painted by Healy that was purchased from
Bryan in 1879, at the instance of William Wilson Corcoran, for The

112. JOHN QUINCY ADAMS.
OIL BY GEORGE PETER ALEXANDER HEALY, 1858 OR AFTER

Corcoran Gallery in Washington. Its size is 30 by 25 inches and it is signed "G. P. A. Healy / 1858."

Another, the same size as the last-named and resembling it most (Fig. 112), is owned by The Brook, New York, but there appears to be no record of its provenance. It is illustrated in Diego Suarez' *The Collection of Portraits of American Celebrities and other Paintings Belonging to The Brook*, New York, 1962, p. 21.

The White House displays a magnificent, but modified, replica (Fig. 113), lifesized, 60 by 45¾ inches, showing the familiar bust and left hand holding a book, but adding the right arm outstretched on a table by Adams' side and continuing downward to include

261

the rest of his chair and the sitter's legs. Although signed on the lower right side "G. P. A. Healy 1864," on the reverse appears the inscription "July 21, 1858—Painted in Chicago." This replica was commissioned especially for the White House, and was received in August 1858, as the following letters written by the Librarian of Congress, John S. Meehan, indicate. The first was addressed simply "George P. A. Healey, Esq., Artist, City of Chicago, Illinois":

Your letter of the 6th instant, accompanied by your bills; No. 3, for Portrait of James K. Polk; No. 4, for Portrait of Franklin Pierce; and bill No. 5, for Portrait of John Quincy Adams, ex-Presidents of the U. States, painted by you for the Executive Mansion agreeably to your contract with the Joint Committee on the Library of Congress, reached me on the 9th instant. The box, that contains the Portraits, has not yet been received, and I will not be able to forward your bills to Mr. Pearce [James Alfred Pearce, Chairman of the Joint Committee] until it comes to hand, and receive instructions from him on the subject. I expect, however, that the box will be received today, and I will then write to him by post mail.[21]

The following day Meehan wrote to Senator Pearce: "The case from Mr. Healy, containing the Portraits of the three Ex-Presidents mentioned in my letter to you, yesterday, came to hand this morning. I will await your order to open the case. I will send to you, tomorrow, his bills and a requisition for the amount necessary to pay them."[22] Two weeks later the Librarian again wrote Pearce:

Mr. Healy was here yesterday morning, and called to see me. He had the Portraits of Ex-Presidents J. Q. Adams, J. K. Polk, and F. Pierce taken from the case in which he had sent them to the Library, and placed in favorable positions in the Rotunda. He was disappointed in not receiving payment for them, but quite satisfied when I reminded him that his contract required that payment should be made after the Portraits were received and approved by the Committee. He was much gratified by your kind offer to pay him, if Mr. Bayard or Mr. Fessenden should happen to visit Washington, see the Portraits, and approve them. He told me that he would go to Philadelphia in the afternoon, and would endeavor to see Mr. Bayard then—or, failing to see him, that he would write to him, and request him, when he next visited Washington, to give you his opinion in relation to them.[23]

But committees do not work with much speed. It was not until January 1859 that Healy's bill, dated 6 August 1858, for $800 for

---

[21] DLC:Letterbook of the Librarian, 5 Jan. 1857–3 Oct. 1859, p. 469.
[22] Same, p. 475.
[23] Same, p. 495.

113. JOHN QUINCY ADAMS.
OIL BY GEORGE PETER ALEXANDER HEALY, 1858

263

J. Q. Adams' portrait, was paid—to Thomas B. Bryan, who was acting as Healy's agent.

There is no ready explanation of the date 1864 which appears on the face of the portrait, as the earlier date, July 21, 1858, endorsed on the reverse is clearly the date it was completed. Years later, in 1884, Healy wrote in his diary: "I went to pay a visit to President Arthur, whom I was to paint. . . . I was shown into the room which forty-two years earlier had been given to me as a painting room by President Tyler. In it hung the portraits of President John Quincy Adams and Martin Van Buren, the first of which I had painted in 1845. . . . It was a singular and very pleasant experience." [24] No doubt the sight of the portrait of Adams which Healy had painted almost two-score years earlier brought up stirring memories—memories of the perceptive conversation of that solemn old man and the unparalleled approval which he bestowed upon the painting. No doubt Healy also felt a certain measure of satisfaction with the enduring quality of the work he had done in his prime.

The New-York Historical Society has a portrait of Adams (Fig. 114) which is undoubtedly another Healy replica, received from Mr. Harry G. Friedman in 1955. Mr. Friedman wrote, "I am happy to give to the Historical Society the portrait of President John Quincy Adams. I am glad it is welcome in your august gathering of historic portraits." [25] Nothing is known of the history of the painting, which is unframed and in bad condition. On the back of the canvas appear the initials "S. D. D." A search of the Adams Papers files reveals a letter to Adams, dated 29 May 1846, from S. D. Dakin, in reference to a sectional floating dock he had developed and which he wished to have the Navy adopt in place of the common stone dock. He stated that he had been introduced to Adams two years before by Judge Bacon of Utica. This was at the time of Adams' 1843 trip, during which he was welcomed at Utica by a committee headed by Ezekiel Bacon, a state judge and United States Representative. Adams' favorable reaction to his warm reception must have been contagious, and Dakin perhaps became thereby emboldened to ask a favor. Perhaps Adams was able to assist Mr. Dakin in furthering his project, and he on his part may have commissioned the replica from Healy as a reminder of Adams' kindness. [26]

[24] Bigot, *Life of Healy*, p. 25.
[25] To The New-York Historical Society, 1 July 1955 (NHi).
[26] It is also possible that the initials "S. D. D." belong to a dealer or earlier owner of the painting. One candidate might be Sussex D. David of Philadelphia, who was active in art matters and who appears to have become known in art circles by the initials "S. D. D." (See Hannah R. London, *Shades of My Forefathers*, Springfield, Mass., 1941, p. 22, 24.)

114. JOHN QUINCY ADAMS.
OIL BY GEORGE PETER ALEXANDER HEALY

The Healy likeness, being one of the "strongest" of Adams, has
been popular and innumerable times engraved, though in any given
case it is not always clear which replica was used as a model. The
earliest—and unquestionably the best—that has come to our notice
was that by Joseph Andrews (Fig. 115), 11 by 9¼ inches in size,
and published in 1848 by George K. Snow of Boston. This engraving
was undoubtedly taken from the original portrait, arranged for by
Healy as explained earlier. Of Andrews it was said that his engraved
"portraits were his best work," and upon them "his claim will rest to
a prominent place in the front ranks of those whom future generations
will term the early engravers of America." [27] Andrews' engraving of

[27] Mantle Fielding, "Joseph Andrews," *PMHB*, 31:113 (1907).

Harper's Black and White Prints

From Harper's Magazine. Copyright, 1884, by Harper & Brothers

JOHN QUINCY ADAMS

1767–1848

After a painting by G. P. A. Healy, Corcoran Gallery, Washington

116. JOHN QUINCY ADAMS.

ENGRAVING BY GUSTAV KRUELL, 1884

John Quincy Adams.

115. JOHN QUINCY ADAMS.

ENGRAVING BY JOSEPH ANDREWS, 1848

117. JOHN QUINCY ADAMS.
ENGRAVING BY
CHARLES KENNEDY BURT, 1870

118. JOHN QUINCY ADAMS.
ENGRAVING BY
CHARLES KENNEDY BURT, CA. 1870

Adams was reproduced as the cover illustration of *Rhode Island History*, vol. 2, no. 4 (October 1943), published by the Rhode Island Historical Society. A similar engraving, derived from Andrews' or from a Healy original, appears in the *Magazine of American History,* 11:102 (February 1884), where it is attributed to H. Wright Smith. They are fine likenesses.

Gustav Kruell engraved a vigorous though not so faithful likeness (Fig. 116) for *Harper's Magazine* in 1884 from the Corcoran replica. The engraver Charles Kennedy Burt reproduced Healy's portrait in 1870 (Fig. 117), apparently using the Corcoran example. Burt's engraving was used on the United States $500 Treasury Note, Series 1869, and a smaller modified example of it on the 1/2-, 2-, 4- (Fig. 118), 8-, and 16-ounce strip Tobacco Stamps, Series 1878, 1879, 1883, and 1891; and on the 50-cent Monroe Doctrine Commemorative Coin issued in 1923, designed by Chester Beach. Burt's larger engraving (Fig. 117) is a creditable reproduction-in-small of Healy's portrait.

267

SAVINIEN EDME DUBOURJAL (1795–1865)

While sitting to Healy in Boston in 1845 Adams recorded his first encounter with Dubourjal. "I walked to Harding's gallery and there met at the door Mr. Healy.... There was also with him a French painter of portraits in Crayons named Dubourjal, who requested my leave to take my head, in his way at the same time while Mr. Healy was at work with his brushes, to which I readily gave my consent. The sitting was of two hours and varied by much conversation upon France at three separate periods of time: Of 1778.... Of 1815 ... and again of now 1845.... Of the first and second of these periods I talked much for I had much to remember."[1] Sittings continued through September, often to both Healy and Dubourjal at the same time. On one occasion Adams saw two miniature portraits of Dr. and Mrs. Nathaniel L. Frothingham done by Dubourjal in water colors the preceding winter; another time he saw a "beautiful miniature of Mrs. Polk, wife of the President."[2]

On 27 September Adams recorded a final sitting at Harding's gallery in School Street, Boston: "Both the portraits of me are greatly different from any that have ever been painted of me before." Next day, returning from church in Quincy, Adams found Dubourjal and Healy awaiting him, the former having brought his finished "portrait in crayons of me, upon which at his request I wrote my name."[3]

A month later: "I gave another last sitting to Mr. Healy, and Mr. Du Bourjal for my portrait."[4] Frequent last sittings were by no means unusual. With his wife, Adams visited Harding's gallery in Boston in October and saw both portraits, praising Healy's but making no mention of that by Dubourjal.

It was in 1835 that Savinien Edmé Dubourjal had become acquainted with Healy, then studying in Paris, and they remained friends for years. The French painter was not long in America, and after his return to his native land, when his health failed him, he was supported by Healy.

The crayon sketch of Adams has disappeared but was exhibited at the National Academy of Design in 1847 as item No. 276.[5] The only clue to its appearance is T. W. Hunt's engraving of the sketch (Fig. 119). If Hunt was true to his original, there is no doubt that Dubourjal fell far short of Healy in getting a good likeness.

[1] Diary, 10 Sept. 1845.
[2] Same, 23 Sept. 1845, 14 Feb. 1846.
[3] Same, 27, 28 Sept. 1845.
[4] Same, 23 Oct. 1845.
[5] *National Academy of Design Exhibition Record, 1826–1860* (NYHS, Colls., 74 [1941]), p. 128.

John Quincy Adams.

119. JOHN QUINCY ADAMS.
ENGRAVING BY T. W. HUNT, 1856

269

MOSES BILLINGS (1809–1884)

In February 1846 Judge Smith Thompson, then a member of Congress from Erie, Pennsylvania, gave his aid to Moses Billings, an artist who, though born in New York State, had settled permanently in Erie. Judge Thompson procured for Billings the use of a congressional committee room for a studio. Two portraits are known to have been painted by Billings—one of Dolley Madison and the other of John Quincy Adams. The artist took a fancy to the pair and would never part with them. They were given by his heirs to Thiel College, Greenville, Pennsylvania, in the 1920's.

The portrait of Adams (Fig. 120) is a pleasing and sympathetic likeness of the old gentleman before his debilitating illness of November 1846, and one of the three last known life portraits of him. He describes the painting briefly, and in an oblique way favorably, in his diary: "I gave a sitting in the Room of the Committee of Territories to Mr. Billings, the Painter from Erie, Pennsylvania, for my Portrait. It was the second sitting of about an hour and he requires only one more." And the last notice: "I gave yesterday the last sitting for my Portrait to Mr. Billings.... He is himself well satisfied with it, as a likeness."[1] And so too should we be after comparing it with the long series available for this period of his life. Some of the usual severity of expression is lacking, and we can perhaps find in Billings' representation what Adams termed "the true portraiture of the heart."

EASTMAN JOHNSON (1824–1906)

One sentence only from Adams' diary tells us all we know about the likeness taken by Eastman Johnson (Fig. 121). In the midst of a busy session of Congress in April 1846 Adams remembered to make a note, though in the hand of an amanuensis, of one more of his many scores of sittings for portraits: "The debate in the House this day was so dull, that I escaped from it, and gave a sitting of an hour to Mr. Johnson, in a Committee Room below for my Portrait."[1]

Johnson was the son of Philip C. Johnson, the Secretary of State of Maine. In his childhood he became proficient in crayon portraits, of which Adams' is a later example; then he became a lithographer and designer of book covers and titlepages. He painted a series of

[1] Entries of 14, 18 Feb. 1846.

[1] Entry of 1 April 1846.

270

120. JOHN QUINCY ADAMS. OIL BY MOSES BILLINGS, 1846

121. JOHN QUINCY ADAMS. PASTEL BY EASTMAN JOHNSON, 1846

portraits of Maine legislators, and, when his father moved to Washington in 1845, the artist continued his career there, taking likenesses of many distinguished members of the Senate. His portrait of Justin S. Morrill, Representative and Senator from Vermont, hangs in the second-floor main corridor of the Senate Wing of the Capitol.

His crayon sketch of Adams is scarcely a likeness, perhaps because it is obviously unfinished. Only one sitting is recorded, though there may have been more. Mrs. Thomas B. Clarke bought it from Mrs. Eastman Johnson, and it was sold at the Clarke sale on 28 February 1938 to Robert Fredenberg for $120, and later to the Harry MacNeill Bland Gallery, New York City, on 27 March 1945, where it was last known to be. It is presently unlocated.

WILLIAM HENRY POWELL (1823–1879)

The best known paintings of Powell the portrait and historical painter are, no doubt, the two in the Capitol. The *Discovery of the Mississippi by De Soto, A.D. 1541*, last of the series of eight monumental panels commissioned for the Rotunda, and painted between 1847 and 1855, for which Powell received $12,000, is striking, imaginative, and romantic. The *Battle of Lake Erie*, his other large canvas, now to be found on the east staircase of the Senate Wing of the Capitol, shows Commodore Oliver Hazard Perry being rowed from his disabled flagship *Lawrence* to his only intact ship, *Niagara*. The likeness of Perry was undoubtedly taken from Stuart's great portrait of the Commodore, and behind him can be seen the excited and eager face of his young brother, Midshipman James A. Perry, who, Admiral Morison tells us, "had slept peacefully below all through the uproar." [1]

Powell was a New Yorker by birth and grew up in Cincinnati. Like so many other artists, he was anxious to obtain the commission to fill the last of the eight great panels in the Rotunda, and like others he also sought advice from Adams, of whom he had earlier asked a sitting. He wrote Adams from Brown's Hotel in Washington in 1847:

Will you do me the favour to let me know how long you will probably remain in Washington? It was my intention to have called upon you, on Saturday last, but illness has Confined me to my room since Friday night. As I expect to be out tomorrow or next day, I should be glad to know, if

[1] Samuel Eliot Morison, *Old Bruin: Commodore Matthew C. Perry, 1794–1858*, Boston, 1967, p. 45.

273

you will remain here long enough, for me to paint the portrait for which I solicited you to sit? I am also desirous to have some Conversation with you in reference to the selection of a subject, for the Rotunda Panel, and shall esteem it a great favour to have your Views on this important matter.[2]

Adams' reply to this letter has not been found, but that they met is established by Powell's portrait of Adams (Fig. 122), which now belongs to the University of Cincinnati Observatory. It was in all likelihood painted at the instance of the Observatory in recognition of Adams' visit to Cincinnati in 1843 for the laying of the cornerstone of its new observatory.[3] The plate on the face of the portrait states only that the artist was William Henry Powell and the date 1847. The painting is signed "W. H. Powell Pinxt. 1847." On 20 November 1846 Adams suffered a stroke while in Boston and did not return to Washington until mid-February 1847. His illness would account for the subsequent omission of many details from his diary. On comparing this portrait with that by Billings a year earlier, we can recognize in Adams' face the traces of his illness. The rugged severity of expression usually present is gone and what we see is the almost pathetic, worried look of an old man whose sand was fast running out. This I believe to be the last life portrait in oil taken of Adams.

The second of the requests in Powell's letter must also have been granted. Because Adams was not backward in offering advice to artists on the subject of their historical paintings or sculptures, there is little doubt that he made suggestions to Powell with respect to his *Discovery of the Mississippi*, and perhaps even aided him in securing the commission.

OTHERS

Alonzo Chappel (1828–1887)

A small handful of likenesses, or unlikenesses, of John Quincy Adams have turned up which are hard to place within the ranks of the documented portraits.

Of least importance and surely the least like, is Alonzo Chappel's portrait owned by the Pennsylvania Academy of the Fine Arts (Fig. 123). It has been said to be "a copy of a portrait by Healy," but bears no resemblance to Healy's or any other presently known portrait of Adams. Chappel used his imagination freely in many cases, and in

---

[2] 8 March 1847 (Adams Papers).
[3] See above, p. 219, 226, 230.

122. JOHN QUINCY ADAMS. OIL BY WILLIAM HENRY POWELL, 1847

275

123. JOHN QUINCY ADAMS. OIL BY ALONZO CHAPPEL

this one it is difficult to see what he used as his prototype. He could never have seen Adams himself at the age depicted.

Albert Newsam (1809–1864)

Newsam, and Duval the lithographer, in concert with C. S. Williams, published a series of lithographs of the Presidents in 1846. Some are recognizable likenesses—several after Stuart, or bad copies of Stuart—but that of John Quincy Adams (Fig. 124) is hard to place. The pose suggests Durand's portrait as a model; the head is older, perhaps after some daguerreotype that has not come to light. This lithograph received considerable circulation but does the old gentleman a disservice and cannot be admitted into the canon of likenesses, though its wide distribution compels us to admit its existence.

276

On Stone by A Newsam.　　　　　　F.S.Duval, Lith. Philad.ª

Entered, according to act of Congress in the year 1846, by C.S.Williams, in the Clerk.'s Office of the District Court of the Eastern District of Penn.ª

JOHN Q. ADAMS,
6ᵗʰ PRESIDENT OF THE UNITED STATES.

PHILADELPHIA.
Published by C.S.WILLIAMS, N.E. corner of Market & 7ᵗʰ St.

124. JOHN QUINCY ADAMS.
LITHOGRAPH BY ALBERT NEWSAM, CA. 1846

277

125. JOHN QUINCY ADAMS.
LIKENESS ON PINT-SIZED BOTTLE OR FLASK
PRODUCED BY JOHN TAYLOR & COMPANY, CA. 1828

John Taylor & Co.

At some time in or about 1828 John Taylor & Company of Browns-
ville, Pennsylvania, glassblowers, produced a "likeness" of Adams on
a clear, light green, pint-sized bottle (Fig. 125). The reverse side of
the bottle bears an American Eagle. This particular bottle or flask is
owned by The Corning Museum of Glass and is one of only five
specimens recorded from this mold.[1]

[1] George S. and Helen McKearin, *American Glass*, N.Y., 1941, p. 459–461.

278

126. JOHN QUINCY ADAMS.
ENGRAVING BY AN UNKNOWN ARTIST

What was followed as a model by the glassblower is hard to imagine. The style of Adams' coat resembles to a degree what he wore in many of the 1820–1830 portraits, but the head and his hair are of a much earlier period, more nearly his father's time, or else purely imaginary. The prototype, freely translated in glass, was probably Stuart's 1818 portrait or an engraving from it.

Unknown

In the print collection of the Boston Athenæum is a small print, labeled on the reverse as being John Quincy Adams, shown here as Fig. 126. It is certainly not a good likeness, but there is just enough similarity between it and, say, Page's portrait (Fig. 86) to make it possible to be of Adams. Nothing more is known of it, but it could be a reproduction of one of the several missing portraits of Adams done during the last ten years of his life.

Honoré Vidal

In 1932 an auction was held in Boston at the Louis Joseph Galleries, then at 14 Newbury Street, advertised by a catalogue entitled *Antiques and Objects of Art, The Property of Frederick Silsbee*

279

Whitwell ... His Marlborough Street House ... His Osterville Estate. The sale was held on 13–15 December 1932, and on page 19 there appeared the following lot:

No. 205. AN EXTRAORDINARILY RARE PORTRAIT OF JOHN QUINCY ADAMS.

President of the United States. Done in pen and ink. The work is so fine that it resembles engraving, and is signed, "Fait a la plume par Honore Vidal." This picture was evidently done for John Quincy Adams to present it to The Honorable Nathaniel Silsbee, between whom there existed a warm personal friendship.

It is true that the men were longtime friends, and when in 1835 Silsbee retired as Senator from Massachusetts, Adams for some time entertained the possibility of standing for election in his place, though nothing came of it. No trace, however, of the origin of Vidal's likeness has been found. The Louis Joseph Galleries have no records of the identity of the purchaser of Lot 205 in 1932 or of the provenance of the pen-and-ink drawing.

VI

Old Man Eloquent in Daguerreotype
1842–1848

"They are too true to the original."
"All hideous."

It was in 1839, the year Adams compiled his oft-mentioned "Rubbish" list of portraits, that Louis Jacques Mandé Daguerre revealed at an open meeting of the Academy of Sciences and the Academy of Fine Arts, in Paris, his revolutionary discovery and invention, the first practical photographic process. Within a short time his name became a household word. A daguerreotype is, of course, a photograph, but of a special kind. It is a unique impression on chemically treated copper and in result produces a reversed or "mirror" image. The word photograph as it is used today has come to mean the positive print (true image) made from a glass or other form of negative.

What family was there, a generation ago, that could not boast of having in its archives (or attic) daguerreotypes of grandparents and children, carefully posed, and preserved in little velvet-lined cases in gilt frames? John Quincy Adams, like so many others, was a frequent sitter before the new camera. His recorded sittings are described below, with reproductions of such resulting likenesses as have come to hand.

PLUMBE'S DAGUERREAN GALLERY

Adams' first recorded experience with the daguerreotype was his visit in 1842 to the Daguerrean Gallery of John Plumbe Jr. in Boston "to have my photograph" taken:

They took me forthwith up to the top of the house where a sort of round house has been erected, with windows like those of a green house, and with a door opening to let in the Sun. I took a seat at the corner of a Settee so that the light of the Sun came obliquely on the side of my face. There was a small telescope nearly in front of me pointed directly at me, and at a corresponding angle on the other side a mirror. A tin or metallic plate was fitted into the telescope, and on that metallic plate the photographic impression was made. Not more than two minutes were required for each impression to be taken during which I was required to keep my head immovable, looking steady at one object. They kept me there an hour and a half, and took seven or eight impressions, all of them very bad for an exposition of sleep came over me, and I found it utterly impossible to keep my eyes open for two minutes together. I dozed and the picture was asleep. I gave it up in despair. How the impression is taken [or] came upon the plate is utterly inconceivable to me.[1]

Four years later on several occasions Adams attended for the same purpose Plumbe's Gallery in the Concert Hall on Pennsylvania Avenue in Washington. In February the result was "quite successful," one full face and one in profile. Still later a Mr. Abel Shawk employed an improved machine at Plumbe's and took more likenesses, sending one to Adams as a present. In June 1846, at the same place, he sat for a daguerreotype likeness for "Mr. Williams, the Swede, from Cincinnati." A month later on his last recorded visit to Plumbe he was accompanied by the artist Healy, but described the results as "both very indifferent." On this occasion he mentioned Healy's desire to include him in his projected canvas depicting Webster's reply to Hayne, and it may well have been one of these "indifferent" likenesses that Healy used for his model.[2]

I have, however, been unable to discover any daguerreotype or reproduction of one that can be identified with any of those taken by Plumbe.

PHILIP HAAS

In March 1843 Adams first visited the shop of Philip Haas in Washington. Haas took "from his camera obscura, three Daguerreotype likenesses of me. The operation is performed in half a minute; but is yet altogether incomprehensible to me." Haas explained that it was "a chemical process upon mercury, silver, gold and Iodine." Adams remarked: "It would seem as easy to stamp a fixed portrait from the reflection of a mirror; but how wonderful would that reflection itself be, if we were not familiarised to it from childhood." A few days later in deep snow he walked to Haas' shop at 9 o'clock in the morning, "my hands in woolen lined gloves bitterly pinched with cold. Found Horace Everett there for the same purpose of being facsimileed. Haas took him once, and then with his consent took me three times, the second of which he said was very good—for the operation is delicate: subject to many imperceptible accidents, and fails at least twice out of three times."

[1] Diary, 27 Sept. 1842.
[2] Same, 14 Feb., 16 June, 20 July 1846.

127. JOHN QUINCY ADAMS.
DAGUERREOTYPE BY PHILIP HAAS, 1843 OR 1844

In May the following year Adams visited Haas' studio several
times, at the request of the artist Lambdin, and had a variety of poses
taken. One of Haas' daguerreotypes of Adams (Fig. 127) cannot be
dated exactly but was probably taken in 1843; it was subsequently
reproduced in the Boston Athenæum's *Catalogue of John Quincy
Adams' Books.*[3] In 1843 Haas published a lithograph of Adams (Fig.
128), an example of which is now in the Library of Congress, with
the pencil notation on its reverse, "Received December 1843 John C.
Davis." It also bears a customary legend, "Entered according to act of
Congress in the year 1843, by P. Haas, in the clerks office of the District Court in the district of Cola.," and in addition the statement,

[3] Same, 8, 16 March 1843; Boston Athenæum, *Catalogue of JQA's Books*, facing
p. 41.

283

129. JOHN QUINCY ADAMS.
LITHOGRAPH BY B. F. BUTLER, 1848

128. JOHN QUINCY ADAMS.
LITHOGRAPH BY PHILIP HAAS, 1843

"Taken from a Daguerreotype by P. Haas," followed by "Lith. & Publ. by P. Haas Wash City." The daguerreotype from which the lithograph was purportedly taken has not turned up. The lithograph and its legends acquire a significance from the clue they provide (as will be disclosed in the discussion of Fig. 130) for dating the touching likeness achieved in the daguerreotype by Southworth.

In Haas' lithograph Adams is shown characteristically with a book in his lap, a finger between the pages, either because that is the way he appeared in the daguerreotype used by Haas as his model or perhaps because Haas was familiar with other likenesses of Adams in such a pose. Haas' lithograph was in turn copied in 1848 by B. F. Butler of New York (Fig. 129) with slight modifications (the chair is different) and with the pose exactly reversed—so that Adams' coat now buttons on the wrong side.

ALBERT SANDS SOUTHWORTH

One of the most striking, and perhaps the most familiar, daguerreotypes of Adams is that taken by Albert Sands Southworth, the Boston daguerrean, reproduced here (Fig. 130) from a plate belonging to the Metropolitan Museum of Art. Adams does not mention sitting to Southworth, and there seems to be no way of determining when this likeness was taken except by comparing it with Haas' lithograph (Fig. 128), known to have been done in 1843.

This likeness is usually thought of as the work of the firm of Southworth & Hawes, although it was not until 1845 that Josiah Johnson Hawes joined Southworth to form that well-known partnership. However, by the time that the plate was made (from which Fig. 130 is reproduced, and which bears the hallmark "Scovill Mfg. Co.," first used in 1850[4]), Hawes was of the firm.

Presumably the daguerreotype is a copy of a daguerreotype, a presumption supported by the fact that it presents a true image and not a mirror image as an original daguerreotype would have done. The likeness confirms the view that Southworth, as has been said of the succeeding firm, "produced portraits far removed from the conventional stiff poses so favored by the majority of [his] colleagues." The effect achieved gives credence to the assertion that the operator "went to the home of John Quincy Adams and there daguerreotyped him with spontaneous informality, sitting by the fireplace, a book-strewn

[4] Beaumont Newhall, *The Daguerreotype in America*, N.Y., 1961, p. 119. The company was formed from the partnership of J. M. L. and W. H. Scovill.

130. JOHN QUINCY ADAMS.
DAGUERREOTYPE BY ALBERT SANDS SOUTHWORTH, 1843

table at his side."⁵ The chair, table, lamp, carpet, and even the mantelpiece can no longer be found in the Old House in Quincy, but the mantels are known to have been removed and replaced over the years, and it is not surprising that after more than a century the other objects have been dispersed.

It has been commonly supposed that Fig. 130 was taken during the last year or so of Adams' life, but a comparison of it with the Haas lithograph of 1843 (Fig. 128) suggests that Fig. 130 antedates the Haas. The similar pose (though the legs are crossed differently), the identical chair, and like carpet cannot all be coincidental. Furthermore, Fig. 130 is a real (photographic or daguerrean) likeness of a living man in actual surroundings. Fig. 128 is (and purports to be) but a lithographic copy of a daguerreotype, with the lithographer free to vary from his original. The likelihood that Haas' own daguerreotype caught Adams in such an identical chair, on a like carpet, and in a similar pose is hard to imagine. Haas, as it appears, worked in Washington; Southworth, in and about Boston. The similarity of the two likenesses can be explained by supposing that during the summer of 1843, or even at some time earlier, when Adams was in Quincy, his "type" was taken by Southworth, perhaps several in the same pose, and that Adams took one with him when he returned to Washington. Haas could well have seen it then and combined some of its features with one of his own daguerreotypes of Adams to make the lithograph, Fig. 128. In any event, the circumstances seem to suggest that the Southworth likeness was taken during Adams' stay in Quincy from May to October 1843.

Whatever its exact date may be, the Southworth likeness is a masterpiece, preserving a magnificent view of the Old Man Eloquent in his aging though still active years. It also affords an interesting vantage point from which to judge his last several painted portraits.

MR. WEST

All we know of West is from the opening of Adams' diary entry for 29 April 1843. "Summer heat—Lassitude and 76. I walked out this morning to the meeting of the Pennsylvania and Louisiana avenues, and sat to Mr. West for two Daguerreotype likenesses; one of which he took for David L. Child, and one for himself. I did not see either of them, nor do I feel any curiosity to see them. They are resemblances too close to the reality and yet too shadowy to be agreeable. I had once

⁵ Beaumont Newhall, *The History of Photography from 1839 to the Present Day*, N.Y., 1964, p. 28.

before been painted by Mr. Charles in the same chamber. Child left the City this morning, not without danger of being Lynched I hear for his pamphlet on the Texan Revolution. The pamphlet smacks of abolition."

Here indeed was a kindred soul; reason enough that he should wish to take with him on his escape from the City a likeness of the great antagonist of the slave power. It is unfortunate that we have no record of Child's memento of Adams. As some compensation, we have from Child a thoroughly informed and informative pen portrait of his favorite statesman, contributed to a volume entitled *Homes of American Statesman*.[6] This is still worth reading as the earliest detailed account of the Adams home in Quincy and an intimate record of J. Q. Adams' character and habits.

CHARLES G. PAGE

Photography by the newly discovered process was proliferating even more than the old-fashioned form of portraiture, and Adams of all people was most in demand as a subject. In May 1843 he records: "I received a note from Mr. Page the Daguerreotype artist requesting me to call again this day as he was not satisfied with the shades taken on Saturday. I did call accordingly twice, and he took my similitude twice but neither time with much success. At one time he and Mr. West took two impressions of me at one sitting, upon two camera obscura's standing side by side, and shewing the face as by two different angles of refraction."[7] Neither "shade" has been discovered.

THE SHADOW SHOP, UTICA

Utica, New York, because it was the home of his nephew Alexander Bryan Johnson, and because of the loyal supporters Adams had there, became a major stop on the trip to Niagara Falls that Adams took in the summer of 1843. The city's warm reception, under the aegis of a committee headed by Judge Ezekiel Bacon, has already been described. Adams recorded that on his way back to "Mr. Johnson's I stop'd and four Daguerreotype likenesses of my head were taken: two of them jointly with the head of Mr. Bacon. All hideous." The following day: "At 7 this morning Mr. Bacon came and went with me to the Shadow Shop, where three more Daguerreotype likenesses were taken of me, no better than those of yesterday. They are too true to the original."[8] So far as is known, none survive.

[6] *Homes of American Statesmen ... by Various Writers*, N.Y., 1854, p. 301–337.
[7] Diary, 1 May 1843.
[8] Same, 1, 2 Aug. 1843.

ANTHONY, EDWARDS & CO.

"I stole an hour," Adams wrote at Washington in 1844, "to have my likeness taken in Daguerreotype." He sat for the purpose, as he had a few days before, to J. M. Edwards, who with his partner, Edward Anthony, had a room for the purpose in the Chamber of the Military Committee. The ordeal was repeated at Mr. Lambdin's request through Edwards and Anthony: "At the request of J. M. Edwards and Anthony, I sat also in their room while they took three larger Daguerreotype likenesses of me than those they had taken before. While I was there President Tyler and his son John came in, but I did not notice them." [9] Photography was certainly in vogue!

A year later, "As I was coming out from the Capitol I met the Daguerreotype printer Edwards who invited me into the Committee room of which he has had the use and shewed me a number of the Portraits recently taken, among which two of the new President Polk—one in a breast-pin reduced from the other, and bespoken for Mrs. Polk." [10] A few weeks later in New York, "Mr. J. M. Edwards, the associate of the Daguerrotype taker and collector Anthony, called on me and invited me to visit their establishment where they exhibit a collection of several hundreds, persons of notoriety of all descriptions. He told me that Mr. Anthony was going to England to carry with him and exhibit there his whole gathering of noted persons of this Country and to procure and bring back a similar collection of European notorieties to exhibit here." [11]

Anthony and Edwards' daguerreotype collection in New York, which became the National Daguerreotype Miniature Gallery, later was owned by Daniel E. Gavit; the entire collection, excepting only the likeness of John Quincy Adams, was destroyed by fire, 7 February 1852. An account of the destruction and the discovery of the single remaining daguerreotype was furnished by Samuel Dwight Humphrey:

The next day, as some gentlemen were looking over the ruins where all seemed a mass of ashes, coals, melted glass, brass, copper, and silver, all were startled by the announcement "Here is a perfect specimen"; and what added more to the happy feeling of all present, it was immediately recognized as the likeness of *John Quincy Adams*, as pure and unspotted as himself. The enthusiasm manifested on this occasion, can be better imagined than described. Should that *good* man appear in person before

[9] Same, 14 March, 12 April 1844.
[10] Same, 27 March 1845.
[11] Same, 2 May 1845.

131. JOHN QUINCY ADAMS.
ENGRAVING BY THOMAS DONEY, 1848

the living Representatives of our country, no greater surprise could be manifested than was on the finding of his perfect likeness in *these* ruins.[12]

We have a good idea of what one, at least, of Anthony and Edwards' likenesses of Adams looked like, from the engraving of it produced by Thomas Doney, in 1848 (Fig. 131). The legend under the engraving states that it was taken from a daguerreotype by E. Anthony, and it shows Adams in profile with his tight-lipped determined expression, far more vigorous than in the later years after his stroke. Doney carried his reproduction even further, publishing a large comprehensive view of the Senate Chamber (Fig. 132), from the legend

[12] *Humphrey's Journal*, 4 (1852):12, quoted in Newhall, *The Daguerreotype in America*, p. 80.

132. U.S. SENATE CHAMBER. ENGRAVING BY THOMAS DONEY

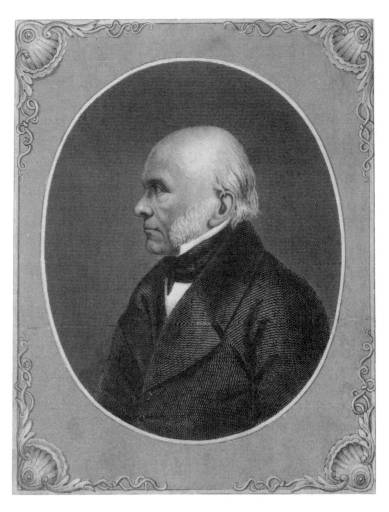

133. JOHN QUINCY ADAMS.
ENGRAVING BY JAMES BANNISTER

134. JOHN QUINCY ADAMS.
ENGRAVING BY AN UNKNOWN ARTIST

under which it appears that the likenesses are taken from examples in the National Daguerreotype Miniature Gallery, which was Anthony and Edwards' creation. Adams can be readily discerned, four likenesses to the left of the Speaker in the far corner of the chamber on a raised seat, the likeness being clearly taken from a prototype of Fig. 131.

Doney's engraving of Adams was copied by James Bannister in 1848 for the *Columbian Magazine* (Fig. 133). Another, and peculiarly ugly, example (Fig. 134) appeared at an unknown date, presumably shortly after Adams' death, inscribed "Sold by Edwd. P. Whaites, cor Cortlandt St. & Broadway," but the engraver is so far unknown.

As the popularity of daguerreotypes grew, Anthony issued large quantities of photographic copies of likenesses in Mathew Brady's daguerreotype collection, in the size called "carte-de-visite." These reverse the daguerreotype image and thereby produce a true rather than a mirror image.

WILLIAM A. PRATT

One mention only of Pratt appears in Adams' diary, in 1846. "This day Mr. William A. Pratt Daguerrean Artist took a type of me, in the

293

135. JOHN QUINCY ADAMS.
PHOTOGRAPHIC COPY OF A DAGUERREOTYPE
BY MATHEW B. BRADY, CA. 1847

Committee Room, of the Committee of Post-Offices and Post Roads of the House. He succeeded tolerably well, at the third trial. The first and second were failures."[13] No known example survives.

MATHEW B. BRADY

Brady, whose name comes instantly to mind as the photographer of the Civil War, started his career as an artist and lithographer, studying under both William Page and Samuel F. B. Morse. Just when he photographed Adams is not known and the occasion has not been noted in Adams' diary. Brady opened a daguerrean gallery in New York in 1844; sometime thereafter, perhaps in 1847, he took one of the most sympathetic and touching likenesses of Adams that has survived (Fig. 135). It is known through photographic reproductions and a fine engraving, and is reproduced here from an example now in the possession of the Massachusetts Historical Society. A comparable one is part of the Signal Corps collection of photographs in the National Archives.

It is not hard to accept the presumed date, 1847, because Adams exhibits the old man's tired, worried expression so well portrayed by Powell in his last portrait (Fig. 122), painted after Adams' stroke. Somewhere in the chain of reproduction a negative has been reversed (a not uncommon incident in the early days of photography), and we see Adams with his coat buttoned on the wrong side as it would have appeared in the original daguerreotype itself.

William Wellstood, the well-known portrait, historical, and landscape engraver, who was born in Edinburgh in 1819 and died in New York in 1900, engraved Brady's daguerreotype in 1857. The engraving (Fig. 136) bears an inscription reading in part, "Engd by W. Wellstood / John Quincy Adams [auto.] / The last Portrait taken from Life." This inscription supports the suggestion that Brady's likeness was taken in 1847. This likeness has been many times reproduced, most recently, perhaps, in the miniature edition of Adams' *The Wants of Man* (written in 1840, first published in 1841), issued in 1962 at Worcester, Massachusetts, with an introduction by L. H. Butterfield. The engraving, which reverses the mirror image, gives us a true likeness.

Alonzo Chappel, the artist and illustrator who painted as many imaginary as real likenesses of prominent Americans for the publishers

[13] Entry of 19 June 1846.

295

John Quincy Adams.

The last Portrait taken from life

Johnson, Fry & Co Publishers N.Y.

136. JOHN QUINCY ADAMS.
ENGRAVING BY WILLIAM WELLSTOOD, 1857

296

J. Q. Adams

137. JOHN QUINCY ADAMS.
ENGRAVING BY AN UNKNOWN ARTIST, 1861

138. JOHN QUINCY ADAMS.
OIL ON CARDBOARD BY JOHN CRANCH, 1853

Johnson, Fry & Co. of New York (including one of John Quincy Adams, Fig. 123), tried his hand on Adams again, using as his model either Brady's daguerreotype or Wellstood's engraving; probably the latter. Chappel's painting has not been found, but a fine stipple and line engraving of it (Fig. 137) made in 1861 has survived, by an artist presently unknown. The standing pose is artistic license, but the upper part of the figure corresponds very closely to Wellstood's engraving (Fig. 136). It shows Adams with a more firm, tight-lipped expression than appears in Brady's daguerreotype (Fig. 135).

Several other painted portraits of Adams taken from the Brady daguerreotype have survived. One (Fig. 138), painted by Adams' cousin John Cranch in 1853, now belongs to a descendant of Cranch,

J. Delafield Du Bois of Greenwich, Connecticut. It is in oil on card-board, 9¼ by 7½ inches in size, and is inscribed on the reverse "John Quincy Adams / Painted from a Daguerreotype by Brady by John Cranch   800 Broadway / New York / 1853." It used to hang in Mr. Du Bois' library with a matching portrait by Cranch of Daniel Webster. Cranch tried to improve on Brady by adding Adams' hands—but failed.

In 1964 an auction was held at Parke-Bernet Galleries of "The Distinguished Collection of Presidents' Autographs & Portraits Formed by Lindley and Charles Eberstadt." Lot 39 in the Catalogue (sale number 2297) was described as follows: "Original Oil Portrait by John Cranch (American: 1807–91). Seated figure, turned to half-right, hands resting on his lap. Framed. Painted when Adams was elderly, probably during his tenure as a Representative. On board: 10 x 8 inches." Having received a copy of the catalogue, I repaired to Parke-Bernet Galleries and inspected the portrait, finding it to be an almost exact duplicate of Fig. 138. The sale was to be held 13 October 1964. On 30 September I wrote to the Galleries, explaining my interest in Adams portraiture, and adding:

> Yesterday I had an opportunity to examine the portrait, No. 39 in the catalogue of sale No. 2297, and found that it is an almost exact duplicate of a portrait owned by Mr. J. Delafield Du Bois of Greenwich, a photograph of which is enclosed. On the back of Mr. Du Bois's portrait there is inscribed "John Quincy Adams / Painted from a Daguerreotype by Brady by John Cranch 800 Broadway / New York / 1853."
>
> The Brady daguerreotype, known to me only from photographs and engravings, was made, I believe, prior to 1847 and shows the bust only of Adams. The hands have obviously been added by Cranch, which perhaps accounts for their rather stiff, unnatural appearance.
>
> Inasmuch as the description of the portrait in your catalogue could fairly be interpreted as indicating that the portrait is an original life portrait, I thought you would wish me to call this to your attention.

The auction was duly held, no mention was made at the sale in explanation of the erroneous description, and the copy fetched $500. Shortly after the sale, I received a letter from an officer of Parke-Bernet, dated 12 October, returning the photograph and thanking me for the information about the Adams portrait, which he said he would remember to pass on to the buyer.

Three other likenesses have been discovered that can perhaps be related to Brady's or to one or another of the earlier daguerreotypes. In 1848 there appeared an engraving by Stephen Henry Gimber, an

Engraved by S.H. Gimber N.Y.

John Quincy Adams.

From a Daguerreotype, taken from life.

139. JOHN QUINCY ADAMS.
ENGRAVING BY STEPHEN HENRY GIMBER, 1848

300

141. JOHN QUINCY ADAMS. OIL BY AN UNKNOWN ARTIST

140. JOHN QUINCY ADAMS.
OIL BY NAHUM BALL ONTHANK

English engraver who settled in New York City about 1829 and moved to Philadelphia in 1842, where he worked as an engraver and lithographer until his death in 1862. This example (Fig. 139) is inscribed in part "Engraved by S. H. Gimber N.Y. / John Quincy Adams [auto.] / From a Daguerreotype taken from life." It could well have been taken from Brady's likeness.

Two oil paintings are so close to Gimber's engraving as to suggest that they are either copies of it or of its prototype. One (Fig. 140), by Nahum Ball Onthank, was presented to the Massachusetts Historical Society in 1928 by the artist's son Arthur B. Onthank; included in the legend written in ink on the back of the painting, the statement that the portrait is "after Stuart" is obviously incorrect. The other (Fig. 141), a more sympathetic likeness by an unknown artist, also belongs to the Massachusetts Historical Society, the gift of Thomas Boylston Adams of Lincoln. If it were not for the inscription on Gimber's engraving (Fig. 139), one might have supposed that he had copied either of these two paintings. In all three instances, Adams' expression lacks the worried look, found in both Brady's daguerreotype and Wellstood's engraving, which I attribute to the effect of his stroke. There is therefore a chance that these three were taken from an earlier daguerreotype than Brady's.

VII

The End

"And when he died in the Capitol, he left
no purer or loftier fame behind him."

On the eve of Washington's birthday, 1848, Adams, then in his eighty-first year, drove to the Capitol and took his seat as usual in the House of Representatives. Early in the day, on a motion to suspend the rules of order to allow the introduction of resolutions of thanks to those officers who had been active in the campaign in Mexico, to which Adams had been heartily opposed, he voted a loud and clear *NO!* The motion, however, carried and the House proceeded to the resolutions.

While the clerk was reading the resolutions Adams was seen to try to speak, to clutch at his desk, and then to fall across it. Cries went up: "Look to Mr. Adams!" "Mr. Adams is dying!" An engraving published at the time by Kellogg & Comstock (Fig. 142), certainly not drawn at first hand but on report of those present, shows the old gentleman slumped in his chair, surrounded by members of the House. However imaginary, it conveys a suggestion of the scene as it must have been. Another version of the scene, somewhat more dramatic, was lithographed and published not long after the event by Nathaniel Currier (Fig. 143). The succeeding events have often been recorded. Mr. Adams was carried into the Speaker's Room, where he revived long enough to call for Henry Clay, to try to express his thanks to the officers of the House, and to say what were to be his last words, "This is the end of earth, but I am composed."[1]

While he lay there, with both Houses of Congress as well as the Supreme Court in adjournment, he was sketched by the New York artist Arthur J. Stansbury. From this sketch, now unlocated, a lithograph was published by Sarony & Major of New York (probably the work of Napoleon Sarony), and an engraving (Fig. 144), taken either from Stansbury's sketch or Sarony's lithograph, was made by Richard Soper, the English-born stipple engraver of New York. As Adams himself probably would have said, these two representations were but *too* like the original.

[1] This is the version given by Samuel Flagg Bemis, who has made the most thorough study of the various accounts and has given his reasons for preferring this version. More felicitous and better known is the phrasing: "This is the last of earth— I am content." See Bemis, *JQA*, 2:536 and note.

142. JOHN QUINCY ADAMS SEIZED WITH A FIT.
LITHOGRAPH BY KELLOGG & COMSTOCK, 1848

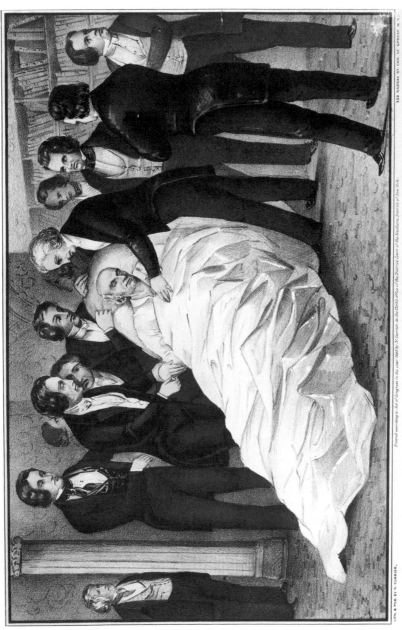

DEATH OF JOHN QUINCY ADAMS,

AT THE U. S. CAPITOL FEB? 23? 1848.

"This is the end of earth...I am content."

143. DEATH OF JOHN QUINCY ADAMS. LITHOGRAPH BY NATHANIEL CURRIER, 1848

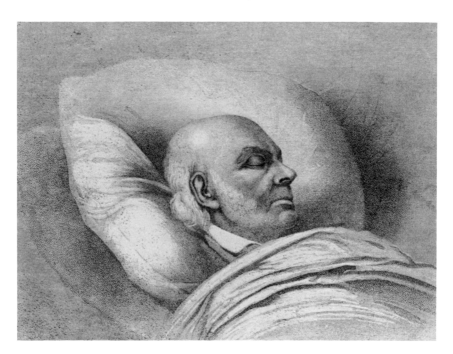

144. JOHN QUINCY ADAMS.
STIPPLE ENGRAVING BY RICHARD SOPER, 1848

On 23 February 1848, in the early evening, Adams died. His body lay in state for two days in the Capitol while thousands of those he had so nobly represented took their last view of Old Man Eloquent. His coffin bore an inscription written, at the request of the Massachusetts delegation to Congress, by Daniel Webster:

John Quincy Adams
Born
An inhabitant of Massachusetts, July 11, 1767,
Died
A Citizen of the United States,
In the Capitol at Washington,
February 23, 1848
Having served his country for half a century,
And enjoyed its highest honors.

After an impressive service in the House, his remains were taken to Boston, placed for a day in Faneuil Hall, and then laid to rest in the family tomb in the churchyard close by the Stone Temple in Quincy. Not since the death of Washington had there been such public mourning and attendance at the various funeral services.

The ceremonies in Boston and Quincy were detailed in the *Boston*

306

Mail in an article entitled "Obsequies of the Dead," [2] which was accompanied by a wood engraving of the cortege (Tailpiece, below). The funeral train was met at the "Worcester depot" by a large number of citizens and the military. Important buildings and vessels at the wharves displayed their flags at half-mast. The account continues:

Shortly before two the train of cars in which was deposited the coffin, arrived. The train was appropriately dressed in black. Soon after the arrival of the cars, the body was borne from the depot by officers from the different companies on duty, and placed on the funeral car.—This was a new one manufactured for the occasion, and drawn by six black horses, trimmed with crape, and with heavy plumes attached to their heads. . . . Leaving the depot, the procession passed through Lincoln, Summer, Washington, Boylston, Tremont, Park, Beacon, Tremont, Court, State, Commercial, South Market streets, to Faneuil Hall. The streets included in the route were thronged with men, women, and children; and it was almost an impossibility to force a passage through the crowds.

The coffin was placed on the Speaker's platform in Faneuil Hall, which was thronged with the public and the military. Joseph T. Buckingham, Chairman of the Committee appointed by the Massachusetts Legislature to accompany the remains to Boston, made a moving speech, which was responded to by the Mayor, Josiah Quincy Jr. On the following day, Saturday, the funeral cortege proceeded to Quincy, stopping for a short time at Mr. Adams' house, then moving on to the Church. After an appropriate service the remains were placed in the family tomb. As the newspaper account states, "The firing of cannon, tolling of bells, and a dirge announced that the Patriot, the Sage, the Statesman had gone to his long rest."

[2] Issue of 17 March 1848, p. 1–2. The copy in the Adams Papers Editorial Files was given by Mrs. S. M. Bristol.

The Funeral Cortege of Ex-President Adams Passing the Daily Mail Building, State Street.

Index

NOTE ON THE INDEX

The principles on which *The Adams Papers* indexes are compiled have been stated in a "Note on the Index," appearing at the beginning of the index in each published unit. Because the content of this volume (like its earlier companion volume, *Portraits of John and Abigail Adams*) is specialized, some devices used in other *Adams Papers* indexes have not been employed here. However, as in all earlier indexes, the compilers have tried to furnish the correct spellings of proper names, to fill out names given incompletely or allusively, to supply at least minimal identifying data for persons who cannot be fully named, and to distinguish by date or place of residence persons with identical names. Wives' names immediately follow their husbands' names. Women who are single whenever mentioned in the text are indexed under their maiden names; women who appear in the text both in single and in married state are indexed under their married names with a *see*-reference under their maiden names. An institution is indexed under its own name with a *see*-reference under the city in which it is located.

The primary locus for each likeness illustrated in this volume is in the entry for the artist who created it; there, in addition to citations to the work in the text, its place in the List of Illustrations and the page on which it is illustrated are given. Mentions in the Index of derivatives from original portraits ordinarily do not include the name of the sitter; it is to be assumed that the subject, unless specifically named, is John Quincy Adams.

The five chronologies included in this volume, intended to provide ready information about John Quincy Adams' occupations and preoccupations when the portraits were done and including therefore much that does not bear directly on portraiture, have been indexed only selectively.

The Index was compiled in the Adams Papers editorial office.

Index

Index

Adams, Isaac Hull (1813–1900, son of TBA), xxv, 146, 150

Adams, John (1735–1826, father of JQA, designated as JA in *The Adams Papers*): on art, x; attitude toward portraiture, 2; Stuart 1823 portrait of, 2–3, 85, 127, 192, 206, 218, 222; on representations of himself, 5; Definitive Treaty signed by, 17; on appearance of JQA, 17; Copley portrait of, 37–38, 55, 78, 122–124, 129, 252; Brown portraits of, 45; Raphaelle Peale silhouette of, 50, 212; Stuart 1798 portrait of, 73, 76, 171–174; on sitting to Stuart, 74; C. W. Peale portrait of, 89; Stuart 1826 replica of, 89; Couché engraving of, 101; Gérard drawing of, 101; King copy of Stuart 1823 portrait of, 102; Sully sketch of JQA wrongly described as of, 112; Leonard medallic likeness of, 122; on pantaloons in Stuart-Sully portrait of JQA, 124–125; Browere bust of, 134, 136–137; Binon bust of, 148, 199, 247; Greenough chalk drawing from Binon bust of, 148; Greenough small bust of, 150; Greenough bust of, 149–153, 185–186, 198; Stuart 1818–1820 portrait of, 165; memorial tablet on, 185; Healy copy of Stuart 1798 portrait of, 256; mentioned, 31, 56, 67, 70, 93, 246

Adams, Mrs. John (Abigail Smith, 1744–1818, mother of JQA, designated as AA in *The Adams Papers*): and Parker miniatures of TBA and JQA, 2, 28, 30, 32; on JQA's appearance, 17; on miniaturists and miniatures, 28; and Shelley miniature of LCA, 31; on Parker miniatures, 31; on Copley portrait of JQA, 38; resemblance of JQA to, 38; friendship of Mrs. Copley with, 38–40; and Copley portrait of JQA, 38, 252; Stuart portrait of, 38, 256; Brown portrait of, 45; Raphaelle Peale silhouette of, 50, 212; Storm engraving of Stuart portrait of, 64; memorial tablet to, 185; *Letters of Mrs. Adams*, 204; Pelton engraving from Blyth pastel of, 204; mentioned, 62, 67, 198

Adams, John, 2d (1803–1834, son of JQA, designated as JA2 in *The Adams Papers*): Hanks silhouette of (Fig. 67, xxv–xxvi, illustrated, 147), 148; birth, 42; in London, 44; H. Williams silhouette of, 50, 212; King portrait

of, 102; private secretary to JQA as President, 116; marriage, 117, 149; death, 155; mentioned, 84, 85

Adams, Mrs. John, 2d (Mary Catherine Hellen, 1806?–1870): Hanks silhouette of (Fig. 67, xxv–xxvi, illustrated, 147), 148; and Parker miniature of JQA, 2, 32; Cardelli instructs in drawing, 73; and Durand portrait of Mary Louisa Adams, 174; mentioned, 63, 85, 104

Adams, John (of South Lincoln, Mass.), and Parker miniature of TBA, 32

ADAMS, JOHN QUINCY (1767–1848, designated as JQA in *The Adams Papers*. For specific likenesses, see under individual artists and the List of Illustrations; see also Lyre and Eagle; Medals; Miniatures; Portraits, lost or unlocated; Silhouettes; Unknown artists): appearance and character of, vii–viii, 17, 38, 59, 108–109, 149–150, 170–171, 182, 193, 199, 217–218, 223, 274; on representations of himself, ix, 2–5, 19, 59, 93, 162, 164, 182, 203, 254; grounding and life-long interest in arts and literature, ix–xi, 8; and design for pediment of Capitol, xiii–xiv, 161; meaning of Lyre and Eagle device to, xiv, xvi, 8–11; seal (Fig. C) used in portraits of, xiv, 8, 12, 58, 77–78, 124, 128–131; public attitude toward, xv–xvi, 198–199, 224–225, 230; address on fiftieth anniversary of Washington inaugural, 1, 202; "Rubbish" list of portraits of, 1–4 (facsimile, 3), 137, 161, 166, 168, 195–196, 202, 240, 281; other lists of likenesses of, 2–4, 182, 253; and Stuart 1823 portrait of JA, 2, 206, 218; "Old Man Eloquent," 4, 12, 155; on his own appearance and character, 6, 19, 95, 182, 253–254; likenesses with opened book, 7–8, 58, 285; motto, from Manilius, 9–10; seal by Silvester (Fig. C), 10–11, 58, 131; on his political principles, 11; papers of Publicola, Marcellus, Columbus, Barneveld, Publius Valerius, 11, 15, 42–43; diary of, 13; at The Hague, 14, 16–17, 28, 34; in St. Petersburg, 14, 17; and Mlle. Dumas, 17; in Paris, 17; LCA wooed and won by, 31, 34–35; in London, 31, 38, 57, 62; and portrait of LCA ascribed to Savage, 45–48; at Ghent, as U.S.

312

Boston *(continued)*
    Historical Society; Museum of Fine
    Arts
Boston Athenæum: and Stuart portrait
    of LCA, 85; Wood miniature of JQA
    (Fig. 48) at, 108; Stuart's paintings
    exhibited at, 127; and Stuart-Sully
    portrait of JQA, 131; 1831 exhibition
    of paintings at, 131–132; and Hard-
    ing portrait of JQA, 139, 141; Green-
    ough bust of JQA (Fig. 68) at, 150–
    152; and Durand portrait of JQA,
    170–171; and Powers 1840 marble
    bust of JQA, 187; example of print
    of JQA (Fig. 126) at, 279; *Catalogue
    of John Quincy Adams' Books,* 283;
    mentioned, 174, 193, 221, 244
Boston Evening Transcript, 250
Boston Mail, 306–307
Boston Patriot, 129
Bowditch, Nathaniel I., 199
Bowyer, Michael H.: engravings of
    Commodores Macdonough and Perry,
    74; engraving from Stuart portrait
    undertaken by, 74–76
Boylston, Edward (1698–after 1723,
    first cousin of JA's mother), portrait
    of, 246
Boylston, Ward Nicholas: on Stuart
    portraits of JQA and LCA, 81–84;
    Stuart portrait of JQA (Fig. 57) con-
    ceived, commissioned, and forwarded
    by, 81, 122–127, 129, 133; and Cop-
    ley portrait of JA, 122–124, 129; on
    JQA's costume for Stuart-Sully por-
    trait, 124–125, 127–131; mentioned,
    85, 128, 246
Boylston, Mrs. Ward Nicholas, 129
Brady, Mathew B.: daguerreotype of
    JQA, photographic copy of (Fig. 135,
    xxxii, illustrated, 294), 295–302;
    mentioned, 4, 293
    Derivatives: Wellstood engraving
    after (Fig. 136), xxxii, 295–298; en-
    graving by unknown artist from lost
    Chappel portrait after (Fig. 137),
    xxxii–xxxiii, 298; Cranch portraits
    after (Fig. 138), xxxiii, 298–299
Brent, Mr. (son of William Brent), 223–
    224
Brewington, Marion V., 243
Brimmer, George Watson, 129
Brinley, Francis, 140
Brock, Mr. (framemaker, of London),
    62
Brook, The, New York City, replica of

Healy portrait of JQA (Fig. 112) at,
    261
Brooklyn Naval Lyceum, and Durand
    portrait of JQA, 179
Brooks, Mr., 241
Brooks, Abigail Brown. *See* Adams, Mrs.
    Charles Francis
Brooks, Peter Chardon (father of ABA),
    140, 224
Browere, John Henri Isaac: plaster life-
    mask of JQA (Fig. 59, xxv, illustrated,
    135), 116, 134, 136–137; bronze
    bust cast from plaster (Fig. 60, xxv,
    illustrated, 136), 135; busts of other
    public figures, 133–134, 137; life-
    mask process, 134; bust of CFA, 134,
    136–137; bust of JA, 134, 136–137;
    C. H. Hart on life-masks by, 135; col-
    lection of busts from life-masks, 135–
    137; mentioned, 4
Brown, Gen. Jacob Jennings, King por-
    trait of, 93
Brown, Mather: portrait of AA2 (Fig.
    14, xx, illustrated, 47), 45; AA2 on
    portrait by, 45; portrait of AA, 45;
    portraits of JA, 45; portrait of WSS,
    45; portrait of LCA (Fig. 13) for-
    merly ascribed to, 45, 48
Brown, William Henry: silhouette of
    JQA, lithograph of (Fig. 101, xxix,
    illustrated, 236), 235–237; *Portrait
    Gallery of Distinguished American
    Citizens,* 235; silhouette of St. Louis
    volunteer fire company, 235; silhou-
    ettes of public figures, 235; men-
    tioned, 216, 217
Bryan, Thomas B., and Healy Presiden-
    tial portraits, 260, 264
Buckingham, Joseph T., 198, 307
Bulfinch, Charles, architect, U.S. Capi-
    tol, xiii–xiv, 69
Bulwer, Edward George Earle Lytton
    (afterward Bulwer-Lytton), *Pelham,*
    160
Burdick, Horace Robbins, copy of Page
    portrait, 201
Burnet, Jacob (U.S. Sen., Ohio), xxviii,
    229
Burns, Robert, 254
Burr, Aaron, 11, 136
Burt, Charles Kennedy: engraving after
    King marble bust for U.S. stamp (Fig.
    107, xxix, illustrated, 250), 250;
    engravings after replica of Healy por-
    trait (Figs. 117 and 118, xxx, illus-
    trated, 267), 267; engraving of Queen
    Victoria for Canadian stamp, 250

Endicott, G., publisher, Ball engraving (Fig. 31), xxii

Essex Institute, Salem, Mass., Osgood copy of Harding portrait (Fig. 62) at, 141

Everett, Edward: Durand portrait of, 174; "American Sculptors in Italy," 183; collection of plaster busts, 188–189; mentioned, 183, 256

Everett, Horace, 282

Ewing, Thomas (U.S. Sen., Ohio), Marchant portrait of, 203

Faneuil Hall, Boston: Greenough bust of JA at, 148; and Page portrait of JQA, 198–201; Binon bust of JA at, 199; Burdick copy of Page portrait at, 201; J. C. King bust of JQA (Fig. 106) at, 247; statuary in, 247; Healy's *Webster's Reply to Hayne* (Fig. 109) at, 256–258; JQA's remains lie in state in, 307

Fay, George (U.S. Repr., N.Y.), 167

Fay, Mrs. George, Rembrandt Peale portrait of, 167

Fessenden, William Pitt (U.S. Sen., Maine), 262

Fifield, H. C., 199

Figureheads of JQA. See Mason, John W.

Fletcher, Richard, 198

Flexner, James T., 40

Foote's Resolution, 256–258

Forbes & Co.: engraving of Powers bust (Fig. 84, xxvii, illustrated, 191), 190; engraving of Leslie portrait of LCA, 64

Ford, Worthington C., 22

Forestier, Sir Amédée, *The Signing of the Treaty of Ghent* (Fig. 21, xxi, illustrated, 56), 55–56

Forsyth, John (U.S. Sen., Ga.), King portrait of, 92

Foster, Dr. Fordyce (of Cohasset, Mass.), xxiv, 108

Fowler, Trevor Thomas or Orson Squire, 196

Fowler and Wells (phrenologists), and Browere busts of JQA, CFA, and others, 136–137

Franklin, Benjamin: Greuze portrait of, 131; Powers statue of, 185; bust of, 253; mentioned, 56, 188

Franquinet, William Hendrik: JQA on lost pastel by, 5, 222; exhibitions of paintings by, 221; portraits by, 221–222; lost portrait of JQA, 222

Fredenberg, Robert, and Johnson crayon sketch of JQA, 273

Freeman, George: LCA on miniatures by, 195; lost miniature of JQA, 195; other miniatures, 195

Freudenthal, David M., owner: Williams silhouettes of JQA and LCA (Figs. 15–18), 50; silhouettes of GWA and JA2, 50; Hanks silhouettes, 50

Frick Art Reference Library, New York City, 98

Friedman, Harry G., 264

Frothingham, Mr., 254

Frothingham, James, King portrait at Lafayette College (Fig. 39, xxiii, illustrated, 96) formerly ascribed to, 95–96, 98, 100

Frothingham, Rev. Nathaniel Langdon, Dubourjal miniature of, 268

Frothingham, Mrs. Nathaniel Langdon: Dubourjal miniature of, 268; mentioned, 139

Frye, Nathaniel, 68

Fryer, Mr. (framemaker, of Baltimore), 47

Furst, Moritz: engraved portraits of JQA on Indian peace medals (Figs. 54a–c, xxiv, illustrated, 120), 118–121; medallic portrait of JQA (Fig. 55, xxiv, illustrated, 121), 118–122; designer, Monroe medal, 118–119; Alexander Hamilton medal proposed by, 121; medal of JQA (Fig. 55), reverse of, 121–122; Jacquemart engraving of JQA medal, 122

Gales, Joseph, 202

Gallatin, Albert: U.S. Peace Commissioner at Ghent, 50, 56; Van Huffel pencil sketch of, 51, 53; mentioned, 203

Gambier, Admiral James, Baron (British Peace Commissioner at Ghent), 50, 56

Gardner, Captain (of the *Lydia*), 30, 31

Gavit, Daniel E., 289

George I, King of England, 246

George Washington University. See Columbian College

Gérard, François Pascal Simon, Baron: tinted drawing after King portrait (Fig. 42, xxiii, illustrated, 100), 101; drawing of JA, 101; portrait of Wellington, 101; mentioned, 149

Ghent, Belgium: U.S.-British peace negotiations at, 50; JQA at, 51, 87; JQA on, 55

Ghent, Treaty of, 44, 51, 55, 57, 67

Gibert, Jean Baptiste Adolphe: portrait of JQA (Fig. 102, xxix, illustrated, 238), 157, 237–239; JQA on portrait by, 5; lost portrait of JQA from Anthony, Edwards & Co. daguerreotype, 237; LCA recommends, 239

Gilbert, Timothy, 199

Gimber, Stephen Henry, engraving of JQA (Fig. 139, xxxiii, illustrated, 300), 299–302

Gimbrede, Thomas: engraving after Stuart 1818 portrait (Fig. 29, xxii, illustrated, 79), 76–78; Lyre and Eagle seal adapted in JQA portrait, 77–78; mentioned, 81

Goodhue, Benjamin (U.S. Sen., Mass.), 12

Goodspeed's Bookshop, Boston, 20

Gore, Mr. and Mrs. Christopher (of Boston), 35

Goulburn, Henry, British Peace Commissioner at Ghent, 50, 56

Gould, Benjamin A., 243

Grand Central Art Galleries, New York City, and Schmidt pastel of JQA, 20

Grant, Annie I., and gouache after Schmidt pastel, 20

Gray, Francis Calley, 48, 133, 199

Gray, John C., 54

Gray, Thomas, 59

Green, Norvin H., 216

Greenough, David (father of Horatio), and Greenough bust of JQA, 150–152

Greenough, Henry, 149, 186–187, 189

Greenough, Horatio: marble busts of JQA (Figs. 68 and 69, xxvi, illustrated, 151, 152), 2, 116, 148–152; small marble bust of JQA (Fig. 70, xxvi, illustrated, 153), 116, 150–152; on Stuart-Sully portrait of JQA, 133; on value of sketches and unfinished work, 133; chalk drawing from Binon bust of JA, 148; on appearance and qualities of JQA, 149–150; busts of JA, 149–153, 185–186, 198; bust of Josiah Quincy, 150; work exhibited, 150; "Forest Children," 152; CFA on, 153; sculpture for U.S. Capitol by, 161; Powers bust of, 183; on Powers bust of JQA, 183; and Powers bust of JQA, 183–188; mentioned, 4, 139, 193

Greenough, Mrs. Horatio, 152, 183, 186–188

Greenwood, Grace (pseud. for Sara Jane Lippincott), 185–186

Greuze, Jean Baptiste, portrait of Franklin, 131

Grinnell, Joseph H. (U.S. Repr., Mass.), xxviii, 229

Groce and Wallace, *Dictionary of Artists*, 137, 196, 202

Grosvenor, Robert, 2d Earl, 57

Guion, David (of Cincinnati), 193

Guizot, François Pierre Guillaume, Healy portrait of, 251

GWA. *See* Adams, George Washington

Haas, Philip: daguerreotype of JQA (Fig. 127, xxxi, illustrated, 283), 221, 282–283; lithograph of JQA (Fig. 128, xxxi, illustrated, 284), 283–287; lithograph after, by B. F. Butler (Fig. 129), xxxi, 285; three daguerreotypes (full-length) of JQA, 219; lost daguerreotypes of JQA, 282–285

Hague, The: JQA at, 14, 16–17, 34; JQA appointed U.S. Minister to, 28

Hall, John E. (editor, of Philadelphia), 109

Hall of Fame for Great Americans. *See* New York University

Hamilton, Mr. (of the British Foreign Office), 54

Hamilton, Alexander, 121

Hanks (Hankes), "Master" Jarvis (Jervis) F., silhouettes of JQA, LCA, and other members of Adams family (Fig. 67, xxv–xxvi, illustrated, 147), 50, 146–148

Harding, Chester: portrait of JQA (Fig. 61, xxv, illustrated, 142), 116, 138–144; portrait of Marshall, 131; portrait of Webster, 131; lost portrait of JQA, 139; portrait of Miss Dehon, 139; portraits of other public figures, 139–140; CFA on portrait of JQA, 139, 141; JQA on, 141, 225; Page portrait of, 197; Gallery of (Boston), 252, 268; mentioned, 4, 149, 182, 191

Derivatives of portrait of JQA: Osgood copy (Fig. 62), xxv, 141; Hoit copy (Fig. 63), xxv, 141–144; copy in pastel by unknown artist (Fig. 64), xxv, 142; D. C. Johnston drawing after, lithograph of, 141–144

Harlan, D., 72

Harper's Bazar, "Mrs. John Quincy Adams's Ball, 1824" in, 106

Harper's New Monthly Magazine, Kruell engraving in, 267

Index

owned by, 51; pencil sketches of James A. Bayard, Henry Clay, Albert Gallatin, and Christopher Hughes, 51, 53; mentioned, 59, 253

Hughes, Mrs. (of Mobile, Ala.), 158

Hughes, Christopher (U.S. diplomat): Van Huffel pencil sketch of, 53; and Van Huffel pencil sketches of JQA and other American peace commissioners at Ghent, 53; mentioned, xxi, 56

Hull, Thomas H.: miniature of Joshua Johnson, 22, 34; JQA and LCA on lost miniature by, 34–35; lost miniature of JQA, 34–36

Humphrey, Samuel Dwight, 289

Hunt, T. W., engraving after lost Dubourjal portrait (Fig. 119, xxx, illustrated, 269), 268

Hurd, D. Hamilton, *History of Norfolk County*, 207

Hyde Park, N.Y. *See* Roosevelt, Franklin D., National Historic Site

Inches, Mrs. Carter (Lois Doolittle): and Parker miniature of JQA, 32; and Shelley miniature of LCA, 32

Indian peace medals: likenesses of JQA on (Figs. 54a–54c), 116, 118–122; discussed, 117–119, 122; likenesses of Monroe, Madison, Washington on, 118–119

Indians, American, King portraits of, 91

Inman, Henry (of New Orleans), 159, 201, 256

JA. *See* Adams, John (1735–1826)

JA2. *See* Adams, John (1803–1834)

Jackson, Mr. (of Philadelphia), 218

Jackson, Andrew: LCA's ball for, 7, 106; King portrait of, 92; likeness after Healy in *Ball Given by Mrs. Adams*, 106; Persico bust of, 162, 164; Powers bust of, 185; S. M. Charles miniature of, 202; Marchant portrait of, 203; W. H. Brown silhouette of, 235; Laban Beecher figurehead of, 243; Healy portrait of, 251, 253–254, 258; mentioned, 108, 168, 169, 179, 226

Jackson, Bernard H., 213

Jackson, Mrs. F. Nevill, 213

Jackson, Francis, 197–198

Jackson, William, 199

Jacquemart, Jules, engraving from Furst Indian peace medal by, 122

James, Henry, characterization of Page, 197

Janes, Miss M. P. (art dealer, of New York City), 137

Jarvis, John Wesley: King portrait of JQA (Figs. 39 and 40) formerly ascribed to, xxiii, 98; portrait of JQA(?) attributed to (Fig. 71, xxvi, illustrated, 159), 158–159; portraits of heroes of War of 1812, 159; mentioned, 107

Jarvis, Leonard (U.S. Repr., Maine), 162

Jefferson, Thomas: and American diplomatic costume, 57; Cardelli bust of, 72; Sully portrait of, 89; Browere bust of, 134; Stuart portrait of, 165; bust of, 165; Rembrandt Peale portraits of, 168; Powers statue of, 185; mentioned, 4, 22, 48, 67, 117

John Quincy Adams (ship), figurehead likeness of JQA on, 243–244

Johnson, Adelaide (d. 1877, sister of LCA): portrait of (Fig. 4i, xx, illustrated, 26); identified, 23

Johnson, Alexander Bryan (of Utica, N.Y.): JQA visit recorded by, 224; mentioned, 243, 288

Johnson, Mrs. Alexander Bryan (Abigail Louisa Smith Adams, daughter of CA), 224

Johnson, Alexander Smith (1817–1878, grandson of CA), 242–243

Johnson, Caroline Virginia Marylanda (1776?–1862, sister of LCA): portrait of (Fig. 4e, xx, illustrated, 24); identified, 23

Johnson, Catherine Maria Frances (d. 1869, sister of LCA): portrait of (Fig. 4g, xx, illustrated, 26); identified, 23

Johnson, Eastman: lost pastel of JQA, photograph of (Fig. 121, xxxi, illustrated, 272), 157, 270–273; portrait of Justin S. Morrill, 273; portraits of Maine legislators, 273; mentioned, 4

Johnson, Mrs. Eastman, 273

Johnson, Eliza Jennet Dorcas (d. 1818, sister of LCA): portrait of (Fig. 4h, xx, illustrated, 26); identified, 23

Johnson, Harriet (1781–1850, sister of LCA): portrait of (Fig. 4f, xx, illustrated, 26); identified, 23

Johnson, John Quincy Adams, and Van Huffel portrait of JQA, 54

Johnson, Mrs. John Quincy Adams, 54

Johnson, Joshua (1742–1802, father of LCA): miniature of (Fig. 4a, xix,

323

Lyre and Eagle (*continued*)
tation of Orpheus myth): meaning
for JQA, xiv, xvi, 8–11; used in portraits of JQA, xiv, 8, 12, 58, 77–78,
124, 128–131; engraved by Silvester
for JQA's seal (Fig. C, xix, illustrated, 12), 10–11, 58, 131; adapted
by Stone for U.S. passport (Fig. B,
xix, illustrated, 11), 10, 78. See also
Vultur et Lyra

MacAllister, John, 89
McClure's Magazine, engraving of
Browere busts of JA, JQA, CFA in,
136
Macdonough, Commodore Thomas,
Bowyer engraving of, 74
McKay, James I. (U.S. Repr., N.C.),
218
McKenney, Thomas L. (of Bureau of
Indian Affairs), Furst employed as
medallist by, 118–121
Macomb, Gen. Alexander, 77
Madison, James: Cardelli bust of, 72;
Vanderlyn portrait of, 89; medallic
likeness of, 119; Durand portrait of,
175; mentioned, 48, 50, 57
Madison, Mrs. James: Freeman minia-
ture of, 195; Billings portrait of, 270
Magazine of American History, 267
Mangum, Willie Person (U.S. Sen.,
N.C.), Lambdin portrait of, 219
Manilius, *Astronomicon*, 8–9
Mankowski, Bruno, 161
March, Mr. (of N.Y.), 127
Marchant, Edward Dalton: 1843 portrait of JQA (Fig. 87, xxvii, illustrated, 205), 157, 204–207; miniature after 1840 portrait (Fig. 89,
xxvii, illustrated, 208), 204–207,
210; Parker engraving after 1843
portrait (Fig. 88), xxvii, 206–207;
replica of 1843 portrait (Fig. 90,
xxvii, illustrated, 209), 207–210;
1840 portrait or replica (Fig. 91,
xxvii–xxviii, illustrated, 210), 209;
modified replica of 1840 or 1843
portrait (Fig. 92, xxviii, illustrated,
211), 210–211, 237; portraits of
public figures, 89, 203; 1840 portrait of JQA, 203–207; Adamses on
portraits of JQA by, 204–206; mentioned, 4
Marchant, Mrs. Edward Dalton, 203
Marcy, William L. (Gov., N.Y.), 201
Marshall, Chief Justice John: Harding

portrait of, 131; W. H. Brown sil-
houette of, 235; mentioned, 188
Martin, Mary, 90
Mason, George Champlin, 95
Mason, Mrs. Henry L., owner, portrait
of LCA (Fig. 13) ascribed to Savage,
48
Mason, John W., lost figurehead like-
ness of JQA, 243–244
Massachusetts Historical Society: minia-
tures of Joshua Johnson family (Figs.
4a–4i) at, 22; Parker miniature of
TBA (Fig. 5) at, 32; Greenough's
"Forest Children" at, 152; Healy
preliminary gouache for *Webster's
Reply to Hayne* at, 256; photographic
copy of a Brady daguerreotype of
JQA (Fig. 135) at, 295; Onthank
portrait of JQA (Fig. 140) at, 302;
portrait of JQA by an unknown artist
(Fig. 141) at, 302; mentioned, 145
Masser (coachmaker, of London), 62
Maubeuge, Jean de, *The Day of Judg-
ment*, 51
Maverick, Peter R., 95
Medals, likeness of JQA on, 116, 118–
122
Meehan, John S. (Librarian of Con-
gress), 165, 262
Memoirs of John Quincy Adams: Forbes
engraving after Powers bust (Fig.
84) in, 190; mentioned, 41, 64
Mercer, Charles F., Persico bust of, 160
Mercer, Dr. William Newton, and
Harding portrait of JQA, 140
Metropolitan Museum of Art: Byron
portrait of LCA(?) (Fig. 37) at,
90; Sully sketch for JQA portrait
(Fig. 51) at, 112; Edouart silhouettes
at, 213, 217; Southworth daguerreo-
type (Fig. 130) at, 285
Michelangelo, 164
Michigan, University of, William L.
Clements Library, Van Huffel pencil
sketch of JQA (Fig. 19) at, 53
Millard, Everett Lee, 137
Millot, M., xxii
Minerva, 121
Miniatures: of JQA, xx, xxiii–xxiv, 22,
28–30, 32–36, 106–108, 195; of
LCA, xx, 22–27, 31–37, 85
Mitchel, Ormsby MacKnight, 226–227
Mitchell, Dr. John Kearsley, 70
Mitchill, Dr. Samuel Latham, Browere
bust of, 137
Monroe, James: and American diplo-
matic costume, 57; Cardelli bust of,

72; Rembrandt Peale portrait of, 89; Wood miniature of, 107; Furst medallic likeness of, 118–119; mentioned, 65, 67, 69, 89, 108

Monroe, Mrs. James, Wood miniature of, 107

Moore, I. W., engraving after Kearney of King portrait, 100

Morehead, James Turner (U.S. Sen., Ky.), Lambdin portrait of, 219

Morgan, W. H., publisher, Durand engraving after Sully (Fig. 53), xxiv, 112–114

Morison, Admiral Samuel Eliot, 273

Morrill, David Lawrence (U.S. Sen., N.H.), King portrait of, 92

Morrill, Justin S. (U.S. Sen., Vt.), Johnson portrait of, 273

Morrow, Jeremiah (Gov., Ohio), 227

Morse, Rev. Glen Tilley, 213

Morse, Samuel Finley Breese: on American artists in England, 58; mentioned, 165, 295

Mote, Marcus: drawings of JQA (Figs. 96 and 97, xxviii, illustrated, 228), 157, 227–229; Daguerrean Gallery, 227; *Indiana Yearly Meeting of Friends*, 227; portraits of Lebanon (Ohio) residents, 227

Mott, Dr. Valentine, Browere bust of, 137

Mount Wollaston. *See* Quincy, Mass.

Munroe, Mrs. Columbus, and Gibert portrait of JQA, 237

Munroe, Seaton, and Gibert portrait of JQA, 237

Musée de la Coopération Franco-Américaine, Château de Blérancourt, Healy portraits of JQA (Fig. 108) and other American statesmen at, 258

Musée Impérial, Versailles, and Healy portrait of JQA, 258

Museum of Fine Arts, Boston: Copley portrait of JQA (Fig. 11) at, 40; and Leslie portrait of JQA, 63; Sully's *Washington Crossing the Delaware* at, 109; Greenough small marble of JQA (Fig. 70) at, 152; Powers bust of Greenough at, 183; Page portrait of JQA (Fig. 86) at, 199

National Academy of Design, New York City: and Durand engraving of Sully portrait, 114; and Harding portrait of JQA, 139; and Durand portrait of JQA, 170–171; and King bust of JQA, 247; and Dubourjal crayon

sketch of JQA, 268; mentioned, 196, 218, 221, 244

National Archives, photographic copy of Brady daguerreotype of JQA at, 295

National Daguerreotype Miniature Gallery, The. *See* Anthony, Edwards & Co.

National Gallery of Art: Stuart portrait of Binney at, 7; Sully portrait of JQA (Fig. 49) in Mellon Collection at, 110–112

National Intelligencer (Washington), 107, 202, 237

National Portrait Gallery, Washington, modified replica of Bingham portrait of JQA (Fig. 100) at, 235

Neagle, John, portrait of Patrick Lyon, blacksmith, 131

Needham, D. (of Buffalo), xxxiii

New Hampshire Historical Society, Wood portrait of Webster at, 107

New Orleans, battle of, anniversary celebration, 106

Newport, R.I. *See* Redwood Library

Newsam, Albert: lithograph (with P. S. Duval) of JQA (Fig. 124, xxxi, illustrated, 277), 276; lithographs of the Presidents, 276

New York American, 217

New York City, JQA in, 65. *See also* American Art-Union; The Brook; The Century Association; Columbia University; Frick Art Reference Library; Metropolitan Museum of Art; National Academy of Design; The New-York Historical Society; New York Public Library; New York University

New York Gallery of Fine Arts, 179

New York Herald, 217

New-York Historical Society, The: JQA address at, 1, 202; and gouache after Schmidt pastel, 20; Cardelli bust of JQA (Fig. 25) at, 70; Greenough bust of JQA (Fig. 69) at, 152; Durand June 1835 portrait of JQA (Fig. 74) at, 179; Luman Reed collection of portraits by Durand and Cole at, 179; Clevenger sculpture at, 193; Marchant 1843 portrait of JQA (Fig. 87) at, 204–207; Edouart silhouettes (negatives and photographs) at, 213–217; Edouart silhouette (negative) of JQA (Fig. 93a) at, 214; replica of Healy portrait of JQA (Fig. 114) at, 264; mentioned, 65, 137

Powell, William Henry: portrait of JQA (Fig. 122, xxxi, illustrated, 275), 158, 221, 274, 295; *Baptism of Pocahontas*, 201; *Battle of Lake Erie*, 273; *Discovery of the Mississippi*, 273-274; mentioned, 201

Powell & Co., printers: Doney engraving of JQA (Fig. 131), xxxii; Doney engraving, *U.S. Senate Chamber* (Fig. 132), xxxii

Powers, Hiram: 1840 marble bust of JQA (Fig. 81, xxvii, illustrated, 184), 2, 155, 182-183, 186-188, 195; marble replica of 1840 bust (Fig. 82, xxvii, illustrated, 189), 155, 188, 195; plaster bust (Fig. 83, xxvii, illustrated, 190), 155, 185, 189, 195; Forbes & Co. engraving of 1840 bust (Fig. 84), xxvii, 190; busts and statues of public figures, 182-185; *Eve* (statue), 183; *Greek Slave* (statue), 183; Greenough on 1840 marble bust of JQA, 183; R. H. Wilde on 1840 marble bust of JQA, 183; busts of JQA as likenesses, 190; mentioned, 4, 191, 193, 246

Pratt, Herbert Lee: and King portrait of JQA, formerly ascribed to Jarvis, 98-100; mentioned, xxiii

Pratt, William A., lost daguerreotypes of JQA, 293-295

Praxiteles, 164

Prescott, William H., 188

Preston, Col. William Campbell (U.S. Sen., S.C.), 166

Price, P., Jr., publisher, Moore engraving of King portrait, 100

Princeton University Library, example of engraving after Chappel portrait (Fig. 137) in deCoppet Collection at, xxxii

Profiles of the Time of James Monroe (1758-1831), 89

Providence, Rhode Island, Public Library, Clevenger bust of JQA (Fig. 85) at, 193-195

Quincy, Edmund (1808-1877), 198

Quincy, Eliza Susan, on Stuart's appearance, 74

Quincy, Mrs. Henry Parker (Mary Adams, daughter of CFA), and Barber miniature of LCA, 36

Quincy, Josiah (1772-1864): and lost copy of Copley portrait, 40-41; Greenough bust of, 150; mentioned, 123, 128, 148, 198, 252

Quincy, Josiah (1802-1882), 133, 198, 243, 307

Quincy, Mass., "Merrymount" at Mount Wollaston, 188. *See also* Old House; Stone Library; Stone Temple; Thomas Crane Public Library

Quincy Patriot, 185-186, 199

Quinn, Edmond T., bronze bust after Durand or Paradise (Fig. 80, xxvii, illustrated, 180), 181

R., H., engraving after Copley portrait (Fig. 12, xx, illustrated, 41), 40

Raeburn, Sir Henry, portrait of Dugald Stuart, 131

Raphael, 167

Redding & Co., publishers, Gimber engraving (Fig. 139), xxxiii

Redwood Library and Athenaeum, Newport, R.I.: benefactions from C. B. King, 91, 95; King portraits of Calhoun, Wirt, Jacob Brown, and Webster at, 92-93; King portrait of JQA (Fig. 38) at, 95, 98-101; Harding portrait of JQA (Fig. 61) at, 140

Reed, Luman: Durand portraits of JQA, Georgeanna Frances Adams, U.S. Presidents, commissioned by, 2, 168-169, 171, 174-179; and Durand June 1835 portrait of JQA, 179; and paintings of Cole and Durand, 204

Reed, Mrs. Luman, 204

Reynolds, Mr. (of Washington), 146-148

Reynolds, Sir Joshua, 202-203

Rhea, John (U.S. Repr., Tenn.), King portrait of, 92

Rhode Island History, 267

Roberdeau, Daniel, 148

Roberdeau, Isaac, 148

Roberdeau, Mary, Hanks silhouette of (Fig. 67, xxv-xxvi, illustrated, 147), 148

Robertson, Archibald, 95

Rogers, B., printer, Durand engraving (Fig. 53), xxiv

Rogers, Daniel Denison, 38

Rollins, Curtis Burnham: "Letters of Bingham to James S. Rollins," 231; and Bingham portrait of JQA, 235

Rollins, George Bingham, and Bingham portrait of JQA, 233

Rollins, James Sidney, and Bingham portrait of JQA, 231-235

Rollins, James Sidney, 2d, owner, Bingham portrait of JQA (Fig. 98), 233

Roosevelt, Franklin D., National His-

❦ The *Portraits of John Quincy Adams and His Wife* was composed on the Linotype by the Harvard University Printing Office. Rudolph Ruzicka's *Fairfield Medium*, with several variant characters designed expressly for *The Adams Papers*, is used throughout. The text is set in the eleven-point size, and the lines are spaced one and one-half points. The printing is by the Meriden Gravure Company, and the binding by the Stanhope Bindery is in a cover fabric made by the Holliston Mills, Inc. The paper, made by the Mohawk Paper Company, is a grade named *Superfine*. The Belknap Press edition of *The Adams Papers* was designed by P. J. Conkwright and Burton L. Stratton. This volume was designed by Burton J. Jones, Burton L. Stratton, and David Ford.